P9-DHL-857

# SLIPPERY SLOPE

# SLIPPERY SLOPE

*Europe's Troubled Future*

GILES MERRITT

OXFORD
UNIVERSITY PRESS

# OXFORD
## UNIVERSITY PRESS

Great Clarendon Street, Oxford, OX2 6DP,
United Kingdom

Oxford University Press is a department of the University of Oxford.
It furthers the University's objective of excellence in research, scholarship,
and education by publishing worldwide. Oxford is a registered trade mark of
Oxford University Press in the UK and in certain other countries

First Edition published in 2016

Impression: 1

Published in the United States of America by Oxford University Press
198 Madison Avenue, New York, NY 10016, United States of America

British Library Cataloguing in Publication Data

Data available

Library of Congress Control Number: 2015952656

ISBN 978-0-19-875786-3

Printed in Great Britain by
Clays Ltd, St Ives plc

*In memory of my mother and mentor*
*Susan Strange (1923–98)*

# ABOUT THE AUTHOR

Giles Merritt was named by the *Financial Times* in 2010 as one of thirty 'Eurostars' who most influence thinking on Europe's future, along with the European Commission's president and the secretary-general of NATO. For fifteen years a *Financial Times* foreign correspondent, Merritt has reported and commented on European affairs since the early 1970s. He went on to found 'Friends of Europe', one of the leading think tanks in Brussels and the policy journal *Europe's World*, of which he is the editor-in-chief. His op-ed columns in the *International Herald Tribune* from 1985 to 2010, and since then in the hundreds of newspapers around the world that subscribe to *Project Syndicate*, have ranged widely across political and economic issues in Europe. His previous books have included *World Out of Work*, an award-winning analysis of unemployment issues, and *The Challenge of Freedom* on the difficulties facing post-communist eastern Europe.

# CONTENTS

# COMMENTS ON *SLIPPERY SLOPE: EUROPE'S TROUBLED FUTURE*

'An excellent and very readable book at the heart of the debate on Europe'
Giles Merritt's excellent and very readable book covers pretty comprehensively the issues which should be at the heart of the debate on Europe. We would be far better served in Britain if the discussion on Europe took Merritt's book as its agenda. Other European citizens, not just the British, would be served by confronting the challenges which Merritt covers.

Chris Patten (Lord Patten of Barnes), EU Commissioner
for External Relations 1999–2004

'Giles Merritt's analysis is first rate—essential reading'
The EU is unique in the world, and so it is hardly surprising it faces unique challenges. Giles Merritt's analysis is first rate—essential reading for those who want to keep investing in this vital project.

Peter Mandelson. (Lord Mandelson), EU Commissioner for Trade 2004–2008

'A warning on the myths Europe must abandon'
This book is a warning to those who are unaware that Europe is no longer the centre of the world, and may even become marginal. But it is still possible for us to have voice, and Giles Merritt's book shows we have to abandon our myths and restore our unity of purpose if we are to move towards the politically rather than bureaucratically integrated Union European of the founding fathers.

Giuliano Amato, Prime Minister of Italy 1992–3 and 2000–1

'A razor-sharp analysis that is underscored by creative solutions and rewarding insights'
Giles Merritt's book offers a crash course on how Europe can master the 'slippery slope' of its uncertain future without falling down. His razor-sharp analysis may not always be flattering to the EU, but it underscores the creative solutions he suggests and his optimistic path towards a better future. The

paths needed to keep our footing on Europe's slippery slopes will demand stamina, but are rewarding because they present valuable new insights.

Franz Fischler, EU Commissioner for Agriculture,
Rural Development, and Fisheries 1995–2004

### 'A distillation of practical experience and clear ideas, in accessible language'

You cannot truly understand Brussels unless you have spoken with Giles Merritt, and his book is a distillation of his tremendous practical experience. With the European project in the throes of an existential crisis, we need clear ideas and Merritt offers just that. He has woven together hard data, narrative examples, and a range of views from academics, opinion leaders, and leading policymakers into extremely accessible language. With Eurosceptics having captured so much of the public debate by framing it in parochial 'them v. us' terms, his book provides a platform for a badly needed broader conversation about the rationale of the European construction.

Ana Palacio, Spanish Minister of Foreign Affairs 2002–4

### 'Giles Merritt's book deals with the EU's challenges, and its tough choices'

The European Union is often misunderstood and its capacities undervalued. Yet the building of the EU is unfinished and its institutions need to be strengthened. At the same time, the EU's legitimacy gap has to be addressed, as do all the weaknesses of its economic, social, and political dimensions. And the EU also has to make its voice heard around the world. Giles Merritt's book deals with all these challenges, and makes it clear that strengthening the EU will involve tough choices as well as greater powers of persuasion when reaching out to Europe's citizens. Unless it does so, he warns, the European future will definitely be on a slippery slope.

Elisabeth Guigou, President of the Foreign Affairs
Committee of France's Assemblée Nationale

### 'A masterpiece that is definitely worth reading by citizens and experts alike'

Can the EU's strengths and weaknesses be addressed in a single book that dispels many predominant prejudices and also looks to Europe's future? *Slippery Slope* does just that, for in his new masterpiece Giles Merritt explores the challenges the EU now faces in a variety of political areas. By setting out facts and figures he critically analyses EU policies, yet does not overlook Europe's achievements of the last sixty years. His book is definitely worth reading by citizens and experts alike because it offers a much clearer understanding of the EU to the former, and useful recommendations to the latter.

Elmar Brok, Chairman of the European Parliament's
Foreign Affairs Committee, and an MEP since 1980

# PREFACE AND
# ACKNOWLEDGEMENTS

This book is not about 'Brexit' or 'Grexit'; its focus is wider than Britain's European Union membership or Greece's future in the eurozone, important though they are. Its message is that Europe as a whole is slipping backwards in relation to many other parts of the world and that, whatever Eurosceptics may argue, the answer isn't a resurgence of European nations' 'sovereignty'.

If we Europeans want our children and grandchildren to prosper, and even to enjoy similar living standards and opportunities to ourselves, we must acknowledge the profound structural handicaps that have developed—some through our own neglect, others through ineluctable global changes. If Europe is to tackle its problems, they must first become more generally recognized. Few of the solutions are purely national, so to recover our economic dynamism we will need greater EU-level political consensus.

This book offers a snapshot of Europe's situation today and its implications for tomorrow. Without getting into the arguments between Brexit partisans on both sides, it aims to help UK voters form a more complete picture of the Europe that Britain is part of, and from which it cannot escape merely by withdrawing from the European Union. There are obvious dangers in generalizing about Europe, but this book nevertheless attempts to assess the EU's strengths and weaknesses. Europe is at a point when the sixty-year drive for closer integration is waning while economies elsewhere are waxing stronger.

The central theme is that no single European nation is capable on its own of defending its interests in today's world, let alone tomorrow's. Whether the EU is able to unify national governments into a stronger and more cohesive force is an open, and indeed vexed, question. That said, it's the only available mechanism.

I have worked in Brussels since 1978, having gone there somewhat reluctantly as a *Financial Times* foreign correspondent who had his eye on Washington. I've never regretted it, though, as I have been fascinated to watch the ups and downs of Europe's great political experiment. I am sometimes asked (usually in the UK by fellow countrymen) whether I am a Europhile or a Eurosceptic, and I say 'both'—I don't think we Europeans have any choice but to unite more closely, but I have long been sceptical about some of the ways the EU conducts itself.

Much of this book reflects the interviews I have been privileged to conduct with prominent politicians across Europe and with influential officials and experts. I am particularly grateful, therefore, to: Joaquin Almunia, Laszlo Andor, José Maria Aznar, Michel Barnier, Roland Berger, Dacian Ciolos, Etienne Davignon, Stefan Füle, Aart de Geus, Karel de Gucht, Angel Gurría, Mo Ibrahim, Leif Johanssen, Pascal Lamy, Andris Piebalgs, Janez Potocnik, Javier Solana, Pedro Solbes, Wolfgang Schüssel, Harry Van Dorenmalen, Hubert Védrine, and Nick Witney.

Where I have drawn on the research of others I have cited them along with sources of statistics and analysis. Errors of fact or interpretation are, of course, entirely my own responsibility. I've stopped short of including detailed notes as this isn't an academic work but rather an appeal to the general reader to take note of, and I hope respond to, Europe's deteriorating outlook.

My thanks go to the many people who gave me their time and advice during the preparation of this book, most of whom but not all are identified. I owe a debt of gratitude to Geert Cami and all our colleagues at Friends of Europe, the Brussels-based think tank

I founded in 1999, for their forbearance and help. Paul Taylor, Thomson-Reuter's veteran EU reporter and commentator, gave me invaluable advice on a number of key points, and most of all I must thank my dear wife Brigid Grauman for her encouragement and expert editorial eye.

Giles Merritt
Brussels, January 2016

# 1

# The Myths Hastening Europe's Decline

*Ten myths stand in the way of Europeans' ability to address their decline and counter it. This opening chapter challenges popular assumptions about Europe's wealth, its voice in world affairs, its outreach, and pressures on society that span jobs and immigration. Until these comforting illusions are exploded, Europe will continue to sleepwalk towards a diminished role in the twenty-first century.*

Europe is in decline; it's a message we hear every day. Sometimes it is expressed in terms of our economic troubles and the bitter debate over austerity policies, and at others through our inability to determine, or even influence, the course of international affairs and conflicts.

We Europeans are increasingly aware of our changing position in the world's pecking order, but we're reluctant to confront these shifts head-on and instead cling to our familiar ideas about Europe's strengths. We know rationally that the new century is bringing drastic economic and geopolitical change, but emotionally we find that hard to accept.

Our inertia also reflects our uncertainty over what practical responses are available to us. Many in Europe may feel that greater unity is the answer, but don't know what that really means. Even those who reject the nationalism overshadowing Europe's politics are unsure about how to translate a vague faith in European integration into clearcut solutions.

Ten persistent myths stand in the way of Europe's ability to address its decline. Until European public opinion can be persuaded that these are false notions it's hard to see vote-seeking politicians taking tough decisions that will hurt now even if they may pay off in the long run. This book looks at ideas and policies that could give us a better foothold on the twenty-first century's slippery slope. First, though, a quick demolition job on the myths that are lulling us into a false sense of security.

*Myth No 1:* **Europe is overcrowded.** Far from it; Europe's population is shrinking and there aren't enough people in the workforce. In terms of population density it's comfortable without being overcrowded. The average of 116 people per square kilometre is about double the density of the United States with its wide-open spaces, but a good deal less than China's 144 people per square kilometre. Rather than too many people in Europe, they are becoming too few; the EU's total population of about half a billion could be down to 450 million or so by mid-century, even with the addition of an expected sixty million badly needed immigrants.

Demographic projections aren't always accurate, but they are far more reliable than economists' forecasts, and on present immigration trends the working age population of the European Union (EU) is due to shrink from today's 240 million people to 207 million by mid-century. If anti-immigration pressures were to prevent the arrival of people from outside Europe, the workforce would then number only 165 million, with devastating effects on the economy. As it is, Europe's ageing population means that the four workers presently supporting each pensioner will by mid-century most likely have shrunk to two.

In terms of elbow-room, Europeans really aren't crowded; the average EU density is about the same as for France, where one of the major headaches is the 'desertification' of its countryside. Britain and Germany are more densely populated, but have about twice as much room per person as countries such as the Philippines or India. Our problem isn't overcrowding, it's underplanning. In most parts of Europe there is a need for more and better housing, and for public transport links that will open up underdeveloped or neglected regions.

*Myth No 2*: **Europe is rich.** This is trickier; European countries are obviously richer than developing ones, and people's savings and higher living standards mean they are likely to remain better off for many years, even if that means we Europeans will be eating our seed corn instead of planting it. As it is, people in the richer Western countries in the EU, not to mention the poorer former communist newcomers, are not nearly as well off as those in the United States; the average income in Europe, or to be more exact, the gross domestic product per capita, is roughly two-thirds of that in America, and by 2025 is expected to have dropped to three-fifths.

Global wealth is roaring ahead, but Europe's share is falling. Bankers at Credit Suisse estimated it at $241 trillion in 2012 and expect it to rise by almost forty per cent to $334 trillion by 2018, thanks largely to Asia's dynamism. China has now joined the US and Japan as one of the top three countries in terms of the super wealthy, overtaking Italy and Germany. The bank also says that the top ten per cent of the global population owns eighty-six per cent of all assets, and that a tiny one per cent of the people on this earth possess forty-six per cent of the wealth.

Europe is becoming relatively poorer and its social inequalities are growing. European society is still fairer, though, than the US, where president Barack Obama has said the average company boss now makes 273 times more than the average worker. But the gap between the uppermost ten per cent of Europeans and the bottom tenth, which had narrowed for much of the post-Second World War era, is now widening fast. Until a few years ago, those people at the top earned six times more than people at the other end of the scale. Today they earn nine times more and it will soon be ten. European society is being more and more split between the very rich and the very poor, and weak economic growth will be hard put to generate the wealth needed to nurse public finances back to health.

It's not all doom and gloom. By some yardsticks, public debt in Europe is amply compensated for by savings; €10 trillion worth of indebtedness, four-fifths of it in the eurozone, should be set against estimates of assets and investments that in some cases are put as high as €21 trillion. Europe's prosperous towns and villages aren't going to be transformed overnight into rundown slums, but nor will its neglected inner cities and immigrant districts be razed and rebuilt. The process of impoverishment will be slow, but it may well be inexorable. European governments increasingly lack the resources to invest in future-oriented projects and have seen a diminishing of the progressive social policies of years past. Rising inequalities of wealth and opportunity are provoking new tensions, and social frictions could contain the ingredients for future political turmoil.

*Myth No 3*: **Europe is strong.** With two million men and women in uniform, more than in the US and almost as many as in China, Europe's armed forces should be the strongest military instrument in the world. As it is, they had difficulty mounting the brief air campaign in 2011 against Libya's relatively outdated defences, and would have been unable to do so without US assistance. Far from that lesson being taken to heart, most national defence budgets in Europe have since suffered further cutbacks.

Europe's military shortcomings are a reflection of its political weaknesses. The ambition that the EU should be able to speak with one voice has been signed up to by all twenty-eight member governments, and that's about as far as it goes. Europe's smaller countries are all in favour, but the bigger ones have their own agendas. Germany has been playing a greater international role since the onset of the Ukraine crisis, but in truth it doesn't yet have a foreign policy that goes much beyond defending its commercial interests, while Britain and France, the two strongest security players, are at loggerheads on many key issues.

The result is not just the absence of coordinated responses to Russia over Ukrainian separatists, the Arab Spring, or Syria's civil strife, but also an incoherent approach to the global governance issues that will determine the new rules shaping the world economy of the twenty-first century. As the biggest economic bloc, Europe's voice could be the loudest, but it isn't.

*Myth No 4*: **Europe is technologically advanced.** Europe accounts for half of all the scientific breakthroughs published in academic papers, so it should be the most powerful technological force in the world. But Europeans are notoriously slow at turning ideas into industrial innovations.

The hottest example of this is the new wonder material known as graphene. A million times thinner than a human hair, extremely strong and supple, and an extraordinary conductor of electrons, this breakthrough at Manchester University in the UK by two Russian-born Nobel laureates is set to revolutionize a rich variety of industries—but not in Europe. Of the 7,500 patents relating to graphene since its invention in 2003, over 2,200 are held by China, followed by the US and South Korea, where Samsung alone has eight times as many as the fifty-odd registered by British interests.

It's just an example, but an instructive one. Europe is lagging further and further behind in the race to dominate new industrial technologies. It's possible that in the years ahead science will transform economic structures around the world, but if so there are real doubts that European companies will be in the forefront of those able to harness major advances commercially. When the twenty-first century dawned, the EU's governments declared their goal was 'to make Europe by 2010 the most competitive and most dynamic knowledge-based economy in the world'. Few if any lived up to their commitments to invest more in research and to finance promising technologies. It's unsettling to note that increasingly Europeans are putting their money into American R&D—the EU accounts for three-quarters of all the foreign investment in US research projects.

Every year sees a flurry of reports warning of the ways in which Europe's industries are falling behind in the global race to dominate new technologies. Each is greeted with serious concern by the relevant authorities, but still are not acted on. A substantial majority of top business executives in Europe surveyed by the Accenture consultancy group thinks that by the early 2020s China will have drawn ahead of Europe on technological innovation.

*Myth No 5:* **Europe is resilient.** Here we should use the past tense; Europe *was* resilient. Reconstruction in the aftermath of Second World War saw a remarkable comeback by shattered industries and ruined economies. The effect was to stimulate new activity and give many industries a fresh start. Even countries such as the UK that suffered comparatively little physical damage proved so resilient that renewed economic growth quickly paid off most of the burden of British war debts. In 1945 these had soared to 200 per cent of GDP—the same level as at the end of the Napoleonic wars in 1815—but had been halved by the end of the 1950s. The decade up to 2015 saw the eurozone members' debt averaging seventy-five per cent of GDP.

Europe has the means to spring back, providing it can summon the will. It has an extremely solid basis to build on, for in the international league table of competitive economies EU countries occupy five of the top ten places and ten of the top twenty. It is still the world's largest trading bloc and the investment portfolios of European companies and wealthy individuals are reckoned to be worth more than $15 trillion. The sinews of resilience are potentially strong.

So much for the good news. The bad news is that so far there have been few signs of Europe rebounding from the impact of the economic crisis now being dubbed 'the Great Recession'. Slow growth is being seen as unavoidable in Europe's generally sluggish economies, where consumer markets are often saturated and demand is depressed. More serious are structural problems such as an ageing population and the alarming shortage of trained and well-educated workers. The focus of public attention is on unemployment and on EU governments' inability to get young people into work, yet it is the growing number of unfilled vacancies that should be ringing alarm bells.

Debate about making Europe's labour markets more flexible has had little impact on the problem. Other than in Germany, where slashing benefits and wage protection has yielded low unemployment but also a new class of the poorly paid, there has been little determined reform. The result has been rising youth unemployment and worries

6

that a 'lost generation' is being created, in southern Europe especially, that may never find regular work.

People in Europe hope that sooner or later the EU's economy will pick up to where it left off in 2008, but realists warn that Europe no longer has the resilience for that. Industrial regions where traditional manufacturing has disappeared, often overtaken by new technologies, are crying out for regeneration. What is needed is the dynamic of a more cohesive Europe-wide economic and industrial strategy, and that means first of all a drive on skills training coupled with more innovation and entrepreneurship. That would do much to strengthen Europe's resilience, but this is still low on the policy agendas of most EU countries.

*Myth No 6*: **Europe is haemorrhaging jobs to Asia.** When Volkswagen, which until its diesel exhaust tests fiasco had been one of the proudest symbols of German industrial success, revealed that a third of its cars are now produced in Asia, the writing on the wall for European manufacturing seemed clear enough. It is a significant trend, even if the overall picture is complicated.

Asia's booming manufacturing sector is creating jobs in Europe too. Low-wage factories in China and elsewhere in east Asia have brought cheaper goods to Western consumers, and that in turn has meant more economic activity. The relationship between the Asian growth spurt and Europe's economic well-being is much more fluid and dynamic than shifts in factory jobs would suggest.

Manufacturing employment in European countries is certainly losing ground, with well over seventy per cent of the EU economy now in services, but the reality is that Europe as a whole has a growing trade surplus in manufactured products. The dwindling number of factory jobs owes as much to productivity improvements through advances in technology as it does to competition from Asia. Yes, Europe's companies need to be sharper and more innovative in the face of Asian competitors who are determined to move up the value chain from the low-profit assembly operations they began with, but in general Asia's industrial revolution has been good for both East and West.

It's hard to measure the ebb and flow of jobs, either locally or around the world. In the decade or so leading up to the financial crisis of 2008 and the subsequent worldwide slowdown, western Europe created around twenty-five million new jobs. And that was at a time when, from clothing to computers, Asia's manufacturing sector was roaring ahead. Since 2008, recession and depressed demand have seen overall unemployment in Europe climb by ten million new jobless to a total of twenty-six million. Analysts at the UN's International Labour Organisation (ILO) in Geneva, nevertheless see Europe's problems as mostly home-grown and are calling for a more 'job-friendly strategy' that would remove barriers to employment.

Services account for nearly three-quarters of European economic activity and that share is growing. The days when EU countries grew rich on steel, shipbuilding, and textiles are long gone, and now it is expertise in areas ranging from sophisticated business services to low-cost air travel that creates wealth. As to Asia, the complaint of emerging economies is that the rich countries, and Europe especially, insist on trade rules that give their service industries an unfair advantage.

*Myth No 7*: **Europeans are losing out to immigrants.** Long before the refugee crisis that broke over the EU in mid-2015, this had been the rallying cry of Europe's increasingly influential populist parties. And it's a drum-beat that is sure to grow much louder, wrong-headed though it is.

The arrival in Europe within less than a year of perhaps a million migrants fleeing conflicts and social collapse is aggravating the picture, and the influx is far from over. Assimilating so many newcomers will be a daunting challenge, and employment issues are sure to unleash waves of increasingly bitter and disruptive anti-immigrant sentiment. The Catch-22 for migrants is that either they are accused of 'stealing' jobs from native Europeans, or if jobless they are accused of benefit scrounging. The furore whipped up some years ago over 'the Polish plumber', when job seekers from the newest member states found work in the West is just a foretaste of far worse to come.

One of the loudest voices in the noisy British debate over immigrant job seekers inadvertently made the case for why they are such an asset for the European economy. An organization called Migration Watch complained that they 'tended to be disproportionately young, well-educated, prepared to work for low wages and imbued with a strong work ethic'. It was speaking of people from the EU's newest member states in central and eastern Europe, and said it would be 'implausible and counter-intuitive' to think their arrival had no impact on Britain's worsening youth unemployment.

Migration Watch was enunciating one of the most enduring fallacies of economics—the 'lump of labour fallacy'. This is the wrongheaded idea that there is a finite number of jobs to be filled, so that each new arrival in the labour market displaces someone else. In reality, each newcomer is also a consumer and brings an extra dynamic. These remarks were promptly slapped down as 'nonsense' by one of the most authoritative of UK economic think tanks, the National Institute for Economic and Social Research, but the myth about immigrants displacing native jobseekers persists, whether the newcomers are from eastern Europe or from Africa and Asia.

Europe needs migrants to strengthen its workforce and its economy. America's economic future looks more robust than Europe's because by mid-century immigration is expected to help lift its population from just over 300 million today to 400 million. Analysts in America working for the McKinsey consultancy reckon that more than nine-tenths of the twenty million new jobs created in the US can be ascribed to the influx of new people.

Europe's politicians should take note of US policymakers' rising concern that America's immigration dynamo may be slowing. Tighter immigration rules mean the labour force in the US is no longer expanding at a rate of over one per cent a year, and the Congressional Budget Office has warned that with IT-fuelled productivity gains also slowing, America's potential economic growth rate has dropped quite sharply to around two per cent a year from its long standing rate of three per cent.

The economic value of immigration is much the same for Europe. But European politicians are unwilling to confront public opinion on the issue, with the result that most of them are extremely cautious about saying so. Over the next thirty-five years as many as six million immigrants are thought likely to make their way to an EU country and that won't be nearly enough. An expert group headed by former Spanish premier Felipe González has suggested that as many as a hundred million foreign-born workers are needed to inject fresh youth into ageing Europe. Convincing the media and thus public opinion that these newcomers create employment instead of stealing jobs away from Europeans seems doomed to remain an uphill struggle.

*Myth No 8*: **Europe's voice is heard around the world.** On a few issues, that's true. When it comes to trade negotiations, the EU's weight as the world's biggest aggregated economy and the largest marketplace for goods and services gives it genuine clout. Diplomats handling sensitive commercial dossiers affecting thousands of jobs tremble when the EU speaks.

These are not just technical issues; setting rules and standards that other nations in this globalizing world have to follow gives European companies a very real advantage. But they're scarcely headline-grabbing matters, and in terms of foreign policy or security crises the EU's voice is rarely more than a high-pitched squeak commanding little attention or respect. And that's when European governments can actually agree on a single message, which on geopolitical questions other than those relating to climate change hasn't been very often.

The disagreements created by EU governments' disparate reactions to world events are a big problem, but not the only one. Another, paradoxically, is that Europe is over-represented in the international bodies that matter. Too many votes for European countries in the International Monetary Fund (IMF) and the World Bank dilute the EU's strength, while the British and French jealously guard their permanent seats on the UN Security Council instead of combining them into a powerful single voice for Europe.

The EU has set up its own diplomatic arm—the European External Action Service (EEAS)—to enable Europe to 'speak with one voice'. It's small, with only 1,600 people of diplomatic rank in comparison to the 50,000-plus diplomats who represent the EU member states, and it is weak. It doesn't have the political muscle to create foreign and security policy strategies that could unite the twenty-eight EU countries behind it, and when reacting to world events it is told to keep quiet by big players such as France, Germany, and Britain, even though they themselves seldom agree. Detractors of the EEAS say it does little more than 'squeak with one voice'.

History is Europe's chief difficulty when it comes to international diplomacy. Almost all the core EU countries have their own legacy of colonial relationships with other parts of the world, and these over-shadow the need for a common approach. That dampens Europe's ability to project a common view on many issues—especially conflicts and security flashpoints—despite the fact that the 'European experiment' of pooling sovereignty in many key areas is so widely admired.

The biggest challenges for Europe's single voice still lie ahead. Global governance, the shorthand term for fixing new rules for the international economy that can accommodate the rising powers of Asia and elsewhere, is going to be the acid test. It is an area where the EU has experience and skill, but it remains to be seen whether it will have the drive and the collective political will to ensure its approach to global issues, ranging from banking regulation to climate change, can prevail.

*Myth No 9:* **Europe is on the same wavelength as America.** In many ways, Europe and the US are in the same boat—both prospered greatly until the close of the twentieth century, but face the twenty-first with growing trepidation. Opinion polls on both sides of the Atlantic show that people fear that their children's opportunities and lifestyles will be inferior to their own. The rise of the world's new economic giants is casting a long shadow.

Having sheltered under the American nuclear umbrella throughout the Cold War, Europeans tend to see security policy as a shared concern. That's why EU countries have felt able to reduce their spending on military capabilities and outreach, even if they continue to rely on their defence industries to develop new technologies and deliver substantial export earnings.

The Ukraine crisis has revived some of the old Cold War certainties embodied in NATO, but until then the twenty-first century had shown that American and European views on security are no longer identical; from Iraq and Afghanistan to Libya and Syria, successive crises have made it clear there is no automaticity in Europeans' willingness to follow a US lead, and in the case of Germany and some others there have been outright refusals to do so.

Trade and investment across the Atlantic is big bucks. The 'bible' on European and North American economic links is an exhaustive report called 'Europe 2020: Competitive or Complacent?' by Daniel Hamilton at Johns Hopkins University's Center for Transatlantic Relations in Washington, DC. Its analysis, along with official figures from the US and the EU, shows how profoundly interconnected the two sides of the transatlantic economy have become.

Two-way trade in goods but not services is worth about half a trillion dollars a year, and is the smallest item on the balance sheet. The buying and selling of services across the Atlantic has risen to around a trillion dollars yearly, and direct investments by US and EU companies in each other's economies total some $2.5 trillion. On top of that, two-thirds of the $13 trillion-worth of foreign assets owned by American corporations are in Europe, and EU companies account for an estimated three-quarters of all foreign direct investment in the US. Finally, private portfolio stakes held by Europeans in America are thought to be worth $3 trillion and those of Americans in Europe some $2 trillion.

These figures dwarf many of the business relationships that make up the global economy, and seem enduring proof of the inextricable common interests of Europe and America. That's true yet not so true, for while the two are bound together in a web of financial and corporate cross-investments they are also very different in terms of business regulation and their mechanisms of government. The two are competitors as well as partners and some of their biggest companies (Boeing and Airbus spring to mind) are bitter rivals.

Washington and Brussels have been trying to bury past differences through a new transatlantic trade and investment pact, known in the jargon as the TTIP. It has the added though undeclared goal of creating a united front on future rules for global governance. In Europe it is having to contend with a groundswell of opposition, not least from NGOs wary of US intentions. In America, the business world sees the need but it is the Congress of the United States that has the last word, and its decision will be driven by the local job concerns of senators and members of the House of Representatives.

An added dimension pushing US and EU interests apart is energy. The shale gas and oil revolution turning the United States into an energy exporter abruptly ended their shared concern over energy security, especially in the Middle East. Europeans' doubts about 'fracking' their own less accessible shale resources are further complicated by all the uncertainties being created by much cheaper oil. In the meantime, American industry's electricity costs look set to remain about half those of European companies, so the relocation to America from Europe of basic energy-dependent industries such as chemicals and aluminium may be an unwelcome feature of the coming years.

The overall picture is very mixed. American politicians continue to see Europe's integration within the EU as highly desirable, and have done so since its earliest days. For Europe, the *Pax Americana* consisting of US diplomatic leadership backed by its fearsome military strength has been a welcome security guarantee. But now the priority America has long given to transatlantic policies and to its EU partners risks being eclipsed by its rising Pacific interests.

The US 'pivot' to Asia isn't so much a strategic ambition as a confirmation of reality. European political and business leaders have had to absorb the lesson that the neocons of the Bush administration a decade ago, with their impatience at 'Old Europe', were not a temporary aberration. The Obama administration, too, has shown that Washington no longer factors Europe's interests into American considerations. European politicians, especially British ones clinging to the notion of a 'special relationship', who believe they share the same geopolitical wavelength with the US, are deluding themselves.

*Myth No 10*: **The EU 'superstate' threatens national sovereignty.** To a good many people in Europe, the idea of 'Brussels' as an all-powerful, all-knowing superstate is a nightmare that is coming true. They can relax, because it's not. The institutions of the EU are small, and while by no means 'know-nothings', they lack the resources and the brainpower to be a superstate. By any stretch of the imagination, Brussels is far from being the 'capital of Europe' claimed by its Belgian hosts.

The EU's institutions are dysfunctional and poorly organized. Far from providing Europe with a well-oiled machinery for collective decision-making and the supervision of fair practices in business and many other walks of life, they are understaffed in some crucially important areas and over-resourced in others. They suffer from a bureaucratic culture that has soured over the years from idealistic visionaries to surly bean counters.

There are about 23,000 civil servants in the largest EU body, the European Commission, which is fewer than in many a national government ministry. Add in the officials at the European Parliament, as distinct from its elected members, along with those who make up the secretariat of the European Council where EU member states confer and decide, and the EU payroll nears 40,000 people.

That may sound a lot, but in reality there aren't enough high-level decision-makers. EU officialdom's rigid hierarchy has suppressed initiative at lower and even mid levels, leaving an overworked layer of around 800 top Eurocrats to try and combine strategic thinking with humdrum responsibilities. The occasional small scandal over misuse of funds (most EU spending is in fact disbursed at national level by national authorities) has also seen the rise of the accountants at the expense of more imaginative officials who in earlier times were able to use Brussels' powers and budgetary resources to push deserving projects.

A more imaginative and less risk-averse EU bureaucracy would be welcomed by many whose work has a European dimension. But that means reaching out to public opinion at large, and that's something the EU has consistently shown itself incapable of doing. It is an Achilles' heel that may yet fatally damage the European project. Distant, remote, inscrutable, politically unanswerable, untouched by the new austerity, and seemingly indifferent to criticism, the EU institutions have increasingly fewer friends or even sympathetic ears.

The mid-2014 European elections emphasized the way in which the EU's waning popularity is an increasingly serious problem. It is largely a reflection of the Eurocrats' inability to articulate in easily understandable language the difficulties Europe faces, and the choices open to it. The European Commission has never been a good communicator, and the European Parliament still has the appearance of a multilingual talking shop, more a Tower of Babel than a tower of strength. Until the commission has the courage to admit mistakes, highlight bad news along with the good, and when necessary denounce member governments' shortcomings, it will continue to slide from being the EU's executive arm to becoming its secretariat. Hardly the stuff of a superstate.

## European Unity to the Rescue...

Blaming Brussels for Europe's weaknesses is to shoot the messenger. The member governments are in the EU's driving seat, and they have been making a poor job of steering. National leaders avoid talking about the tough choices that could eventually improve Europe's global position in the fast-changing political economy of the twenty-first century. That's because these choices involve pain to achieve gain, and pain loses elections. The Paris-based Organisation for Economic Cooperation and Development (OECD), the 'rich man's club' of thirty-four countries, has calculated that most of the overdue reforms needed to streamline European economies would take at least five years to bear fruit.

Five years is, needless to say, the average mandate of a government. The example that many politicians are uncomfortably aware of has been Germany's social democrat Chancellor Gerhard Schroeder's reforms of the country's labour market in 2003; although widely seen as having transformed the then-ailing economy into today's powerhouse, those controversial reforms lost him the 2005 elections.

Failing to make the right choices isn't just about the self-interest of politicians. It also involves European society's willingness to question its prejudices, and for opinion-formers to be more clear-sighted about Europe's strengths and weaknesses. The strengths still outweigh the weaknesses, but that balance is altering. No single European nation will prosper alone amidst the harsher global pressures of the twenty-first century, yet solidarity and the need to rely on one's neighbours is a lesson that European governments learned fifty years ago but are now forgetting.

It's easy enough to talk of reforms that will streamline Europe's economies and make them competitive and successful in the years ahead, but putting that talk into practice is another matter. The brunt of cutbacks and tough austerity measures is borne by the less privileged sectors of society. Europe needs better strategies for spreading the burden, both within EU countries and between them. The Greek debt tragedy is an example of the absence of both—the 'solidarity' that was Europe's watchword is no longer on the lips of Germans or others, and Greece's rich seem to have been insulated from their country's economic misery. The constructively pro-European stances of political leaders in the 1960s and 1970s contrast sadly with today's nationalistic finger-pointing.

All is far from lost. Comparatively small though they are in population and size, the nations of Europe still exert a great deal of collective muscle. The EU is by far the world's biggest exporter and importer of goods and services, and its investments and savings are far bigger than those of any other region of the world. A third of the biggest international businesses are European, a third of the world's top universities are in Europe, and half of all Nobel prizewinners have been Europeans.

The question this boils down to is whether the rise of other parts of the world automatically means the decline of Europe. Not necessarily is the answer; if Europeans can keep their balance on the slippery slope, they will retain much of their wealth in a thriving global economy. Decline relative to rising living standards elsewhere will be acceptable. But if decline becomes absolute rather than just relative, Europe will suffer economic stagnation and social discontent. Its fate may be to become a geopolitical backwater with less and less say in international affairs.

Europe's salvation lies in economic and political integration. A fragmented Europe made up of countries pursuing beggar-my-neighbour protectionist policies was never able to compete with giants such as the United States or Japan, and will be even less capable of doing so now that fresh challenges are coming from such competitors as China, India, or Brazil. Yet the tide is running strongly against further integration. Public opinion has turned against Europe, and people increasingly say they prefer the devil they know in the shape of national politics to the devil they don't, which is decision-making in far-off Brussels.

Successive opinion polls point to a steady fall in support for the EU, yet that hasn't produced a corresponding rise in people's faith in national governments. A global survey conducted every year since the beginning of this century by the US-based Edelman public relations consultancy shows that trust in governments is falling in China, Japan, Brazil, and India as much if not more than in Europe or

America. But that's no consolation for the EU, whose waning popularity saps its ability to introduce measures that could turn the European economy around.

## ... Once There is Unity of Purpose

For the EU to come to the rescue requires, in the first place, a greater unity of purpose. Europe's governments need to agree on what has to be done, when, and by whom. The sovereign debt crisis in the eurozone was, after the initial disarray, tackled in a constructive manner, with subsequent reforms and the initiation of a banking union being considerable achievements. But there is also consensus among many observers that Europe still lacks drive and leadership.

Where there is far less agreement is on the overall policy approach that could revive the EU's fortunes. The eurozone crisis and its legacy of austerity cutbacks on social spending is pitting northern Europe against the south, and those who believe in deficit reduction against those who warn it has been aggravating debt problems by stifling growth. Angel Gurría, the former Mexican finance minister who is the OECD's tough-minded secretary-general, says 'policymakers have never been so much at odds on what to do'. Gurría sees the EU's outlook as worrying but not impossible. 'Yes, we should be worried', he agrees, 'but it's not "the sunset of the west" even though the problems that are affecting countries around the world have become particularly acute in Europe'.

Aside from the continuing problems of the eurozone and the imbalances within it, Gurría believes the EU has serious structural shortcomings. As well as Europe's problems with education, immigration, and competitiveness, he thinks taxes affecting employment and corporate investment must be lightened, with the burden shifted towards taxing consumption and property. Green growth and a major effort to reduce inequalities in European society are also important goals. 'We are headed towards a 4°C, if not 6°C, temperature rise, and at the OECD we think green growth will bring new ways of addressing major problems. As to the growing inequalities in Europe afflicting the young, the elderly and women, they clearly have to be reduced.'

Gurría rattles off a list of deep-seated problems that European governments have yet to resolve, though he thinks of himself as an optimist. 'I'm reminded', he says, 'of the scaffolding that used to cover the facade of the cathedral of Notre Dame here in Paris. It dismayed tourists from around the world, but once removed the spectacular results attracted even more visitors. I like to think Europe is covered in scaffolding, but that beneath it is reinventing itself'.

Among the seasoned political figures who see Europe's challenges in a bleak light is Hubert Védrine, a former French foreign minister who at a crucial period was diplomatic adviser to socialist president François Mitterrand. 'The shrinking and ageing of Europe's population', he warns, 'and the irreversible geopolitical shifts under way, mean an end to the Western monopoly of power. We'll still be comparatively wealthy, but the implications for Europe, and for America too, are enormous. The question is how to face up to this without collapsing in despair'. Védrine believes the highly sensitive question of managing immigration to satisfy Europe's labour needs is crucial, but he fears that EU policymaking will be inadequate. 'European politicians are tired. We need a shake-up in the way EU decisions are taken'.

Much the same view is shared by his country's current president, François Hollande. 'My duty is to get Europe out of the lethargy gripping it', he has said, 'and ease the disaffection that can only compromise the European Union's future'. Hollande's record-breaking lack of popularity in France has sadly eclipsed the interesting ideas for Europe he has put forward, notably that of 'an economic government that would meet every month around a real president, who would be appointed for the long term' to tackle such issues as tax harmonization, social convergence, and energy.

Not all of Europe's political thinkers share the vision of a continent steeped in gloom and despair. Someone with a very long institutional memory of Europe's economic problems is Belgium's Etienne Davignon, who in the late 1970s was the European Commission vice-president responsible for industrial policy. He's unimpressed by comparative studies showing a slide in Europe's share of the global economy. 'If we're selling more, even if our overall market share shrinks, then we're getting richer', he says.

Davignon is one of the doyens of EU policymaking and an informal adviser to successive leaders. He thinks personalities are as important as policies: 'The human factor in the EU is more important than anywhere else, especially when compared to national politics where leaders at least have democratic legitimacy. The EU needs leaders who can explain complicated things simply, and then deliver'. He added a piece of advice for former Luxembourg prime minister, Jean-Claude Juncker when he took the reins of the European Commission. Drawing on his close association with Jacques Delors, widely seen as that body's most effective president to date, Davignon recalled Delors's dictum that the key was to concentrate on everything the member states found most difficult.

The mood around Europe is very different today. The standstill endured since 2008 by many northern European economies and the savage shrinkage of southern ones was reflected in the results of the mid-2014 European Parliament elections. About a quarter of the new assembly's 751 members are Eurosceptic in one sense or another. They are probably too disparate to become a concerted political force, but they certainly represent the widespread doubts among Europe's voters that bode ill for closer integration in the foreseeable future.

Some very dubious calculations have been produced, most notably in Britain and in the Netherlands, purporting to show that leaving the EU would yield economic benefits. Few take them at all seriously, since these figures are generally based on the unlikely premise that exiting nations would remain an integral part of the EU single market. But they strike a chord with a good many politicians and their supporters whose resentment against the EU's apparent fondness for regulation and its inability to curtail its own red tape is fuelling Euroscepticism.

Explanations from Brussels that many of the EU's rules are levelled against unfair trading practices and hidden protectionism tend to fall on deaf ears. Even the most moderate critics of the European project are beginning to demand that some of the EU's powers should be returned to member governments. In early 2014 the Dutch government drew up a list of fifty-four 'competences' it believes should be in the hands of national authorities.

There is clearly room for manoeuvre on all sides. European governments, when not panicked by Eurosceptic challenges of various kinds, know that cautious rather than sweeping reform is needed if the EU's economic integration is not to unravel. And in Brussels realists concede that the European Commission has been compensating for being sidelined on many major policy areas by stepping up its creation of non-essential projects.

A prerequisite for reforming the EU, and redefining what it should and shouldn't do, is that Brussels must no longer be seen as so powerful that it is answerable to no one. It is in any case a myth that the EU institutions 'are out of control'. The truth is that while the European Parliament has gained more power, EU governments have over the past two decades steadily wrested the political initiative away from the commission. That isn't at all well known, so it doesn't alter the widespread view that Brussels' unelected Eurocrats are high-handed, arrogant, and out of control. What's needed is a realistic shift in public perceptions.

The difficulty is that two separate debates are taking place, with little chance of combining them into a single, wider discussion. The question of how to restore European electorates' faith in the EU is entirely separate from that of strengthening the EU to protect Europeans' interests in a rapidly changing world.

## Business as Usual is Not an Option...

The message that business-as-usual policies simply won't deliver and therefore have to be replaced by radical change, is to be found in a number of reports on the outlook for Europe. These have been put together on both sides of the Atlantic and set out a range of scenarios that span the most likely trends and developments.

An unusually frank and hard-hitting analysis called 'Global Europe 2050' has come from the European Commission itself. The commission's publications are all too often banal and self-congratulatory, with undistributed leaflets clogging the corridors of its buildings. But this study by outside experts working with officials in the commission's research arm used three scenarios to drive home the point that EU countries simply can't afford a comfortable business-as-usual attitude.

Their first scenario is called 'Nobody cares' and paints the depressingly familiar picture of Europe muddling through without clear vision or direction. The result is low growth and unstoppable global decline. The second, 'Europe under threat', is worse, with the EU's share of global GDP almost halved by mid-century as its economic and political fragmentation accelerates; instead of accounting for over a quarter of the global economy, the EU's share dwindles to fifteen per cent. Scenario three is 'European Renaissance', and of course points to the innovation and integration policies the commission has been advocating. It promises a near doubling of the European Union's GDP by 2050.

The absence of a concerted and headline-grabbing European strategy owes much to the comforting idea in capitals such as London, Paris, and even Berlin that the biggest European countries can leapfrog the EU's dysfunctional policymaking and go it alone. Their thinking is that if unhindered by Europe's smaller and poorer member states, they can each be a global player and will prosper accordingly. It's a delusion tackled forcefully in another valuable analysis, this time by the EU's Paris-based Institute for Security Studies.

Entitled 'Global Trends 2030', its message is that 'the future role of the EU as an international actor stands in the balance'. The EU's chances of remaining one of the world's great powers in 2030 depend on its countries joining forces, says the institute, emphasizing that the status of middle-rank powers such as Germany, Britain, and France will depend on the evolution of the EU as a whole. The in-depth report warns that China already sees the EU as a key market, but not as a relevant strategic actor.

A third significant report, this time by the US National Intelligence Council and confusingly also called 'Global Trends 2030', sees Europe's economy continuing its slow relative decline, along with those of Japan and Russia. In a world where it expects the population to number 8.3 billion people by then, the report forecasts that demand for food will rise by thirty-five per cent, for water by forty per cent, and energy by fifty per cent. The American analysts expect that 'the current, largely Western dominance of global structures such as the UN Security Council, World Bank, and IMF probably will have been transformed by 2030 to be more in line with the changing hierarchy of new economic players'.

Among the scenarios the National Intelligence Council posits there is one that may have a familiar ring to European ears; called 'Stalled Engines', it advances the idea that Asia's security tensions and even conflicts could begin to reverse the process of economic globalization, with the US and Europe then both turning inward. 'Under this scenario,' says the report, 'the eurozone unravels quickly, causing Europe to be mired in recession'.

The message that all these experts are sending is that Europe must play a much more influential role in world affairs. To maintain the living standards of its citizens, the EU must first maintain international stability. When European policymakers discuss foreign affairs they still see their policy responses in largely twentieth century terms, combining a heavy emphasis on trade and commercial interests with a security dimension that reacts to events but doesn't seek to shape future developments.

The model for European foreign policy in the twenty-first century should be that of the US in the aftermath of the Second World War. For all of Washington's blunders and despite the lunacies of the Cold War, *Pax Americana* was win-win for much of the world as well as for the US itself. Europeans are still grateful for the way the Marshall Plan helped kick-start their post-war recovery, and even called for another in the wake of upheavals such as the war in the Balkans, the Arab Spring, and the need to stabilize Ukraine. They forget, perhaps, that the Marshall Plan wasn't so much about the cash transfers it involved but America's enlightened self-discipline in limiting its own exports so as to encourage inter-European trade. That sort of far-sighted and selfless approach to nations in need should be the hallmark of Europe's common foreign and security policy.

## ...But Muddling Through Has Become the EU's Habit

Calling for a strategic rethink is one thing; bringing it about is quite another. The difficulty is reaching out to Europeans and seizing their imaginations. Europe's very distinct national political cultures may look broadly similar to Asian or African eyes, but they are different enough to stand in the way of a shared approach not just to international affairs but also to economic management. Driven as they are by national electoral considerations, European governments see the notion of 'European public opinion' as frail and untrustworthy, if it exists at all. This makes finding EU-level solutions to problems, shared though they are, far less attractive than fashioning national policies.

That doesn't mean that finding Europe-wide policies is impossible. If there is a key to engaging Europeans' support for EU-wide policies it is to translate rational arguments into emotional convictions. It's a view neatly summed up by former Dutch social affairs minister, Aart de Geus, who now heads the Bertelsmann Stiftung think tank in Germany. De Geus believes that the lack of 'emotional shine' on the EU's endeavours is a potentially fatal weakness. 'I see a huge risk that false promises that are not delivered on will mean trouble in store', he says. 'People would accept higher taxes, lower pensions and constitutional change if they were to be convinced that these would bring their children a better future'.

He's right; the sensitive emotional nerve that the Brussels Eurocrats and all involved in EU policymaking haven't attempted to touch is the fate of today's children and tomorrow's grandchildren. Warning that it is voters' young families who will suffer if Europe doesn't shake itself out of its lethargy is the card the EU must learn to play. It could be the only argument that will sway public opinion in favour of tough reforms whose brunt would inevitably be borne by the poorest and least privileged sections of society.

It is a danger put succinctly by Paul Taylor, the Thomson-Reuters news agency's chief commentator on European affairs. Taylor warns that 'the problem with "elite prescriptions" like more immigration, more open markets and tearing down barriers to trade in services is that at a macro-level they may be win-win propositions, but in the real world of the here and now they create plenty of losers among Europe's low-skilled poor living in social housing. 'The question', he adds, 'is how to mitigate those side-effects and avoid the political fall-out that is already driving working class and anxious, downwardly mobile middle class voters into the arms of xenophobes and extreme right-wing Eurosceptic politicians'.

That view is shared by the University of Oxford's Paul Collier, author of *The Bottom Billion*, which analysed the failures of development aid for the world's poorest. He sees serious political unrest ahead unless these fears are addressed, writing of the UK's highly charged immigration debate that 'public policy clearly needs to lower the temperature before popular discontent metastasises into something ugly'.

Immigration is an issue that the EU has consistently failed to tackle. Warnings to the British government that any attempts to stem job-seekers from eastern Europe would violate the basic EU principle of free movement are perfectly correct, but they are far from an adequate response to the questions that surround migration. For more than twenty years Brussels has tried somewhat half-heartedly to promote a common immigration policy and failed. Now, with the political pressures against immigration and the economic needs for it having greatly intensified since the early 1990s, the EU should return to the fray with redoubled vigour.

Caution over interfering in the domestic politics of EU states has been the chief brake on a common European approach to immigration, but that no longer seems very valid. Surging illegal immigration across the Mediterranean from conflict zones in the Arab world, and from Afghanistan, Africa, and Asia is placing intolerable burdens on southern European countries that will have to be shared by the EU as a whole. That should open the way to a broader and more constructive EU-wide discussion, not only on the costs and benefits of immigration, but on the wider dimension of the structural difficulties beginning to crowd in on Europe. Once powerful but disunited, Europeans must wake up to the realities of a twenty-first century in which only their collective strength will count.

Exploding the ten myths outlined in this chapter is key to awakening European public opinion to our increasing vulnerability to change and decline. We cannot know whether that decline will be relative in a world of accelerating prosperity, or whether it will be absolute. Either way, we can be fairly sure that unless there is a determined policy shift, the widening wealth gap within European societies will hit first the young and the elderly, the unskilled and the underprivileged. Europe is proud of its enlightened approach to greater social cohesion, but now it risks going into reverse.

The array of policy shortcomings to be tackled, and therefore the barriers to be overcome, are daunting. Centuries of global power, and more recently long decades of prosperity, have lulled Europe into a false sense of security. This has led to a very limited understanding of how quickly the world is changing. We Europeans will be unable to confront our challenges if we retreat into outdated nationalistic rivalries, and that is the message the political, business, and civil society leaders in the countries of the EU should all be sending to voters.

Solidarity between nations was the bedrock of European integration and won the admiration of the world. The term didn't solely mean financial transfers between richer and poorer countries; it also referred to their willingness to agree common decisions and then defend them. It served Europe well for half a century, but in the more fraught times of the twenty-first century it has acquired an old-fashioned and almost quaint feel. The European Council, whose summit meetings have become arenas for discord and disagreement on issues ranging from foreign security threats to the eurozone's future, would do well to restore 'solidarity' to its pedestal.

The EU's leaders should lay the foundations for a European reawakening and revival by publicly pledging their renewed commitment to solidarity. This would be a message that public opinion can readily understand and a signal that Europe is shaking itself awake to its shared future.

# 2

# The World in 2050

## A Glimpse into the Future

*Europe will no longer enjoy a privileged and dominant place in tomorrow's world.*
*Each of the four European Union countries still among the ten richest in the world*
*will drop from the list in each decade to mid-century. Intensifying competition for*
*natural resources and skilled manpower will demand concerted European policy*
*responses, while development and global poverty reduction will still be in Europe's*
*long-term interest.*

We'll be wealthier, smarter, and more international in our thinking. We'll also be thirstier, more crowded, and a good deal older, with the average age of humanity over forty instead of today's late twenties. Our mid-twenty-first century world is going to be reassuringly familiar yet disconcertingly different. It's probably not going to be the 'Asian century' so many predict, because a worldwide pattern of increasing migration will make it the 'global century'.

The diminished weight of Europe in a world of well over nine billion people is clear enough, but less so is the degree to which its importance will have dwindled. Bewailing Europe's shrinkage to less than five per cent of the global population is fruitless; what's needed is to look at the trends and the most likely developments to see how the European nations can retain a central role in this globalized world. That sounds obvious, but Europeans will need to be quicker and much more alert to change than over the past half-century.

There's a long standing jibe that if Europe doesn't wake up and become more competitive in world markets it will be reduced to little more than a quaint tourist destination. If that turns out to be true, it may be nothing to be ashamed of; urbanization is going to be such a feature of development around the world that Europe with its shrinking population will, in comparison, very probably be a haven of peace and tranquility. The Common Agricultural Policy that has long been reviled could well be blessed in years to come for safeguarding our rural environment.

The green and pleasant European countryside with its contrasting national architectural and cultural heritages is going to stand out against the urban sprawl engulfing so much of Asia, Africa, and Latin America. China is already building skyscrapers at an astonishing rate of one Manhattan every two years, and has plans to construct 50,000 more high-rise buildings. By mid-century, about three-quarters of humankind will be city dwellers, whether in China's impersonal metropolises or in Africa's teeming slums and shanty-towns. Forget sprawling Tokyo or the US East Coast 'megalopolis' stretching northwards from Washington, DC, through New York to Boston, it's Kinshasa's ten million people and Jakarta's thirty million that are the signposts to the future.

The coming strain on the earth's resources is hard to imagine, but it's real. Two-thirds of the global population will be living in what the experts term 'water-stressed regions', with the Middle East and much of Asia particularly affected. The World Bank warns that half of China's 660 cities already suffer from water shortages, yet the country's urbanization drive will increase its water needs by a factor of two and a half. The world is heading for a forty per cent shortfall in fresh water because we're increasing our use of water at twice the rate of population growth.

More mouths to feed and major changes in eating habits are the root problems. Africans are eating much more rice, and by 2035 it will have overtaken maize as the chief staple. Global rice consumption is rising twice as fast as rice production despite the introduction of more efficient new strains. In Asia, rising living standards are prompting a shift from rice-based diets to meat eating, and this demands much more water because of the extra crops needed for animal feed. The Chinese used to consume a modest nine kilos of meat per head every year but now it's fifty kilos, and for the developing world as a whole, meat consumption that averages sixteen kilos per person is forecast to double by 2050.

It's no surprise that feeding the world's growing population is going to present difficulties, but there's little awareness of the scale of the problem. There are still about 2.5 billion people around the world engaged in agriculture of some sort, and although farm productivity has generally improved it hasn't kept up with the demographic explosion. The groaning supermarket shelves of the Western world hide the reality of food scarcities that send about a billion people hungry to bed nightly, and are certain to become more critical in Africa, the Indian subcontinent, and parts of Asia. When the G8 leaders met in the Italian city of L'Aquila in 2009 they committed to a $20 billion agricultural investment plan for the developing world, but only a fortieth of that has been paid over.

Food production needs to rise by at least seventy per cent over the twenty-five years to 2040, and perhaps to have doubled by 2050. That may be less daunting than it sounds because a solution to the problem is readily at hand—tackling wastage. Homi Kharas at the Brookings Institution, a Washington, DC, think tank, points out that inadequate storage and distribution in poor countries and sheer waste in rich ones mean that almost a third of the food the world produces goes uneaten.

City planners, too, will have to become far more aware of the resource limitations they must contend with. Justin Yifu Lin, for four years the World Bank's chief economist, is among the voices urging a structured international approach to these difficulties. He has suggested a 'global infrastructure initiative' to tackle the lack of physical infrastructure such as roads and ports that is holding back development in many countries and condemning others to nightmare cities of the future. The Asian Development Bank has put a figure of $8 trillion on Asia's infrastructure needs up to 2025.

Much of this may sound like the notoriously rash undertaking of futurology, and it's true that attempts to peer into the years ahead often look bizarrely wrong before the ink is even dry on the page. But a good many of the projections (rather than predictions) being made for the first half of the twenty-first century are based on measurable quantities, whether people or resources. The proportion of young people in the populations of Asia, Africa, the Arab world, and to some extent Latin America—and of older people in Europe and America—gives a good indication of what the world will look like by mid-century.

The UN's projections now see 9.6 billion people by 2050—with other scenarios varying between those that suggest 10.5 billion rising to 11 billion by 2100, and those that detect a slowing in the growth rate that could see the global population peaking by as early as 2030. What none of these figures tell us is whether the developing world's youthful and dynamic workforces will have created the extra wealth needed to satisfy not just people's needs but their ambitions. The most encouraging signpost so far has been the speed with which a new global middle class has been created in the emerging economies, especially Asian ones, in the space of thirty years or so. On the other hand, much of the coming population growth will be in sub-Saharan Africa, where poverty is as pervasive as ever.

A positive overall indicator is that the value of the global economy in 2020 is being forecast by EU economists to reach $121 trillion, up during a single decade from $69 trillion in 2010, with seventy per cent of that increase in the emerging economies. The US and the EU will still be far ahead, with GDPs in 2025 of around $21 trillion each, compared to China's $15 trillion. Unsurprisingly, there's a wealth of different and contradictory projections, with some econometricians even suggesting that China will draw level with the Western economies and possibly overtake them before 2030. But that doesn't mean the average Chinese will be richer. Projections for incomes per person show Americans at $60,000 a year by 2025, Europeans at $42,000, Chinese at $10,000, and Indians at just under $3,000.

If the populous new economies fail to deliver—and by mid-century the world's ten biggest countries will include Nigeria, Pakistan, Bangladesh, and Ethiopia—the world will be a progressively more dangerous place. Economic and trade tensions, together with resource competition for energy and scarce materials, are certain to push security much higher up the international agenda. Europe's wealthy and privileged lifestyle means that, just like the United States, it has a vital interest in creating new political mechanisms that can help to defuse crises and find compromises that will resolve national, ethnic, and religious rivalries.

There's little sign that Europeans yet think of themselves collectively as a force in international politics. The emphasis in the foreign ministries of most EU governments is on trade and economic diplomacy. Only Britain and France have a strong sense of being major players on the world stage, and that's in part due to being, like the US, Russia, and China, among the five permanent members of the UN Security Council.

## Resource Competition and Conflict

What sort of conflicts might arise in the years ahead, and why and how should Europe have a hand in preventing them? It's likely that Africa will be as much of a flashpoint as the Middle East, and perhaps more so. The development of shale oil and gas around the world as well as in North America is going to transform the oil politics of the twentieth century. Governments everywhere will be striving to reduce their import dependency, hopefully making the Gulf and other regions of the Arab world less volatile.

The snag is that the process of 'fracking' shale to release oil or gas requires enormous quantities of water. That's not a problem in northern parts of the US or Canada, but it's certain to aggravate water conflicts elsewhere. And because major rivers so often either run across frontiers or are natural borders between countries, the likelihood of disputes over them is inescapable.

The water needs of China alone are alarming. Each Chinese at present uses only a quarter of the average amount of water consumed per person worldwide. But over the thirty-five years to mid-century China's consumption is expected to more than double, even though climate change and desertification have already been reducing the flow of vitally important Chinese water arteries such as the Yangtze and Yellow rivers. There are promising new desalination techniques for taking the salt out of seawater, but so far they have either been so expensive that only countries such as Saudi Arabia can afford to experiment with them, or they've been confined to the laboratory.

What we don't know is the extent to which these and other environmental constraints are being taken into account by policymakers. In 2050, there will be eight billion people living in what today are developing or emerging countries. If the world is indeed headed towards a rise of 3°C global warming or more, with average temperatures last seen three million years ago, what impact will that have?

Chandran Nair, a Hong-Kong-based analyst and author of a book entitled *Consumptionomics*, has warned that the five billion people living in Asia by mid-century cannot possibly consume at the same level as, say, people in the US. His message has been that Asians must create economies that constrain resource use through what he terms 'true pricing' that will inevitably make energy, fisheries, forests, water, and land more expensive. That sounds like common sense, but it also sounds like political dynamite in countries whose leaderships are struggling to meet their peoples' rising expectations.

It's much the same message as UK economist Nicholas Stern conveyed in his celebrated *Stern Review* back in 2006, when he warned that dealing with climate change is going be a major brake on growth. Stern has said that even if the rich countries grouped in the Organisation for Economic Co-operation and Development (OECD) were at last to bite the bullet and reduce their greenhouse gas emissions to zero by 2030, the developing world will also need to make enormous sacrifices.

The leaderships of Asian and other developing countries might be more inclined to listen to Western analysts if they felt that their own concerns were better appreciated. From their standpoint, the rich world's narrative is that poorer countries should slow down growth and industrialization so as not to imperil the West's comfortable living standards. They've got a good point, and the figures speak for themselves. To meet the climate change targets that scientists are urging, average greenhouse gas emissions worldwide must by mid-century come down from seven tonnes of $CO_2$ equivalent per head of population to only two. Right now, every American produces twenty-two tonnes a year, each European over nine, the Chinese seven, and Indians two.

The pressure that will really determine the developing countries' approach to the environment is self-interest; pollution is costing them dear. As part of its drive to encourage 'green growth', the World Bank has tried to calculate the cost of environmental degradation as a percentage of the GDPs of twenty-one developing countries. It found that on average the economies of these countries were eight per cent smaller than need be, with bad sanitation and water pollution imposing huge costs and actively discouraging investment and growth.

It's a message some governments seem to be taking to heart. Nicholas Stern hailed China's five-year plan for 2011–15 as 'the biggest contributor to greenhouse gas reduction by any country', and Ethiopia intends to double the size of its economy by 2025 while pegging greenhouse gas emissions at their 2015 level. Making sure that the twenty-first century world won't repeat the mistakes of the past is going to be an uphill struggle. Although the clean energy industry is doing a roaring business worth $260 billion a year and rising, that has to contend with the $1.2 trillion being spent every year by governments everywhere to subsidize what the World Bank classifies as environmentally and economically harmful activities.

If Asia risks being riven by water rivalries, Africa's dangers are more likely to be over minerals. The endless, bloody, and disastrous war in the Democratic Republic of Congo, the DRC, that involves rival militia forces is fuelled by competition to control a greatly prized mineral called coltan. Short for columbite-tantalite, it's used in most lightweight electronic devices to regulate voltage and store energy. The DRC has four-fifths of the world's known reserves of coltan, and until such time as alternative technologies emerge, it seems certain to be Africa's most explosive powder keg. Meanwhile, volatile South Africa has the lion's share of the world's platinum, and similar ingredients for conflict are present in a good many other African countries.

Trying to look over the horizon at the security tensions that will dominate the mid-century world is foolhardy, but it's probably safe to say they won't be much like those of today. Rather than localized conflicts such as in the DRC, it may be that non-African countries whose industries badly need a scarce mineral and have invested in its extraction will be drawn into resource struggles, in much the same way that the Cold War bred proxy conflicts that pitted Soviet-backed regimes against those supported by Western nations.

Africa's trouble spots—whether across the Maghreb region, in the Sahel, or in sub-Saharan countries—are capable, despite their small scale, of breeding huge humanitarian crises. As a threat to global security, though, they pale in significance when compared to developments in Asia.

## Asia's Accelerating Arms Race...

China and India have not been alone in pouring money into military hardware, training, and even the development of 'blue seas' naval power. Smaller Asian countries such as Singapore now have powerful deterrent forces, and larger ones such as Indonesia and South Korea are keen to reduce their dependence on America's protective shield. Seoul has plans to build 128 warships of various types, and Japan is backing away from its post-Second World War stance of total pacifism with a shipbuilding drive for its Self-Defence Force that is almost as large. In 2010 the Japanese abandoned their long standing fixation with a Russian invasion of northern Japan in favour of a scenario with plans for protecting Okinawa and its other southern islands against China.

India is now the world's largest arms importer according to the Stockholm International Peace Research Institute (SIPRI), a think tank that monitors defence spending and the international armaments market. Its main supplier is Russia, and in New Delhi the military planners have embarked on a twenty-year programme to spend $45 billion on over a hundred new warships ranging from destroyers to nuclear submarines. That's almost double China's ambitious naval modernization plan.

The London-based Institute for International Security Studies (IISS) think tank notes that Asian defence spending has overtaken the investment level of NATO's European members, and is set to keep on rising. China accounts for almost a third of all Asian defence spending, and has moved rapidly past the stage at which it was reconditioning second-hand warships. Beijing is investing large sums in 'dual use' R&D programmes that will help develop new generations of weaponry.

Why are the Asian nations pouring resources into military power that could be invested in so many other areas? And what are the implications for US-led Western security thinking that has been such a dominant feature of geopolitics during and after the Cold War? Asia's rising powers are aware that when more than half of the world's population lives in their region, fresh security problems will inevitably arise; more people are unlikely to equal less trouble.

Identifying the issues that will spark trouble is less obvious, but it's unlikely to be the conflict across the Pacific between China and America that the military top brass in the United States plan for. At the Pentagon they believe China has become capable of blocking American access to Asia's strategic waters and have developed their 'Air/Sea Battle' computer model in preparation for the hostilities they envisage between the two great powers. It seems much more likely that for the foreseeable future both countries' economic dependence on one another will dampen any pressures for confrontation.

The Chinese defence ministry nevertheless complains openly of America's 'Cold War thinking', even if its senior soldiers seem mildly flattered by the idea that they could directly challenge the US At China's Academy of Military Science, General Yao Yunzhu has put the gap between Chinese and American military power as 'at least thirty years, maybe fifty'. China's short- and medium-term aims are not to directly challenge the US but rather to blunt the projection of American might in Asia, where it understandably sees itself as the dominant regional power. Beijing has rejected overtures from Washington that there should be a 'permanent dialogue' between the US and Chinese armed forces, and the reason it has refused is that the Chinese see the idea as a ploy to underwrite a security status quo that they do not accept.

Another of Beijing's security concerns is the need to safeguard its fast-growing expatriate workforce. The speed and efficiency with which it airlifted 35,000 Chinese workers out of Libya in 2011 was no lucky fluke—protecting its nationals in far-flung parts of the world is high on China's agenda. In 2010 there were some five million Chinese working abroad, many of them in construction, and by some estimates that mobile labour force may have risen to a hundred million by 2020.

A major factor in China and elsewhere in Asia is disputed territory, notably the various islands claimed by two or more countries. There are the hundred or so islands of the Spratly chain in the South China Sea, where Vietnam and China have long been at odds even though the rich oilfields thought to be there remain unproven. Some of them are also claimed by Taiwan, Malaysia, Brunei, and the Philippines. Then there are the Paracel Islands, also thought to be energy-rich, that China seized from South Vietnam while the Vietnam War raged. To their east lies the Scarborough Shoal off the Philippine island of Luzon that has seen naval confrontations between Beijing and Manila.

And north of Japan there are the Dokdo islets off the coast of South Korea that Tokyo lays claim to under the name of Takeshima.

Above all, though, there's the Senkaku chain of uninhabited islands in the East China Sea that the Japanese administer but which the Chinese call Diaoyu, and over which both countries have been alarmingly belligerent. The reason all these lonely outcrops of rock provoke such high emotions isn't just nationalism, there's also a strong commercial interest. Nobody can be sure that, quite apart from oil and gas, there isn't something valuable there. Japan's discovery in 2010 of up to a hundred billion tons of rare earth elements in the Pacific has concentrated minds wonderfully. These deposits lie in seventy-eight different locations in mud that is 3,500–6,000 metres below the ocean's surface, and to complicate matters further are in international waters east and west of Hawaii and east of French Polynesian Tahiti. It's nevertheless a significant find, in geopolitical terms at least.

## ...and the West's Changing Security Role

The point is not that Asians in the twenty-first century have plenty to squabble about, but that America and its European allies need to rethink their security role in Asia. They will need to be engaged, but at the same time be respectful of the major regional powers there. Sooner or later, NATO must stop seeing Atlantic security and the European 'theatre' as the likely crisis point. The onset of the Ukraine crisis and Russia's belligerent involvement in it has shifted attention back to Europe, but the NATO allies nevertheless need to recognize that Asian countries, too, are going to be major security players, and adapt their planning accordingly. They should turn their eyes eastwards and find ways of extending to Asia the security framework that has successfully defused tensions and maintained peacekeeping since the fall of the Berlin Wall.

NATO is constructing an extensive new headquarters complex in Brussels, and until the Ukraine crisis and Russia's annexation of Crimea in spring 2014, its huge domed buildings looked an extravagant architectural memorial to an alliance that had served its purpose. The years following the 1991 dissolution of the Soviet Union saw NATO become little more than a waiting room for former communist countries that aspired to European Union membership. Its continued existence seemed to reflect its member governments' inertia and unwillingness to create a different security structure more suited to the twenty-first century.

It may be that Russia's nationalism and fears of a renewed threat from Moscow will reinvigorate NATO. Until Russia's overt support for Russian-speaking Ukrainian separatists, the alliance had, in the eyes of many Americans, chiefly become a convenient device for providing Washington with political cover when needed, notably in the case of Afghanistan in the wake of 9/11. For its European members, it has been an alibi for inaction because being part of NATO was a good excuse for failing to develop the EU's own military outreach. As it is, only Britain and France can claim to have real defence clout, with most other European allies increasingly resigned or content to be free riders.

That attitude relies on the assumption that US and European interests would be broadly shared, so that America's taxpayers will continue to pay substantially towards Europe's defence and security. And Russia's assertiveness not only toward eastern Ukraine but other 'frozen conflicts' in eastern Europe and the Caucasus region could indeed ensure that US involvement will be little changed.

But Europeans' vulnerability to Mediterranean instability following the Arab Spring of 2011 has also underlined their need to act independently of the United States. European policymakers know they must help create new political structures in the Arab world and in Africa. That would mean bringing governments regularly around a table to discuss both economic and security questions, and some European foreign policy experts believe EU countries should also be working with the US to involve Asian governments in a similar arrangement.

The history of European integration shows that creating frameworks for international cooperation can be extremely positive. It's an area where Brussels has a great deal of experience and enjoys international credibility. Looking to the future, Europe should be preparing itself for a global diplomatic role. That, of course, demands more troops and the means to deploy them, but even more important are the links the EU has with almost 200 national governments and international bodies that can be used to build stronger mechanisms for consultation and cooperation.

The UN's extended family of agencies each have a role to play, but no one really believes that the United Nations itself is up to the job of ensuring international security in a world that by 2050 risks being so much more insecure than today. Instead of arguing over ways to reform representation in the UN Security Council, the time has surely come for an institutional reset in which Europe would have a single and louder voice.

## The New Global Economic Landscape

Economic development will be the key to security, and there are no prizes for guessing that the corporate world will be very different by mid-century. There are already big corporate newcomers in the developing economies, and over the next decade or two we can expect them to become world leaders. Analysts in the US at the Boston Consulting Group have developed a list of a hundred 'Global Challengers', the new multinational corporations being created by the BRICS nations (Brazil, Russia, India, China, and South Africa) and by other thrusting economies.

To give a flavour of how little known they are, the most recognizable names include Asia's biggest agribusiness, Wilmar International of Indonesia, India's aluminium giant Hindalco, and a host of Chinese companies such as Geely for automobiles, Sany for heavy machinery, and Zoomlion for construction equipment. Soon they'll be household names, as familiar to our ears as are China's Huawei and Lenovo, or India's Tata, and they are just the advance guard of a new generation of world-class businesses.

Their arrival on the international scene is greatly to be welcomed for a number of reasons. The first and most obvious is that they will bring wider prosperity by fuelling the world economy. The new global challengers have been more profitable and far better job creators than most of their longer-established Western competitors. The second is that they will also improve the chances of peace, because prosperous people are far less likely to generate political turmoil. Investment by these big corporations in markets around the world is a powerful stabilizer; few governments will ignore the economic repercussions of conflict on their own big corporate employers and taxpayers, however much nationalists or religious extremists in their country may be baying for blood to be spilt.

The response of Western multinationals to these tough new competitors is going to reshape large parts of the global economy. General Electric (GE), the US engineering-to-banking giant that is the world's largest industrial company, expects to undergo radical change itself. It foresees half of its entire business coming from the growth markets of Asia and Latin America by 2020, up in just a decade from around a third. Those numbers more or less track the shift in the global economy as emerging markets now account for half of global GDP, while twenty years ago their share was just thirty per cent.

It's the sort of strategic thinking that big business in Europe and America will have to adopt to survive. That means it will present Western politicians and governments with some tricky choices. The pressure on US and EU corporations to safeguard jobs at home instead of outsourcing looks certain to get fiercer than ever, yet to protect their global market shares these companies will need to shift a growing proportion of their domestic activities abroad.

## Workforce Shortages in an Overpopulated World?

One of the chief features of the changing global economy is going to be competition not just for markets but also for employees. Europe already has a labour shortage—although few politicians dare say so—and it's set to spread and become a major international problem. Much of the growth that over the last thirty years or so has lifted billions of people out of poverty has been fuelled by population growth. The global workforce in 1980 numbered about 1.2 billion people, and today it's close to three billion. Although the population explosion is still at work, the world's labour force is now growing more slowly and the global economy is beginning to be weighed down by an ageing population.

A study by McKinsey consultants reckons that by 2035 when the world's workforce reaches 3.5 billion there will be a shortage of about forty million highly skilled university-trained people. Of these 'missing' workers, twenty-three million will be in China, and almost eighteen million in advanced economies such as Europe, America, and Japan. Dominik Ziller, who heads the migration service at Germany's GIZ international development agency, puts the figures higher still, saying there will be over 200 million unfilled jobs for skilled workers around the world, with fifty million of them in Europe, and that the competition for people with advanced technical qualifications is going to be a salient feature of the coming years.

As well as these shortages of people to fill very high-tech jobs, there's expected to be a further shortage in the developing world of about forty-five million workers who possess a secondary education and medium-level skills. At the other end of the spectrum, meanwhile, there will be a surplus of at least ninety million low-skilled workers, meaning that they are likely to become the chronically unemployed.

The lesson is plain enough. If China and other Asian countries are investing so heavily in technical training and education in order to face serious skills shortages, the problem will be all the greater for the Western economies. European governments are already wrestling with the conundrum of rising unemployment and increasingly serious skills shortages, and it's a problem that seems certain to become more acute. There are reckoned to be about four million unfilled vacancies across the EU, despite there also being some twenty-six million registered unemployed. Employers' organizations see Europe's overall deficit of people with high-tech qualifications of around 900,000 now rising to upwards of a million by 2020 and beyond.

The implications for European society are discouraging, to say the least. What life for most Europeans will be like by 2050 no one can tell, but there's a strong sense that unlike during the post-war years—what the French call 'les trentes glorieuses' and the Germans their 'wirtschaftswunder'—successive future generations in Europe are going to find life much tougher. When the US-based Pew Research Center asked people in thirty-nine countries whether they thought their children would enjoy better lives, they got a positive answer from only twenty-eight per cent of Germans, seventeen per cent of Britons, fourteen per cent of Italians, and in France only nine per cent. Americans were a bit more optimistic, with a third hopeful for their children's living standards, while in China eighty-two per cent believed in a more prosperous future, in Nigeria sixty-five per cent, and in India fifty-nine per cent.

The United States shares many of Europe's problems of adapting its comfortable twentieth century lifestyle to the rigours and uncertainties of tomorrow. But it has one major advantage; a growing population fuelled by immigration and also by higher fertility rates among its immigrant communities. The early twenty-first century US population of 300 million is expected to reach 400 million by around 2050, even though there are new concerns that stricter immigration rules mean the workforce may not be expanding as fast as had been hoped. Another plus that America has, and that Europeans have yet to wake up to, is the huge economic contribution of its highly educated immigrants. Half of the exciting start-up ventures in California's Silicon Valley since 1995 have been founded by immigrants; the foreign-born engineers and scientists who stay on after graduating from American universities are now thought to account for half the country's high-tech PhDs.

Far from emulating the US, Europe has been contributing its own scientists to America's talent pool. Every year, says Manjula Luthria, who heads the World Bank's international mobility programme,

1.7 million highly educated Europeans move to the US, but only 200,000 comparable Americans head the other way. And leaving them aside, the overall quality in economic terms of people who migrate to Europe is poor; less than a fifth have a secondary education or better. Even so, there quite simply aren't enough of them, and the OECD has warned for some time that from 2015 onwards the working age populations of EU countries will dwindle, with Germany's situation particularly worrying because by 2025 it's going to see its export-led industries hit by a shortfall of six million skilled workers.

It would take a determined political drive by EU governments to address these big structural problems, and there's little sign of European politicians having the courage to tell their voters that instead of limiting immigration they must increase it. The alternative, they should explain, is to lose more economic activity to other countries. If Europe won't bring the people to the jobs, then the jobs will move abroad to the people. And as the communications revolution lengthens its stride, these jobs won't just be industrial ones. Services that span medicine, law, architecture, accounting, and financial services will all be extremely mobile. In the United States, Princeton University economist Alan Blinder reckons that thirty per cent of American jobs are now potentially 'offshoreable'.

## Energy Will Determine Our Policy Options

People and their jobs will shape tomorrow's world, but it is energy that will determine many of the choices available to them. And here the crystal ball is cloudy and even very dark. The two big factors at play are, unsurprisingly, politics and technology. On the political side, oil-based energy prices are far too low and discourage the development of alternative energy sources. On the technology front, the shale gas revolution is opening up new vistas that could address the economic development needed to feed our exploding global population.

Measured in constant dollars, energy has been getting steadily cheaper since the start of Britain's coal-based Industrial Revolution.

Even when price hikes at the petrol pump or of heating bills were fairly frequent they failed to put a dent in that curve, with energy prices lower in real terms than thirty years ago. The danger for Europe is that popular opposition combined with energy's relative cheapness means there isn't a powerful enough incentive to develop shale energy with much vigour.

The shale revolution in North America has been dramatic and its implications inescapable. The US has become a major energy exporter, and is already looking forward to the much sharper competitive edge its industries will enjoy thanks to cheaper electricity generated by shale gas. And we may see similar developments in China, where geologists reckon that their country's potentially recoverable shale resources amount to twenty-five trillion cubic metres of gas—in other words about 200 years' worth at present consumption levels. The problem for China, and another reason Europeans are so reluctant to start 'fracking' for shale energy, is that the process pollutes large quantities of water. It's possible that new technology will some day be able to fix that, but not quickly enough. French scientists, for instance, are working on a method using electrical charges as an alternative to the hydraulic fracturing of shale rock.

Where shale gas may prove to be a game changer is in the transportation sector. Automobile industry forecasters are divided and uncertain about growth in demand for cars and commercial vehicles, with some arguing that urbanization is reducing travel needs. But even in the fairly short-term there's likely to be a sizeable jump in the present global market for eighty million new vehicles a year to around 110 million in 2020. That will mean a big rise in fuel needs, and that's where shale comes in.

When Royal Dutch Shell first unveiled its $19 billion 'gas-to-liquids' (GTL) plant in the Qatari desert outside Doha, the idea of treating gas chemically to produce clean diesel fuel was seen by sceptics as a spectacular feat of engineering but a commercial dead-end. GTL needed so much cheap gas that experts put it into much the same category as hydrogen-powered cars whose clean fuel is produced via processes involving fossil fuels. But if shale is going to be a plentiful source of cheaper gas, then GTL may yet come into its own.

Energy will be crucial to the way the world of 2050 will look. In Paris, International Energy Agency chief Fatih Birol has been warning that Europe is at a crossroads on its energy policies: 'energy can either be an engine of growth', he says, 'or a drag'. He fears that the outlook for Europe on developing shale energy is 'in the foreseeable future, bleak'. By 2035, electricity in America may cost forty per cent less than in Europe—and in China half as much.

For the developing world, it's possible that solar energy may transform peoples' lives, either through the massive industrialization of solar panels or through scientific breakthroughs that lie just around the corner. At the Massachusetts Institute of Technology (MIT) near Boston, American researchers believe they have found a way of concentrating the sun's rays to produce electricity. The device they've been working on is a suntrap made of thin sheets of heat-resistant tungsten and manufactured by the same photolithography used for computer chips.

A more industrial approach is the half billion-dollar solar park that Gujarat province in India has built at Charanka. Its one million solar panels produce 200 megawatts of electricity, and although that's comparatively small, Indian experts say that potentially it offers an affordable answer to the country's daunting energy shortcomings. The Charanka project took only sixteen months to build and cost less per megawatt than a highly polluting coal-fired power station. By 2022, the Gujarat authorities plan to expand its capacity tenfold to 20,000 megawatts (enough to power something like thirty or even forty million homes), and see Charanka as a pilot for other parts of India where solar power at present accounts for only a few percentage points of the country's energy needs.

## The Wild Card is Future Technologies

This chapter began by making the distinction between projections and predictions—the extrapolation of measurable trends as opposed to outright guesswork. But the wild card that can reduce the work of the econometrists to the same level as fortune-tellers is technology.

So far, the information revolution and the electronic age haven't had that much of an impact on living standards. Not, at any rate, when measured against the way steam power and later the internal combustion engine changed the world. The age of coal produced steamships, railways, and mass manufacturing, and that of oil revolutionized road transport and created an era of air travel. For all the hype, the semiconductor has yet to do more than create greater efficiencies.

But that doesn't mean it won't, and it's possible that some major advances lie ahead that will do much to relandscape the global economy. As well as bio-sciences that can feed the world there are desalination methods that could make water shortages a problem of the past and open up new solutions to global warming. If shale and new energy-efficient technologies can bring energy costs to levels that are affordable for the poorest countries, then that would open the way to their industrial development in a manner that aid programmes have never aspired to.

Then there are the information and communication technologies that are beginning to transform the business environments of poorer countries. East Africa has seen the rapid changes made possible by the M-Pesa money transfer system for mobile phones. Farmers and merchants in rural Kenya can use this Safaricom service to conduct business that previously involved long journeys and complicated arrangements. And the spread of the Internet is also capable of transforming education right around the world; Swedish telecoms giant Ericsson reckons that by 2017 there will be twenty-one times as much data traffic on mobile phones as five years earlier, and that the number of smartphones in use will have jumped fivefold to five billion. In the US, Cisco is forecasting that by 2020 there will be fifty billion electronic devices linked by the Internet.

Another technology that has the potential to revolutionize the economies of rich and poor countries alike is 3D printing. At one end of the scale, layering techniques based on Internet-borne information transfers can use advanced metals and materials to construct sophisticated machinery faster and cheaper than with conventional means. China's civil aviation bid to catch up with Boeing and Airbus is using 3D printing to make complex aircraft parts, and Chinese experts say they can now produce a prototype car engine in less than a fortnight instead of several months. At the other end of the 3D scale, small printers that use powdered plastics cost as little as $500 and can turn out objects that previously needed lathes, milling machines, and cutting tools. The implications may be worrying for high-tech industries, but for people in poorer and less developed parts of the world they are very encouraging indeed.

What all these technological changes will mean for the years to mid-century no one can tell, but perhaps it helps to look back at where we've come from. Humankind tends to focus on looming problems, with all the doom and gloom that inevitably generates, so we should also count our blessings, as they too may point to the future.

In the quarter century since 1990, says the United Nations Development Programme (UNDP), forty of the world's poorest countries have seen substantial progress that goes far beyond simple GDP growth. Looking at health, education, and the overall well-being of people, the UNDP's Human Development Index shows South Korea at the top, followed by Iran, China, and Chile. It reflects the way that since 1980 there have been astonishing reductions in poverty levels; today less than a quarter of the global population has to survive on less than $1.25 a day, whereas in 1980 over half lived in such truly miserable conditions.

As to the rich countries, much as their people may bemoan the economic crisis and the West's smaller share of the global economy, the truth is that in the thirty years from 1980 to 2010, average disposable income in the United States rose by sixty per cent, and increases in Europeans' per capita incomes had until recently kept pace with those of Americans. Much is made by some commentators of the far-sightedness of German philosopher Oswald Spengler's century-old analysis in his book *The Decline of the West*, but so far it has chiefly been a warning against the perils of forecasting.

# 3

# Managing the New Global Economy

*Europe's Chance to Take Centre Stage*

*Pressure from the emerging economic giants for a new global rulebook is less a challenge to Europe than a great opportunity. The EU countries' voluntary pooling of so many powers could be a model for new consensus-based global governance mechanisms, but Europeans have yet to waken to this. Economic and monetary arrangements that suit the developing world as well as the richer countries will be vitally important, and Europe could lead on creating them. First, the European Union must seize the initiative.*

Globalization, we all know, is creating an ever-growing global economy, and that in turn will mean more global rules. So far, there's been little sign of an economic rulebook that can meet the conflicting demands of rich and poor countries, or of East and West. Yet the political elites of the world's 200 or so nations seem in growing agreement that only concerted action on an unprecedented scale can address the dangers of the twenty-first century. It's an area of particular interest for Europe, which needs to protect its own interests but can also claim to be the model for far-sighted cross-border cooperation.

Global governance is the shorthand term for a framework of common rules governing the ways people, governments, and companies interact and do business with one another. Although it's never likely to mean global government, it does add up to sovereign nations committing to policies fashioned elsewhere. For developing economies intent on access to the global marketplace, it will increasingly mean that they must accept a web of international standards and regulations.

There have been international agreements over the centuries on a wide range of issues, and these expanded dramatically in the wake of the Second World War. But they are now seen by many of the emerging economic powers as rules conceived by the industrialized Western nations that too often are to the disadvantage of developing countries.

That's not entirely true, because those rules kick-started the huge growth of international trade that is raising living standards around the world. Trade across frontiers and between continents has gone from almost zero in 1947, when the General Agreement on Tariffs and Trade (GATT) was born, to the present yearly level of over $18 trillion. But it's also fair to say that freer trade benefited the industrialized nations first and foremost, so Europe accounts for over a quarter of global trade in goods and services.

The need for a more coherent international rulebook has become a pressing concern of the richer countries since the near-meltdown of financial markets in 2008 and the ensuing worldwide economic slowdown. Until then, for the few people who thought about global governance at all, it meant little more than the distant concept of the Bretton Woods institutions—the World Bank and the International Monetary Fund.

Conceived in the summer of 1944 in a New Hampshire mountain resort hotel at Bretton Woods just after the Normandy beaches had been stormed, they were part of an Anglo-American vision for the post-war world agreed principally between famed British economist John Maynard Keynes and his US Treasury counterpart Harry Dexter White. The deal they struck served the new post-war era well by providing mechanisms for managing the international monetary system, introducing development policies, and creating wealth through freer trade.

But by the closing years of the twentieth century it had become clear these sexagenarian institutions and their rules were in dire need of rejuvenation; they were no longer suited to a world in which the North–South divide between rich and poor is being overtaken by the East–West relationship between the profligate debtor nations of the industrialized West and their creditors in thrusting Asia.

The IMF and the World Bank occupy imposing adjoining buildings just off Pennsylvania Avenue in Washington, DC, a short walk from the White House. Their physical location symbolizes their widely perceived roles as the instruments of the developed world—the head of the World Bank is always an American and the head of the IMF a European. For many years other countries have complained of Europe's glaring over-representation—for example, Belgium had a larger IMF voting share than India—and although there has been a slight rejigging of key jobs and votes, it hasn't been nearly enough to still resentments.

The answer will have to be sweeping reform and a new approach to global governance. That's easier said than done. Pascal Lamy, a former French EU commissioner who in 2013 stepped down after eight years at the head of GATT's successor, the World Trade Organization (WTO), sums up the problem neatly: 'Managing global problems by using traditional models of national democracy has important limitations. Yet the credibility of our national democracies is at risk if global governance fails to establish its own democratic credentials.'

Another WTO veteran, French economist Patrick Messerlin, points to the difficulty of persuading them that more global governance is in their interest. 'It is fashionable these days', he wrote in the Brussels-based policy journal *Europe's World*, 'to look to stricter international rules as "the solution", but that's not a strategy well suited to times like ours that are dominated by an ongoing shift of the tectonic plates in international economic relations. The combined emergence of new world powers with the diminishing influence of the current powers is not propitious for stricter disciplines'. He added that while they will not accept anything that looks like US or EU 'tutelage', 'they themselves are still far from being able to exert leadership or introduce more discipline'.

The question now is whether the World Bank and the IMF are a firm enough base to be built on, and whether the G20 (which group's emerging economic giants, together with the biggest industrialized countries) is a viable platform for adapting existing global governance structures and constructing new ones. Some politicians think it most definitely is not; in mid-2010, just as the G20 leaders were gathering in Toronto, Norway's then foreign minister Jonas Gahr Støre denounced it as 'one of the greatest setbacks in terms of international cooperation since World War II'. His point was that a small self-appointed group that excludes more than 170 of the world's nations will be incapable of resolving global problems.

## The Key Role Europe Could Yet Play

If Europe can get its act together internally, it could hold the key to new global governance mechanisms. Multilateralism and international cooperation are deeply engrained in Europe's political DNA, and the EU also has a strong motive to create improved global rules because the uncertainties of the eurozone crisis are calling into question the European Union's own structure and integrity. As Pedro Solbes, a former EU economic affairs commissioner and before that Spanish finance minister, puts it: 'We need to reshuffle the global governance system, and where we Europeans have a big advantage is that, despite EU bureaucracy, we've abandoned conflict and discovered consensus-building'.

Before getting on to Europe's role, it would be useful to look at what global governance can reasonably be expected to deliver. There are arguably three distinct elements, and therefore three phases. First, there's the firefighting job of trying to knit back together the potentially dangerous unravellings of the financial and trading aspects of globalization. Then there's the longer-haul task of updating existing global rules on trade, investment, banking, and intellectual property protection to accommodate the aspirations of the five BRICS nations—Brazil, Russia, India, China and South Africa—along with all the other emerging economies.

The third element is game-changing new developments, of which the bitcoin is a striking example and signpost to the future. Controversial and somewhat dodgy, the new digital crypto-currency seems to point to a digital economy over which individual governments will have far less control. Like the Internet itself, the bitcoin and its growing number of competitors raise uncomfortable questions about global supervision and regulation.

Right now, global regulation already has some very thorny problems to address. There are persistent worries that 'the Great Recession' that continues to grip many countries in the wake of the global economic crisis could yet trigger waves of protectionism that might lead to another 1930s-style Great Depression. These concerns have so far proved largely unfounded, not because politicians and diplomats have averted trade wars but because the global supply chains of so many multinational corporations mean those powerful lobbyists remain committed free-traders.

Free trade can't be taken for granted. The failure of the decade-long Doha Development Round of trade liberalization negotiations to deliver a deal is raising doubts about the future of the Geneva-based WTO. It took over from the post-war General Agreement on Tariffs and Trade—the GATT—in 1995, but Doha's lingering death has seen the goal of an ambitious multilateral deal giving way to bilateral trade pacts that threaten the WTO's existence and could open the way to future trade conflicts. The warning signals may already be visible; analysts at Global Trade Alert at the Swiss university of St Gallen say they have tracked tariff increases, export restrictions, and regulatory dodges hitting ten per cent of trade between G20 member countries despite all their pledges to refrain from protectionism. The WTO acknowledges the problem, but puts the figure at nearer four per cent.

Unless an acceptable new model for global governance can be found, there's a risk that the spirit of multilateralism that predominated for so many years and led to economic globalization will evaporate. In the United States, foreign policy analysts such as Princeton University's John Ikenberry are increasingly aware of the need for the post-Second World War institutions to be overhauled. 'Washington will need to envision a global governance system', he has commented, 'in which it will increasingly share authority and leadership with other states…America continues to have an overriding incentive to build and strengthen global rules and institutions'.

When it comes to firefighting, the most immediate global governance challenge is to calm the world's financial markets. The crisis that began on Wall Street in autumn 2008 was such a near-catastrophe that the search was initiated among G20 members for a more uniform global regulation of banks and financial institutions to ensure greater stability. The result so far has been a disastrous mess.

Regulators in the United States are at odds on key details with their UK counterparts, and the 'Anglo-Saxon' financial centres of New York and London are separated culturally and historically from those of continental Europe. The EU is itself divided internally between the eurozone 'ins' and 'outs', but has very different priorities and concerns to those of Asia's booming markets, especially Hong Kong and Singapore. The situation was summed up by a former UK regulator, Jon Pain, when he told the *Financial Times*: 'There is a mismatch between the brave G20 announcements of global solutions and the messy practicalities of national authorities scrambling to protect their own national interests'.

The gap between the G20's ambitions and its achievements has been widening. G20 leaders have repeatedly committed to reforms aimed at forcing private derivatives (in essence bets on rates and prices) into 'clearing houses' to make them easier to monitor, but with negligible results. The volatile 'shadow banking' sector made up of hedge funds, money market funds, and what are euphemistically known as 'special purpose vehicles' or SPVs, is the fastest growing sector of the whole financial services industry. Its pre-crisis peak of $50 trillion, around a quarter of global financial dealings, had by 2014 rocketed past the $70 trillion mark, warns G20's Financial Stability Board (FSB).

The G20 has been making a real if inadequate effort to introduce reforms that would stabilize the markets. It created the FSB in April 2009 to mastermind global reform, and since then it has raised capital charges and required 'living wills' from the thirty or so GSIFIs—global systemically important financial institutions—that would greatly soften the impact of any future collapse by one of them. An effort is also being made to stabilize the highly volatile $19 trillion over-the-counter trade in derivatives with a new set of global standards drawn up by an American-led body called the Committee on Payment and Settlement Systems.

Bankers warn that the G20 reform effort is being undermined by G20 members' own uncoordinated and sometimes contradictory actions. Around the world, 'regulatory announcements' by various authorities concerned with financial services have been running at around sixty a day. They are made up of the many tentacles of the Dodd-Frank Act in the US as it reaches into almost every aspect of financial transactions there, the Volcker Rule that aims to stop retail banks from gambling with depositors' funds, the EU's planned 'Emir' (European Market Infrastructure Regulation) on derivatives, and both its Alternative Investment Fund Managers' Directive (AIFMD) on hedge funds, and its Solvency II insurance rules, to say nothing of the more global Basel III package of global capital adequacy rules created under the auspices of the Basel-based Bank for International Settlements.

Just as worrying are the disagreements within the EU itself, because financial markets reform is inextricably linked with the twists and turns of the eurozone crisis. The European Banking Authority set up to rebuild confidence in the eurozone's commercial banks quickly found itself being undercut by national regulators in Germany, France, and Spain who moved to create new standards for their own banks.

The European Commission has been trying to prevent individual EU member states from creating chaos by imposing their own tougher standards, but non-eurozone countries such as the UK and Sweden have been joining the fray to rally support against the commission's efforts.

The EU is certainly not finding regulatory and supervisory reform easy. The European Securities and Markets Authority set up in 2011 to regulate the rating agencies has been accused of creating confusion with its decision that ratings from agencies in the US, Hong Kong, and Singapore can be used in EU financial markets. Although this appears a laudable step towards the greater internationalization of regulation, it has come under fire because the move is said to impose a heavier administrative burden on the banks.

The EU's efforts are at the same time being criticized for falling short of Europe's own needs. The many calls by industry spokespersons and others for an EU-wide deposit guarantee scheme as the best way to support the development of cross-border banking have not been taken up by the commission, and deposit guarantee arrangements will therefore stay in the hands of individual member states.

The EU banking union agreed between European governments in early 2014 is a major though incomplete step towards making banks less vulnerable. But sadly its creation of a powerful new agency called the Single Resolution Board that can wind up or restructure big banks that look like failing is an EU-centric reform. Europe's banking union concept could, say its proponents, have been a cornerstone for a wider global structure. Instead, the US, the continental EU countries, and the UK are each pushing ahead with their own reform measures, while accusing one another of watering down or delaying bank capital adequacy measures. The US is particularly reproached, with Tokyo, Ottawa, and London all warning that their own sovereign bond markets are increasingly under threat from the impact of new US rules limiting banks' risks.

It's not just the way these rules compete with one another and impose expensive administrative burdens that is raising concerns around the world; it's the way the US and EU regulators insist on extraterritoriality—the application of their rules internationally—that financial operators elsewhere, and in Asia particularly, find increasingly annoying.

## It's True; Only Global Solutions Will Do

The longer-term case for improved global governance mechanisms extends much further than tougher rules on financial services and transactions. From global warming to cyber-security, from intellectual property protection to the free movement of goods, services, and people, most countries need a framework of clearer rules. And it would be wrong to believe that the Western nations are the supporters of more virtuous liberalization measures and that the emerging economies are not. Patrick Messerlin, an economics professor at Sciences Po in Paris, points out that 'China's trade liberalization has done more to convince the other developing countries of the gains from trade than all the OECD countries' exhortations. China has undertaken over the last 20 years a liberalization process it took 40 years for the US and Europe to do.'

Beijing has long been accused of allowing if not encouraging Chinese companies to steal the technologies of foreign investors, but now China is actively seeking an improved global system of patent and copyright protection. It has overtaken the US and Japan to top the list of applicants for international patents, and files almost half a million international patent applications a year, against America's 400,000 or so.

In just about every area of economic activity, Asian policymakers are aware that their interests lie in cooperation rather than in head-to-head competition because their low wage advantage is being so rapidly eroded by pay increases. Issues such as climate change remain divisive because the newly industrializing countries have very different views on what constitutes fair burden-sharing, but by and large the emerging markets know how essential it is to rethink the global rulebook on trade, investment, technology transfers, and, of course, finance and monetary policies.

Their problem is to agree amongst themselves on what they want from a redrawing of these international rules, and how to ensure that they exert their collective strength in the face of European and American opposition. France's former foreign minister Hubert Védrine points out that the lack of unity amongst the five BRICS countries means it could be up to the Europeans to manage the reorganization of global governance.

The BRICS countries may indeed have very different development needs, but Asian nations are uniting around their shared problem of inadequate infrastructure ranging from transport links to telecommunications. The announcement in Shanghai in late 2014 of the Chinese-inspired Asian Infrastructure Investment Bank, the AIIB, has seen twenty-seven governments ranging from Jordan and Saudi Arabia in the West throughout the Far East to Australia and New Zealand flocking to join. With a starting capital of $50 billion, it is designed to compensate for the shortcomings of the World Bank, which Beijing sees as excessively dominated by the US. The infant AIIB has also had the effect of driving a wedge between America and Europe, for the UK's decision to join, while hotly criticized by Washington, was nevertheless soon followed by membership applications from Germany, France, and Italy. In all, fifty-seven countries are now AIIB members.

Such divisions characterize the industrialized and industrializing camps alike. The ten countries in the Association of Southeast Asian Nations (ASEAN) may have failed to reach common positions on many key questions, but the nations of the OECD 'rich man's club' cannot be said to have a shared agenda themselves. The US political elite continues to be embroiled in a debate about whether as the sole superpower it whole-heartedly embraces multilateralism, and the EU will for the foreseeable future remain caught in a chronic eurozone crisis that isn't just about sovereign debt but increasingly about the union's future political and institutional architecture.

The BRICS nations' New Development Bank (NDB) based in Shanghai has got off to an impressive start, even if some analysts saw that launching it was the easy part and now it must deliver. The NDB is headed by an Indian chief executive, with a Russian chairing its board of governors, and a Brazilian leading its board of directors. It is a common lending institution for its five member nations with an initial $50 billion in capital and a planned $100 billion fund. The evident aim is to bypass the World Bank, but it is its wider significance that's the subject of much speculation; the BRICS bank could either help to strengthen the structures on which global governance can be built, or it could do much to destroy them.

When he was the World Bank's president, before stepping down in 2012, the American economist Robert Zoellick gave his backing to the idea of a BRICS bank, providing that it could be established within the framework of the World Bank group. But if it were to be outside, he warned that pushing middle-income countries such as China and Brazil out of the World Bank system 'would be a mistake of historic proportions'. In Europe, others such as Italian commentator Marta Dassù have seen the BRICS bank question more darkly still, saying it will mark the end of the Bretton Woods era and that the G20 will be unable to produce a new global order to replace it. 'The very notion of global order will become obsolete', she has warned. 'Variable geometry will be the rule, not the exception. And regionalism will prevail over global agreements.'

Westerners may worry that the BRICS are undermining hopes of a new consensus on global governance, but Asians have not forgotten what they saw as the IMF's high-handedness back in 1997–98 when many countries in the region were hit by a severe financial crisis and needed bail-outs. That resentment gave rise to calls for an 'Asian Monetary Fund', and in 2000 a meeting in Thailand's northern city of Chiang Mai saw the unveiling of the Chiang Mai Initiative (CMI), a bilateral currency swap arrangement led by the Asian Development Bank that grouped the ten-nation ASEAN bloc along with China, Japan, and South Korea. In 2010 it was beefed-up into a multilateral arrangement with a $120 billion fund, and two years later that amount was doubled.

In parallel with the setting up of the BRICS bank for funding development projects, the BRICS leaders have agreed a Contingent Reserve Arrangement (CRA) consisting of a $100 billion pool of foreign exchange reserves that once operational will offer standby credits to the BRICS countries themselves and probably to other developing countries, and will have no links with the IMF. Indian economist Kavaljit Singh working for an NGO called Madhyam explained the thinking shortly after agreement on the CRA was reached. 'In a western-dominated financial world', he said, 'the idea of a BRICS reserve fund looks very exciting and promising. In a post-crisis world full of financial risks and uncertainties, the reserve pool could potentially reshape the global financial architecture of the 21st century'.

On trade, much as the emerging economic powers are aware of the benefits they derive from the boom in international commerce, they also feel that the West hasn't dealt fairly with them. When the WTO replaced the GATT in the mid-1990s it brought in new trade disciplines as well as liberalizations; these ranged from ways of banning non-tariff barriers such as special technical requirements or awkward customs procedures to ending subsidies. For developing countries striving to compete with the rich industrialized ones, the WTO rules could be particularly onerous. As Jeffrey Schott at the Peterson Institute for International Economics in Washington, DC, put it, 'the WTO milestone became a millstone' around the necks of poorer nations.

The EU, meanwhile, complains that it, too, suffers unfair treatment, saying that many of its trading partners operate restrictive government procurement methods that discriminate against European companies when they bid for public contracts. When he was the European commissioner for the EU's internal market, French politician Michel Barnier spoke bluntly of Brussels's demands for greater transparency when EU bidders lost out to suspiciously low local offers: 'The EU should no longer be naive', he said, 'and should aim for fairness and reciprocity in world trade'.

Many of these conflicting perceptions of fairness came to a head in the Doha Round, and help to explain its failure. Developing countries demanded payback for earlier concessions they had made in the Uruguay Round of trade negotiations that concluded in 1994 and marked the end of the GATT era. They believed that they'd been given a raw deal on subsidies, intellectual property protection, employment and labour laws, environmental standards and, above all, on their openness to services ranging from banking to civil aviation. They dislike the WTO's legal architecture and its mechanisms for settling disputes, believing these favour the richer trading nations.

## Pinning Hopes on the G20

In the face of all these pressures, the questions about the value of the G20 have been multiplying. Is it capable of delivering the goods on global governance? Should it be beefed-up through the creation of a permanent secretariat instead of the present system of rotating presidencies? Or is it already dying from a fatal mixture of neglect and disagreement?

The G20 is a strange hybrid beast. It sprang to prominence in the autumn of 2008 as the forum for rescuing the world from financial collapse, but its birth dates back long before, to 1999. The idea came from Canada, because at that time Ottawa saw the need for a much wider grouping than the G7 of the world's richest nations so as to include the rising economic powers. The G20—which in fact numbers nineteen countries plus the EU—was for almost a decade a low-profile consultative body on technical financial matters, attended by finance ministers rather than heads of government, and viewed by many as no more than a sop to the emerging markets' ambitions for a seat at the top table.

The Washington G20 summit in late 2008, and that in London a few months later, did much to calm global panic and establish the G20's authority. A good deal of the credit for the actions that restored relative calm in the financial markets belongs to the then UK prime minister Gordon Brown and his fellow G7 leaders. But since then the

G20 has seemed to be running out of steam even though the world economy's systemic ills are as serious as ever.

Spain's former prime minister José Maria Aznar says: 'When it comes to global governance, the international system doesn't work. The G8 (the G7 plus Russia) is no longer relevant, but the G20 has no capacity for setting common goals'. It has also been derided as lacking legitimacy. When Norway's Jonas Gahr Støre called it 'the greatest setback for the international community since World War 2', he added: 'We no longer live in the 19th century, a time when the major powers met and redrew the map of the world. No one needs a new Congress of Vienna'.

Others disagree and think that is precisely what's needed. The creation of a permanent secretariat that would manage the G20 agenda in a much more organized manner was first proposed by Nicolas Sarkozy when still France's president. It foundered for a variety of reasons, many of them symptomatic of the jealousies and rivalries that beset the whole notion of global governance. Gordon Brown remains to this day deeply sceptical of the creation of another international bureaucracy, and countries as different as Japan and Italy have formally blocked the idea. But China and Brazil favour it, and South Korea has put forward an original and technologically advanced suggestion for a virtual secretariat that would not be based physically in any of the G20 members' national capitals but would operate in cyberspace.

Politically, the more interesting question would, in any case, seem to be how a G20 secretariat would be manned and what its mandate might be. The present system of revolving group presidencies and only an annual summit meeting is quite evidently failing to maintain the G20's earlier momentum, with the result that it is regressing back towards its original and uncontroversial technical character. Yet with so much frustration among the emerging nations over the way the Americans and Europeans still dominate the Bretton Woods institutions, choosing a G20 secretary-general from one of the BRICS would do much to allay that discontent. It would also create a mechanism for encouraging the emerging economic powers to define exactly what they believe the new global rulebook should contain.

## The Transatlantic Dimension

Where do the United States and the European Union stand in the search for global governance mechanisms capable of addressing twenty-first century challenges? Neither of them is in anything that looks like a leadership stance. Washington has seemed preoccupied with its 'pivot to Asia' strategy and hasn't wanted to address the issue. The US foreign policy community of diplomats, think tankers, and so on seems in little doubt that America needs to think carefully about its own vulnerabilities in the global economy, not least because upwards of forty cents in every dollar spent by the federal government at present has to be borrowed from abroad. Almost half of its debt is held by foreign investors, notably in China and Japan.

The eurozone crisis has underlined the US dollar's unassailable position as the world's main reserve and trading currency, but that isn't quieting growing fears that America's runaway debt problem means it will in future have to dance to the tune of its Asian creditors. The sheer scale of US debt is breathtaking; the tax cuts introduced a decade ago by George W. Bush's administration will have reduced revenues by $2 trillion over ten years, while the Iraq and Afghanistan wars have cost another $2 trillion. On a GDP of roughly $17 trillion a year, the US government deficit is now running at about ten per cent of that, so by 2020 its cumulative deficit could top $9.5 trillion.

Back in the late 1990s, Bill Clinton's administration ran a healthy surplus equivalent to one per cent of America's GDP, but since then federal spending has surged to two and a half times the rate of the 1990s, and the post-2020 scenarios for the country's economy are being described as 'truly apocalyptic'. And because the US Treasury has to refinance maturing debt as well as cover its current deficit, its borrowings are set to run not at a yearly $1 trillion-plus but at a staggering $5 trillion.

The US economic outlook is the subject of admiration and much debate. Thanks in part to the fillip of shale gas and tight oil, America's impressive resilience saw it bounce back from deep economic recession while most European countries have remained stuck in the doldrums. Slowly but surely, though, the effects of globalization and surging Asian growth across the Pacific are making Washington's policymakers more reliant on international cooperation. At the same time, the US is seen as less generous and imaginative than before in its dealings with the outside world. A good deal of the blame for the collapse of the Doha Round is being laid at the door of American 'rejectionism', and that together with its obduracy on climate change issues may be just a foretaste of US behaviour in the years ahead.

Europe is itself in no better shape to exert leadership on global governance. The EU should be a shining example of how to reconcile competing national interests and forge collective policies to the benefit of all, and that was certainly its narrative until it was engulfed by the crisis over the euro. Now, the growing unpopularity of the EU and even of European integration has become a major obstacle to safeguarding the single currency and reforming EU decision-making, and also to finding a way forward on global governance.

'We Europeans need a strategic agreement with the US on handling the BRICS', says Hubert Védrine, and ironically that's what Beijing and other emerging economic giants believe is the hidden agenda of the ambitious Transatlantic Trade and Investment Partnership (TTIP) that American and EU officials have been putting together. It's an attempt to clear away as many of the barriers and legal obstacles that still limit economic cooperation across the Atlantic, issues on which both sides have long agreed to disagree. The notion that Washington and Brussels are using TTIP to cook up a common position on global governance reform is somewhat flattering, for so far there's been little sign of such far-sightedness.

Europe's internal squabbles and the lack of a wider vision on the part of the EU's national leaders are such that Europe has not advanced at all on global governance issues. It hasn't proposed a strategy and has not even begun to draw on the expertise of the commission's specialist directorates-general to put together a detailed plan. The EU is missing a great opportunity to recover much of its lost credibility and prestige. The challenges that call for greater global governance are the very problems that the EU institutions have long been grappling with, and where Europe has earned international respect.

Europe has led the world on development aid and in trying to organize concerted responses to the planet's environmental problems. That should leave Europeans well positioned to exert fresh leadership in the key areas of infrastructural investment and resource management, both of which are integral parts of the global governance question. Yet to date there's been little sign of this.

It would be hard to overstate the importance of adjusting Europe's mindset on future relations with Asian and African countries. Europeans need to focus on sharing the fruits of rapid growth there instead of seeing threats. The EU's political focus is inward-looking, yet the key to recovering public support for the European project is quite obviously external. The length and breadth of the EU, we Europeans know in our hearts that no single European nation is big enough or rich enough to influence the global agenda, and that the tide has begun to run strongly against us. Europe made itself a globally admired model for international cooperation, and now it's time for the EU's policymaking elite to put forward a more global vision of that.

## European Voices: Cacophony not Chorus

Opinion on what an EU-backed global governance agenda should look like is divided. When the policy journal *Europe's World* questioned a panel of twenty-six prominent politicians and policy analysts, it found substantial disagreement on the reform steps that should be taken. On the plus side, an overwhelming majority of twenty-one of them favoured radical reform of the IMF, seventeen backed changes at the WTO, and nineteen called for reform of the UN Security Council.

But when it came to other institutions, notably the chief UN agencies, there was little consensus.

Ideas such as an International Climate Change Agency or a Carbon Tax Global Coordination Authority were voted on, with the former receiving substantial (seventy-nine per cent) support and the latter a good deal less (fifty-eight per cent). The suggestion for an International Financial Derivatives and Hedge Funds Authority seemed attractive (sixty-two per cent) but notable amongst those opposing it were a serving EU commissioner and a former finance minister, both of whom were perhaps led by personal experience to doubt its viability.

One idea that hasn't received the attention it deserves is to establish an international statistical agency—WorldStat—to make sense of the welter of confusing and at times contradictory national statistics that handicap international discussions. From trade to climate change to bank failures, negotiators know that a major bugbear is the absence of readily acceptable statistics that prevents them from cutting to the chase and clinching a deal.

Suggestions for such innovative mechanisms to smooth the path towards global governance are few and far between. More plentiful are criticisms of what isn't being achieved, especially by the EU and its member governments. Pedro Solbes, who is now president of the Madrid think tank FRIDE, sees little evidence of a more coherent and forward-looking approach by the EU to the new forms of global governance that G20 leaders committed themselves to. 'The comparatively large number of European countries in the G20 serves little purpose in the absence of systematic coordination', he says, adding that 'there also appears to be little deep reflection over what should be the long-term global role of the IMF. This body still lacks legitimacy yet is being mandated with powerful new surveillance functions by the G20'.

The reason for Europe's inability to seize the initiative on global governance isn't hard to find. The largest EU countries want to retain their voice in international affairs. Politicians, diplomats, and even business leaders in Britain, France, and Germany, and a handful of smaller countries do not wish to hand the reins over to Brussels's unelected Eurocrats. It's a deadlock that reflects the short-sightedness of EU governments, but also EU officialdom's lack of imagination and charisma.

There's still room for imaginative thinking; the need for greatly improved global governance rules and structures will not go away. In France, Pascal Lamy has suggested a longer-term approach that would involved the G20 and the international agencies such as the IMF and World Bank 'reporting to the "parliament" of the United Nations'. He believes a revamping of the UN's Economic and Social Council would be a step in that direction, and that in time the development of the G20 could provide an answer to the knotty and long standing problem of reforming the UN Security Council.

The eastward shift of the world's economic activity is sure to be accompanied sooner or later by some sort of political and security upheaval. That certainty has made little impact on the thinking of Western leaderships and the political elites. The question we are so reluctant to address is whether it's better to meet change halfway, or to wait to be engulfed by it.

# 4

# Europe Need Not Fear Asia's Rise

*In what's billed as the Asian century, Europe and America are suspicious and resentful of the success and growing assertiveness of Asia's 'tigers'. The answer isn't to contest or try to block their growth, but rather for Europeans to engage more closely with their Asian competitors. This will demand courageous political leadership at national and EU levels, and so far that's been signally absent.*

The single-mindedness of Asian countries determined to catch up with Western living standards attracts admiration and unease. That shouldn't prevent Europeans from remembering the old adage 'if you can't beat them, join 'em'.

A glimpse on an empty pre-dawn Vietnamese highway in the mid-1990s captured the spirit of that war-torn country's disciplined approach to carving out a better future. Travelling south from the ancient Annamese capital of Hue at 5 am, the car's headlights picked out the rhythmic cadence of a crocodile column of small children in white and blue sailor-suit uniforms heading to school. That generation of early-rising high achievers is today fuelling Vietnam's impressive growth.

Asia's rise doesn't automatically mean the decline of Europe and America; the world economy isn't a cake that has to be cut into smaller pieces to accommodate newcomers to the feast. Or if it is a cake, it's one that grows with every baking and can offer bigger slices and new opportunities for all.

The coming thirty or so years should be seen in their historical perspective. In 1750, Asia accounted for more than half the world's wealth, even though this was during Europe's 'Age of Enlightenment' when its cultural and political influence was reaching out around the world. In terms of economic output and population, Asia easily outpaced Europe, and had done so for centuries. China began making steel during the Han dynasty (200 BC to AD 200), and the king of what is now the Punjab is said to have presented the briefly conquering Alexander the Great with a sword of finest steel yet undreamt of in Europe.

But the mid-eighteenth century marked the rise of Europe's nation states, the development of trade links that were to become colonial chains, and the onset of Europe's Industrial Revolution. By the late nineteenth century, Asia's share of the global economy was to fall to around twenty per cent.

That's more or less where it stands today; at the end of the first decade of this century Asia's share of the global economy was 22.5 per cent and Europe's was thirty-four per cent. By 2050 the tables will have been well and truly turned, with Europe's share projected to fall to only eighteen per cent and that of Asia rising to fifty-four per cent. Three centuries of Western economic hegemony will have been just a blip.

The question that Europeans and Americans have to address is how to make sure their own living standards are not diminished by Asia's rise. Theirs will, after all, be only a relative decline. It has become commonplace to speak of the 'Asian century', as if that signals the eclipse of the West, but it's not going to be a zero-sum game in which the advantage of one part of the world is at the expense of the others. Asia's rise in a globalized economy will be a far more complex process than that, requiring big changes in Western thinking and the abandonment of cultural and racial prejudices.

Explaining this to European voters and their elected politicians is going to be tough. The mistaken idea that countries compete in the same way as companies is deeply rooted, so it will require progressive thinking and greatly improved communication to persuade people in

Europe that resenting Asia's rise, or even trying to resist it, is fruitless and self-defeating. Europe's strategy must be to cooperate so closely with Asian businesses that their success will be Europe's too.

This is going to demand a mindset change of monumental proportions. In his perceptive 2010 book *Why the West Rules–For Now*, American historian Ian Morris advanced persuasive reasons why Western civilization overtook both Asia and the Arab world in spite of the early technological head-start enjoyed by both. Morris sees 2103 as the year when Asia will once again be the undisputed top dog.

But does this picture of the rise and fall of continents really hold true for the globalized world of the twenty-first century? It seems more likely that we stand on the threshold of an international economy that will not have the same characteristics as today. The interdependence of national economies has been underlined by the global economic crisis and the submerging of national identities is a growing feature of the corporate world. Household names such as US automobile maker General Motors or Britain's BP energy giant are still seen as national champions, but in fact are increasingly multinational.

The multinational corporations, which since the Second World War established subsidiaries and operations around the world while retaining their national identities and headquarters, are changing. The multinational of the twenty-first century is becoming just that—a business that must answer to many different governments, whose executives are drawn from as many countries as its factory payrolls, and which raises the finance for its investment programmes on international capital markets that are linked around the world and around the clock. And it's going to be an increasingly digital global economy, with Asians already proving very adept at digital innovation.

The coming changes are going to relandscape the world we know. Forecasts that the global economy will almost double its present $70 trillion to top $120 trillion by 2020, with seventy per cent of that growth in the emerging economies, may even prove overly conservative. Some estimates are bolder still; researchers at Credit Suisse looking at global wealth as distinct from economic output, said in 2013 that they 'expect global wealth to rise by nearly 40 per cent over the next five years, reaching $334 trillion by 2018'. The European Commission's 'Global Europe 2050' report looks further ahead to mid-century and sees a sixfold increase in the world economy by 2050.

As the world's population expands, with economic growth powered by the many young people in Asia and Africa who'll be joining the workforce, Europe's relative shrinkage will be impossible to ignore. Javier Solana, who was the EU's first foreign policy chief, believes that in each decade up to mid-century one of the four European countries presently on the list of the ten biggest and most powerful economies will drop from it. Germany will be the last to go, he says, but by 2050 the major newcomer economies will all be larger than any single one within the EU.

What we don't know, of course, is how the living standards of Europeans will be affected by this shift. Can Europeans, with their expensive social security systems and growing shortages of highly skilled workers, hang on to their comparatively rich lifestyles?

What we *do* know is that Asian countries are determined to improve the lot of their own peoples. The last quarter century has seen them accept the need to tighten their belts and constrain consumer spending so as to invest in education and technical skills. They have boldly executed growth strategies and breathtaking industrialization programmes. The result has been to transform the once sleepy economic backwaters of Asia into a region that is becoming more vibrant and self-confident by the day.

## Asia's Patchy Growth Outlook

However, it is a very patchy development picture. Asia's impressive high-rise cities are generally ringed by noisome slums and shantytowns. This picture is characteristic of many parts of Asia and a reminder that Asia's political and business leaders have daunting development problems to tackle. Economic growth in Asian countries is counted in impressive billions of dollars, but their infrastructural needs rank in the trillions. And funding won't be easy given the under-development of Asia's financial markets; only fifty-five per cent of Asian adults have a bank account and in south Asia that drops to a third.

The sheer scale of Asian infrastructural planning can nevertheless be breathtaking; the city-state of Singapore is to move its huge port area, the world's second busiest, fifteen miles westwards from its present situation next to the high-rise business district. It is a project no European government would contemplate nowadays, but in Asia the need to think ahead and think big raises few eyebrows.

At the same time, the patchiness of development in Asia is a constant reminder of the region's huge challenges. A short hydrofoil ride from Singapore across the Straits of Malacca to Sumatra and the archipelago of Indonesian islands takes the traveller back half a century in time; to teeming Asia with narrow traffic-choked streets, buzzing hordes of motor bikes and scooters, and the heady mix of energy, optimism, and pervasive poverty. The same can be found a short distance from almost any Asian city centre, be it Kuala Lumpur, Bangkok, Manila, or Jakarta.

India's future will be as crucial to Asia's development as that of China, and perhaps more so. It has the brains and the people to become a dynamo for much of Asia. The average Indian family's income has doubled in the twenty or so years since a host of restrictive business regulations were swept away, and the country's growing population, always an economic driver, is due to overtake that of China. India's ambition is to create a hundred million new industrial jobs by 2022, boosting manufacturing's share of the economy to a quarter from its present level of around sixteen per cent.

Standing in the way is the woefully inadequate state of India's infrastructure. Until that is addressed it's hard to see those ambitions being realized. The contrast between new India and old is encapsulated in New Delhi's satellite city of Gurgaon twenty miles south of the capital. Not far from the international airport, Gurgaon's skyscraper office blocks and hotels are host to a rapidly expanding core of Indian and foreign corporate headquarters. A fast highway, much of it carried on soaring overpasses, links Gurgaon's thriving business hub with the wide avenues of New Delhi that recall the British Raj's imperial grandeur. But Gurgaon is also where the motorway abruptly ends. A mile or two beyond its toll booths the four-lane highway narrows to a pot-holed road, and the vista of attractive modern buildings gives way to ramshackle single-storey workshops served by open sewers. Modern, go-getting India becomes timeless, backward India.

The Asian Development Bank (ADB) puts India's immediate infrastructure needs up to 2020 at a minimum of $1 trillion. And it's obvious that if it is to do more than scratch the surface of its deeply ingrained rural and urban poverty, India must industrialize much faster and more widely. The advanced software strengths of Bangalore and the business verve of Mumbai need to generate manufacturing investment, and that means a revolution in India's nineteenth century road and rail networks.

These are not insuperable difficulties for India or for the rest of Asia, even if the ADB reckons that by 2020 Asia as a whole needs to have ploughed $8 trillion into improved infrastructure. Asian governments understand very well that to sustain their enviable rates of growth they must make a more determined assault on their infrastructural shortcomings. That is why they have unhesitatingly backed China's idea of an Asian Infrastructure Investment Bank that will help fund new projects in the region.

Attracting investment funds to Asian countries is becoming easier, thanks in part to the global economic crisis and the eurozone's difficulties. Previously, there had been a considerable gap between the credit ratings of the emerging markets and those enjoyed by the developed economies; but reviews by Moody's and other leading ratings agencies in 2011 and again in 2013 saw the downgrading of twenty-nine countries, including the US, the UK, France, Spain, and Italy, and the upgrading of twelve others, notably China and some other Asian borrowers.

The economic slowdown in Europe and America helped to push funds towards Asia's bond markets, making it easier for big projects such as deep-water ports and new business parks to attract financing. There are fears, though, that the influx of money from outside Asia could create a credit bubble similar to that of the mid-1990s when the Asian 'tiger economies' spectacularly overheated and boom turned overnight into bust. The bursting of that bubble led to the Asian financial crisis of 1997–98 that brought economic activity in much of the region to a near-standstill.

Asians are understandably wary of a rerun of that scenario, but this time there are grounds for believing that the region is much more robust. Deep-seated reforms were implemented in most countries and generally the picture looks bright. Two blips on the radar screen are rising levels of private debt and insufficient investment in domestic infrastructure. Many Asian households have been on spending sprees, buying cars and property, so consumer indebtedness is increasingly a cause for concern. The other worry is that cash-rich Asia should be doing more to funnel investment funds away from foreign capital markets and into the infrastructural projects at home that are badly needed as well as being comparatively safe.

China's expanding financial services sector is looked to by investment-hungry Asian entrepreneurs as a major source of funding, with the China Development Bank and the Export-Import Bank of China seen as key players in Asia's infrastructural development. Some cautious voices warn, however, that China's financial services sector has been developing at an extraordinarily rapid rate, and may risk going from boom to bust. Over the five years from 2008–13, reported the *Financial Times*, China created new credit roughly equivalent to the entire US banking system.

## Asia's Bargain Hunters are Investing Worldwide

The temptation for Asian investors of all shapes and sizes has been to go for the easier pickings in Western countries that resulted from the global crisis. Of 800 big Asian companies surveyed by the Florida-based group FTI Consulting, whose global affairs chairman is Mark

Malloch-Brown, a former head of the United Nations Development Programme (UNDP), forty-five per cent of them were planning to buy up companies in Europe because the eurozone crisis has meant cheap assets for sale. In the UK, the Chinese government's $400 billion-plus sovereign wealth fund, the China Investment Corporation, made headlines and created a political stir when it bought a large stake in Thames Water, a major utility serving the greater London area.

So far then, Asian investors have generally ignored the calls that they should first concentrate on their own countries' infrastructural projects. Three-quarters of all the big deals in Asia are in the mining and resource extraction sector, according to the accounting firm Ernst & Young. And the trend is towards more and more investment in business ventures outside Asia, especially by Chinese companies. Their spending on stakes in European businesses has been growing by roughly twenty per cent year-on-year, and these range from the sale of Sweden's Volvo car company to China's Geely brand to much smaller deals in the high-tech or specialist services sectors. In almost two-thirds of these, Chinese buyers have settled for a minority stake.

The formerly communist countries of central and eastern Europe that are the EU's newcomers seem particularly attractive. In 2005, total Chinese investment in them amounted to only $66 million, and now it's running at close to a billion dollars a year. In Bulgaria another leading Chinese automotive group, Great Wall Motors, is investing $100 million in a plant that will produce SUVs, in Poland road machinery producer Liu Gong is spending about the same on a new factory, and Hungary has succeeded in attracting a third of all the Chinese investment spending in its region.

Not just Chinese companies are bargain-hunting in Europe. In Seoul, Jun Kwang-Woo, the chairman of South Korea's National Pension Service—the world's fourth largest—comments: 'As a long-term investor, we look for interesting opportunities coming out of this ongoing turmoil in Europe'.

These investments by Chinese and other Asian companies inevitably raise hackles in Europe and America. As well as being a reversal of the long standing business pattern that has seen Western money and power flow eastwards, they are seen as attempts to 'steal' technology. They should instead be welcomed because they bind the West's Asian competitors firmly into the global economy.

The more inter-investment there is around the world, the less likely are conflicts that might jeopardize those assets. From a purely security viewpoint, the more cross-border investment between Asian countries the better, because that will reduce the chances of military confrontation between them. And from a European or American standpoint, there will clearly be great advantages in being embedded ever more deeply in the fast-growing Asian economy.

It isn't just Asia's increasing share of manufacturing output that Western companies should be thinking about. When it comes to technology, the popular myth of Asians as the followers and copiers of US and European innovations no longer fits the facts. In key parts of the information technology sector, Asian companies are drawing ahead.

China's Huawei is the shining example; in the space of thirty years it has come from nowhere to overtake Sweden's Ericsson as the world's biggest manufacturer of telecoms switchgear equipment. Founded in 1983 by engineer Ren Zhengfai who had been employed by the People's Liberation Army, today it has yearly sales of $32 billion to 140 countries worldwide and employs 150,000 people, almost half of whom are engaged on research and development work. And in contrast to China's many state-owned enterprises, it has a distinctly capitalistic feel to it; its chief financial officer, Cathy Meng, is Ren Zhengfai's daughter, and thanks to the employee stock-option plan that Huawei introduced in 1997, more than half of its workforce are shareholders.

## Feeling the Hot Breath of Asia's R&D Spending

The Huawei story says much of China's industrial rise and of its ambitions for the future. Mr Ren had been 'let go' at a time of cutbacks in the Chinese military and decided to set up his own small company in Shenzhen, the development zone established by the Chinese authorities close to Hong Kong. With his $5,000 capital investment he sold second-hand telephone-exchange equipment to Chinese buyers that he had imported from Hong Kong. By the late 1980s he had moved on to begin developing his own digital switchgear. Huawei has since launched a consumer electronics range that includes smartphones and tablets, and in the words of the *Financial Times* it 'is no longer a cheap copycat'.

That's also the view of managers who run Europe's leading companies; they fear that within ten years they will have fallen behind China in the innovation race. When 500 of Europe's top business executives were surveyed by the Accenture accounting and consultancy firm, two-thirds said that Europe now risks losing its competitive advantage in the development of new technologies by as soon as 2023. The study was conducted on behalf of the EU-wide employers' organization BusinessEurope, and found widespread concern and alarm in boardrooms. As well as a growing innovation deficit, these business leaders pointed to skills shortages, with more than half saying that Europe's industrial workforce no longer represents a competitive advantage.

The relationship between Beijing and Chinese corporations such as Huawei or other big high-technology groups such as ZTE, one of the world's largest mobile phone producers, seems somewhat opaque to Western eyes. In Brussels, the European Commission's competition watchdog lawyers receive a steady stream of complaints from EU companies that state aid from Beijing in the form of subsidies and other types of financial support give the Chinese newcomer corporations an unfair advantage. In industrial sectors spanning microelectronics to solar energy and renewables, there are doubts that China's understanding of market economy disciplines is the same as that of the EU or the US. There's little doubt, too, that China uses its near-monopoly of rare earths and other scarce minerals as part of a wider long-term strategy that isn't just industrial but geopolitical.

Whatever Western companies may say, the advances made by their Chinese and other Asian competitors owe their success to much more than a friendly push from their governments. Nor is it just in manu-facturing and the high-tech sector that competition from China is making inroads into markets that have long been dominated by Western companies. Five of the world's ten biggest construction companies are now Chinese. In 2003 there wasn't a single Chinese name on that top ten list, and now those five companies have com-bined yearly sales of $300 billion and work on huge contracts in Moscow and New York and deliver turnkey projects such as a giant tourist complex in the Bahamas. Chinese companies, as the Japanese and Koreans before them, have shown energy and vision when setting out to conquer new markets.

Many of these Chinese competitors are rapidly becoming more like Western companies, thanks to rising labour costs and the pressures of the international marketplace. Wage costs in southern China are rising fast; when the London-based Standard Chartered Bank surveyed 200 manufacturers in the Pearl River delta, it found their wage costs had increased by ten per cent in a single year. In Guangdong province, close to Hong Kong, blue-collar workers have been getting twelve per cent average annual pay rises, and in the Shanghai region the figure is reportedly nearer fourteen per cent. The EU Chamber of Commerce in China has forecast a doubling or possibly tripling of labour costs by 2020.

If China's currency, the renminbi usually known as the yuan, appre-ciates in value and shipping charges rise in line with wages, then Chinese manufacturing costs are going to align more with those of other parts of the world. Not necessarily Europe, where it is hard to see the three million industrial jobs lost since 2009 being replaced very soon, but perhaps in North America once the huge advantage of cheap shale-based electricity costs clicks into place. In any case, busi-ness analysts no longer point to China's lower wages as a major strength but to the reliability of its supply chains and its improving productivity.

China's investment-driven, export-dependant growth model is already running out of steam, say economists such as Lu Ting at

Bank of America–Merrill Lynch. Beijing's new strategy is to focus more on domestic consumption, particularly green energy-efficient products and services. It's an approach that has long been urged on China, particularly by governments elsewhere that have seen the Chinese manufacturing juggernaut cut swathes through their own industrial payrolls.

Consumer purchasing by Chinese people has changed out of all recognition over the decades since the early 1980s and Deng Xiaoping's opening up of Mao Tse-tung's brand of rigid communism to the market economy. But still only a third of China's economy is accounted for by consumption, whereas in most countries it's over half. How China will be able to sustain the rapid growth that its people now expect at a time when its industries become more like those of other countries, especially Western ones, remains to be seen. Beijing's plans at present are centred on urbanizing a further 400 million people by 2030, with the aim of tackling rural poverty and backwardness while boosting the industrial workforce and enjoying the stimulus of a huge construction drive.

As recently as 1990, only a quarter of Chinese were city dwellers. That proportion has already risen to almost forty-five per cent, and the target to be reached within fifteen years is seventy per cent, or a billion people. Shanghai and other major hubs are each to be ringed by up to a dozen satellite cities of a million apiece, and the planners foresee a further 50,000 miles of highways to link the cities and industrial zones. The high-speed rail network will by 2020 have grown by over 4,000 miles, connecting every city with a population of half a million or more.

The internal political effects of this huge development strategy seem very positive, despite Western criticisms of China's shortcomings on democracy and human rights. More than eighty per cent of Chinese questioned for the global attitudes survey by the Pew Research Center said the country's economic outlook is good, and the same proportion told Boston Consulting Group researchers that they believe the next generation of Chinese will have a better life than themselves. By contrast, only a fifth of Europeans and Americans expect that for their own descendants.

## Do We Want a Billion-plus Angry or Happy Chinese?

What if the Chinese were to be disappointed? There are serious difficulties to be resolved in China, and it is important that Europe and America should not be seen by the Chinese people as responsible for setbacks to their progress. That could all too easily create frictions and conflict that would threaten global security. Javier Solana, who nowadays spends a good deal of time in China teaching at Beijing's elite Tsinghua University, warns that 'beneath China's boom there still lie many unresolved nineteenth- and twentieth-century problems'. He's referring to the century-long humiliations heaped on China between the Opium War with Britain and Mao Tse-tung's establishment of the People's Republic in 1949, and he believes that Europe rather than the 'less sophisticated' US has a major role to play in dealing with Beijing.

The threats to China's rise are partly manmade and partly natural. On the natural resources side the challenge is water, the essential ingredient of everything from agriculture to manufacturing. In 2015 Beijing will for the first time be introducing water quotas for each of China's twenty-eight provinces in an attempt to confront the growing shortages. The proximity of eight of China's provinces to the Gobi and Inner Mongolian deserts means they are as parched as many Arab countries. And China's industrialization, its urban development strategy and the shift towards higher protein meat diets are together placing unbearably heavy pressure on water resources. 'Beijing's great moment of choice will be over GDP or the environment', comments Javier Solana.

The policy choices could prove more complicated still, as water constraints together with the inefficiencies resulting from China's appalling levels of pollution are said by the World Bank to be costing it 2.3 per cent of its GDP. On top of that, other threats to China's economic future range from its internal economic management, which is not nearly as surefooted as the Chinese authorities would like the world to believe, to labour shortages resulting from the famous 'one child policy'.

When China's decade-long growth spurt of around ten per cent a year began to falter in the wake of the global financial crisis of 2008, Beijing launched a determined nationwide stimulus programme. The result has been a sharp rise in government debt that may well come to haunt China. Provincial governments' debt levels trebled in just a few years, and because the stimulus projects were so hurried much of the money was spent indiscriminately. About a quarter of all these projects don't generate any revenue at all, and that means many local authorities in China are going to be saddled with bad debts for a long time.

The demographic outlook worries Chinese policymakers as much if not more. There is already tough competition for labour between China's major employers—a survey of 200 top companies saw them able to fill only seven in ten of their job vacancies. The labour shortages that brake corporate growth are going to get worse because China's working age population recently stopped growing and is starting to shrink by roughly 2.5 million people every year. In the decade up to 2025 the workforce of under-thirty year olds will contract annually by 1.4 per cent, and that's raising a host of questions about the nature of the Chinese economy in the fairly near future.

As China isn't going to remain the low wage manufacturing exporter of recent years, it's going to be importing more goods and services to satisfy the demands of its new middle class. It is also going to see the business models of its huge manufacturing sector assailed by new technologies. No one yet knows what the impact of digitization and such techniques as 3D printing will be, but the effect doesn't even need to be revolutionary to disturb the delicate equilibrium of China's economic growth and the mass improvement of living standards.

Some scenarios see a dramatic reversal of the trend that shifted so much manufacturing to China; the Boston Consulting Group has speculated that in sectors such as transport, computers, and machinery, somewhere between ten and thirty per cent of the goods China currently produces for American customers could by 2020 be 'repatriated' and produced once more in the United States.

These and many other factors add up to huge headaches, and when Western competitors complain about China's trade practices, its 'manipulation' of the renminbi to slow its appreciation against other currencies, its apparently more tolerant approach to protecting intellectual property rights, its failure to control cyber-espionage, and all the other perceived inequities, they should remember one thing; China's dynamo has been a driver of the global economy. Without it, the ripple effects of the worldwide economic crisis that began on Wall Street would have been truly devastating.

The Chinese and most other Asians will, in any case, be levelling the industrial playing field themselves. Their ageing populations together with the pressures for improved social policies are set to alter the balance, even if this will probably take a good many years. The question being asked by some analysts is whether improved welfare policies in Asian countries will expose them to the 'European disease'.

EU countries account for half of all the social and health benefits paid out by governments around the world. But the ageing phenomenon is changing such calculations, and the democratization of Asian countries has also meant that voters are demanding and getting better healthcare. In Indonesia, for instance, 2014 saw the introduction of what is being called the world's biggest 'single-payer' health insurance scheme, to be followed by pensions, death benefits, and accident insurance. In the Philippines, well over four-fifths of people are signed up for health cover, and China has a special rural health insurance scheme that is claimed to cover 97.5 per cent of the eligible population.

It's not going to be easy for Asian governments to pay for these schemes. The growing proportion of old people in Asian countries will place enormous strains on their economies. By 2030, Asia will be home to half the world's elderly population and will also account for half the patients afflicted by non-communicable diseases ranging from diabetes to cancer. In South Korea, Singapore, and Hong Kong the ageing phenomenon will be so acute that by 2040 there will be fewer than two working-age people for every pensioner.

The solution that Asian governments look to is for their companies to move as fast as they can up the value chain, even if in the short term that creates fewer jobs. The Asian Development Bank has warned that cheap labour cannot sustain Asia's manufacturing boom, and that high-value activities such as financial services and information and communications have to be developed as quickly as possible. Less than half of Asia's economic activity is in these service sectors, whereas in the rich Western 'industrialized' countries the proportion is over three-quarters.

Although Asian companies have made impressive inroads into markets that were once dominated by Americans and Europeans, they have a number of inbuilt weaknesses. There's the low profitability of many of the sectors they are in, and there's also the very Asian characteristic of family ownership. Credit Suisse analysts say that half of all the listed companies in the ten leading Asian economies are family-controlled, and that family disputes and succession squabbles when a company's patriarch retires or dies often cause its value to plummet.

Samsung Electronics in Korea, which is run by the Lee family dynasty, is now the world's biggest-selling high-tech company, having overtaken such rivals as California-based Hewlett-Packard HP and Japan's Hitachi. But its profit margins are about half those of its main competitors, as are those of that other great Asian success story Hon Hai, the Taiwan-based assembler of Apple devices better known as Foxconn. Both are considered innovative but not inventive, and both are typical of many of Asia's new industrial giants. Samsung has great ambitions to develop products in solar energy, batteries for hybrid cars, biopharmaceuticals and medical equipment, but its return on capital is about half that of Apple and other American or European competitors. It's a similar story for Foxconn, which employs approaching a million and a half people on mainland China and is growing at a rate of almost twenty per cent yearly. But market pressures have seen its profit margin shrink from six per cent a decade ago to about two per cent.

The fear in Asia is that these highly successful but very young industries will not be as resilient and durable as long-established industry leaders such as, say, Siemens in Germany or Philips in the Netherlands. They are uncomfortably aware of the fate of Japanese consumer electronics companies such as Sony and others that failed to move up the value chain and so were overtaken by low-cost newcomers.

Corporate Japan's answer has been to focus at home on new technologies and materials, and to invest heavily abroad, especially in South East Asia. Fujitsu and Panasonic are merging their chip-making sides, and to some extent their prized corporate identities, to create a new Japanese semiconductor giant able to fight back against Taiwan's dominance. Investment in countries such as Vietnam and now Myanmar is booming, so much so that total Japanese foreign investment is now ten times greater than a decade ago. That's also a reflection of Japan's own demographic nightmare; it is estimated that by 2060 its population will, at about ninety million, have shrunk by thirty-seven million people.

## Wake Up, Brussels!

Where do European companies fit into this fast-moving picture? The answer is far from clear. They could become much more engaged than at present, but require a political kick-start. Just as US president Barack Obama's 'pivot to Asia' both confirmed and stimulated American companies' interest in Asian markets, Europe, too, needs to put down a marker signalling new economic priorities there.

In Brussels, the EU Commission's ponderous bureaucracy has been slow to engage with the ten-nation ASEAN bloc. The Association of South East Asian Nations has modest origins dating back to 1967, when Indonesia, Malaysia, Singapore, the Philippines, and Thailand cautiously began to emulate the European Economic Community.

Since then they've been joined by Vietnam, Cambodia, Brunei, Laos, and Myanmar, making ASEAN much more muscular politically as well as economically. The EU's unaccountable delay in appointing an ambassador to the ASEAN secretariat in Jakarta—it at last decided to do so in autumn 2014—had long been taken by Asians to speak volumes about Europe's attitude to them.

The pace and vigour of Asia's development has been the envy of the world, and Asians are inclined to be dismissive of the opportunities Europe can still offer them. They would be wrong to do so, for in terms of wealth its internal market is the largest in the world, and thanks to the EU's huge eastward expansion much of it has exciting growth potential.

The combined economic clout of EU countries is a powerful political instrument if wielded properly. Europe's national diplomats and civil servants prefer, though, to cling to their traditional bilateral relationships with individual Asian governments. And for their part, the Brussels bureaucrats have shown little flair for presenting the 'big picture' of a new Euro-Asian strategy. EU officials are happier with the detail of administering established policies than with the uncertainties and dangers of creating new ones that might incur the wrath of the bigger member states. The consequence is a paucity, indeed an absence, of European initiatives in vibrant Asia.

Asian countries have transformed themselves and their peoples' living standards and future prospects in a remarkably short space of time. Yet they still face serious difficulties, and many of them live with the threat of dangerous political instability should their economic growth falter. On top of that there are security frictions and national rivalries that risk flaring up and disrupting the region's economic development. These are all problems that would be greatly reduced by a stronger European political engagement. It is not too late for Europeans to take a second look at their twentieth century patterns of trade and investment in Asia and replace them with a more strategic and less haphazard model, but it is long overdue.

# 5

# For Europe, Africa Spells Trouble and Opportunity

*The resources and potential of Africa as a huge market are of fundamental importance to the European Union. But the volatility of Africa's fifty-four states poses security problems that their population explosions seem likely to compound. Yet 'Rising Africa' will be a global game changer, and Europeans' links with African states promise win-win economic partnerships. First, EU policymakers must review the trade and development policies that many Africans see as wrong-headed.*

E urope's freebooting explorers and traders had since the fifteenth century been largely responsible for shaping Africa's future. Now, Europeans are introspective and self-absorbed and seemingly indifferent to Africa's beckoning opportunities. Yet on their doorstep lies a continent whose potential for economic growth and wealth creation is enormous. Asians see this clearly—most notably the Chinese—but Europe's focus has been more on the difficulties created by the fractious politics of Africa's fifty-four nation states and its myriad ethnic and tribal divisions.

*

There's still room for imaginative strategies by European businesses as well as governments that could help to shake EU countries out of lethargic acceptance of their own decline and falling living standards. What's needed is a resetting of Europe's geopolitical compass, an abandonment of the many prejudices about Africa, and a fresh look at what is being achieved there.

Rocking gently in the French Riviera's pleasant winter sunshine, Mo Ibrahim's ocean-going yacht commands a fine view of Monte Carlo's harbour and the high-rise buildings that climb the hillside behind it. Its billionaire owner is one of Africa's best-known success stories and he's also among its most vocal champions. Ibrahim made his fortune bringing mobile phones to Africa, and in doing so helped to trigger a social and economic revolution that promises to transform the lives of hundreds of millions. The question is, though, what could Europe do to accelerate the improvement of the world's least developed continent, and how can it benefit from Africa's growth?

Africa is trouble and opportunity, and not only for itself. Its population is set to more than double in the next few decades and its mineral riches will be the focus of even greater global resource competition and unrest. Europe is going to be on the frontline if Africa's volatile and unruly politics are not tamed. 'Africa's future is still an open question', says Mo Ibrahim. 'If we can manage to train and educate the coming generation we will have the world's largest available workforce. China won't necessarily remain the workplace of the world.'

But that's a big 'if', as Ibrahim readily acknowledges. Half of the global population explosion up to mid-century will be in Africa, taking the continent's population of about a billion to over two billion, and placing huge strains on African governments' abilities to feed and house their people. How to prevent the rapid growth of African cities from creating sprawling, unmanageable, and crime-ridden slums is one headache, and another is finding ways to boost food production when the continent as a whole is today producing less food per head than in 1960.

In the face of all these woes, there's a persuasive school of thought amongst some economists that Africa's demographic growth will be the driver of wealth, not the harbinger of doom. Mo Ibrahim agrees, and sees a not-too-distant future in which European know-how combines with Africa's expanding marketplaces to transform the economic outlook. He should know, for his championing of cheap, no-frills mobile phones in Kenya and other parts of East Africa has had a dramatic impact. More and more people in isolated rural communities now conduct their modest financial transactions through the Safaricom system operated by Vodafone, and it's transforming the agricultural economy.

Sudanese-born Mo Ibrahim has a wider geopolitical view of Africa's future. Looking at the way Africa has begun to breed 'tiger' economies similar to those of Asia twenty years ago, he remarks: 'It's no coincidence that things started to improve in Africa after the Cold War ended. The civil conflicts that were in reality proxy wars between the West and the Soviet bloc did much damage, politically and economically.' The challenge for Africa, he believes, is to bring about the regional integration of African states. 'There are 54 of them,' he says, 'and many are sub-skilled, landlocked and have relatively small populations. Political union of any description is out of the question, but more open borders are essential to encouraging trade and investment.'

Africa's economic turnaround has been taking place right under Europe's nose and at Europe's expense. A report by the Johannesburg-based Standard Bank has shown that in the ten years since 2002, China's exports to African countries tripled. They now account for approaching a fifth of all imports into Africa. Those from Britain, Germany, Spain, Italy, and Japan have all been falling. Few Europeans have taken much notice, and probably fewer still know that since the new century began, six of the world's ten fastest-growing countries are in Africa, and that in eight of the ten years between 2002 and 2012, Africa as a whole grew faster than East Asia, including Japan.

There is obviously an important difference between the Maghreb countries of northern Africa and sub-Saharan Africa. But with the former still suffering the aftershocks of the Arab Spring, it's the sub-Saharan countries that have been chalking up an economic turnaround. The average growth rate in African countries, IMF monitors say, is running at a fairly steady six per cent; that's roughly the same as in Asia, and at least a dozen African countries have enjoyed that level of growth since 2008 or so. If the ready availability of African labour can be coupled with revolutionary new technologies and the continent's huge and still largely untapped natural resources, then the sky would seem to be the limit.

## Europe Hasn't Yet Registered 'Rising Africa'

Where does Europe fit into this potentially rosy future? It's a very mixed picture, but the short answer is not nearly enough.

American corporations often shy away from African projects because they fear political risks. European companies tend to be less worried, perhaps because former colonial links make them more familiar with local conditions. Asian investors are among the most active and far-sighted, and that doesn't only mean the Chinese. It says a lot that Mo Ibrahim's pioneering Celtel company that brought mobile phone services to fourteen African countries is owned nowadays by Indian telecoms giant Bahrti Airtel, number three in the world.

The world's rising economic powers are seizing opportunities in Africa with an enthusiasm that should ring warning bells in corporate boardrooms across the EU and US. A generation ago, the BRIC nations—rather than BRICS, which now includes South Africa—accounted for a tiny one per cent of Africa's total foreign trade. That share has grown by 200 per cent since the new century began and is expected to rise from today's twenty per cent to fifty per cent by 2030. The old post-colonial patterns of African economic life are being torn up and discarded forever, but Europeans remain only dimly aware of this.

For now, though, it is the trends rather than the absolute figures that matter most. The small and middle-sized countries of sub-Saharan Africa receive only a very small share of foreign investment in the continent because the lion's share has been going to South Africa, followed closely by Egypt before it succumbed to political turmoil, and then by oil-rich Nigeria.

For all the excitement over Africa's new-found economic dynamism, it's still a backwater of the global economy; it currently attracts only three per cent of the more than one trillion dollars spent worldwide every year in international investment projects, and its share of world trade is just two per cent. To put those figures in context, populous and vibrant Africa's total economy of some $1.6 trillion yearly is reckoned in terms of purchasing power to amount to no more than 2.5 per cent of the world's economic output.

It's more important to look at Africa's potential and at the gathering momentum of development there. Some observers think the commodities boom explains the faster growth rates and the tenfold increase in foreign direct investment (FDI) over the past decade, but that's not the case. A closer look shows that raw materials spanning minerals, energy, and agriculture accounted for less than a third. African countries' manufacturing and services sectors are picking up, too, although often from a low base and very patchily.

The good news is that foreign investment is surging ahead. The predicted 2015 level of $150 billion in FDI is almost three times greater than the $55 billion five years earlier and the mere $5 billion that foreign investors spent in 2000. Perhaps the most significant milestone is that 2015 has also been the point at which private sector investment from businesses based outside Africa overtook the development aid that Western governments have long poured into Africa with such mixed results.

These are all encouraging details, but the big question mark over Africa's future is whether its population growth will stifle economic development instead of fuelling it. That's of more than academic interest to Europe, because a future of grinding poverty for African youth in slum cities stretching from Cairo to the Cape would pose a direct threat to Europeans' own security. The Arab Spring that spread so rapidly in 2011 across the Maghreb countries of Tunisia, Libya, and Egypt showed that in the information age young people will not remain passive. The protests of the Arab Spring were not only directed at repressive and autocratic regimes but at the lack of jobs and opportunities.

Mobile phones and greater familiarity with relatively opulent Western living conditions may have helped trigger upheavals in the Arab world, but religion has been the explosive charge. Now, Islamic militancy is taking hold in large parts of Africa, with profoundly disruptive effects. The Libyan conflicts between rival militias and jihadist groups quickly spread south to the Sahel region that stretches from the Atlantic to the Horn of Africa. The fairly modest French-led military intervention in Mali has since been beefed-up to three times its original size, and the 3,000 soldiers engaged in 'Operation Barkhane' have wide-ranging orders from Paris to counter jihadist terrorism. Meanwhile, the militant Islamists of Nigeria's Boko Haram movement have been defying attempts to suppress them and halt their depredations.

Security is seen as an increasingly worrying problem by many European politicians with first-hand experience of Africa. 'Mali, Chad, Niger, and Sudan are all going to present long-term peacekeeping and security problems', says Karel De Gucht, the former Belgian foreign minister who was Belgium's member of the 2010–14 European Commission. His view is shared by Michèle Alliot-Marie, who as France's defence minister warned back in 2007 that Europe should pay greater attention to buttressing Africa's precarious security. 'What we in Europe would see as a moral imperative', she said, 'also happens to be in our strategic interest because unchecked violence has a proven tendency to spin out of control and spill over elsewhere. Benign neglect is not an option for Europe'.

The cost of these security threats to Africa's struggling economies is growing. Measuring economic loss is hard, but the absence of normally export-hungry German companies from African markets serves as an illuminating example. Asked why Germany's trade with the whole of sub-Saharan Africa is, at €26 billion, only a sixth of its trade with the Netherlands, a spokesperson explained that the *Mittelstand* companies that are the backbone of German foreign trade 'are wary of conflict and corruption'.

Deteriorating security conditions in northern and sub-Saharan Africa are a very real threat to African governments as they try to harness the encouraging upsurge of economic growth to create jobs while improving education and healthcare. And the backdrop to these efforts is the runaway growth in population and the burning question of whether it will eventually prove a blessing or a terrible curse.

It is certainly not going to be easy in most African countries to absorb the huge population growth by local labour markets, or into the changing fabric of society. Africa's population explosion by mid-century is certain to create huge problems of adaptation, and could possibly be even more dramatic than the doubling to two billion being forecast. If the average lifespan of Africans that today averages less than fifty years is extended by better healthcare, then the continent's demographic tsunami wave will be even higher.

The sheer size of the African population is probably less important than the other major change taking place. Urbanization is altering the face of African society, yet it's still very unclear what its eventual impact will be. Four out of ten Africans no longer live in rural communities, inhabiting instead the cities and townships, and all too often Africa's teeming slums.

The drift away from the countryside has really been more of an exodus and is clearly irreversible. At the turn of the century less than thirty per cent of Africans were urban, with over two-thirds of the population in most countries rural and living only off the land. But subsistence farming holds fewer attractions than ever, so forecasts now suggest that by as soon as 2025 half of Africa's people will be urban, which is more or less the same as in Asia today where it is fifty-two per cent.

Worrying as this huge shift of people to Africa's often ill-planned and chaotic cities would seem, the Asian experience holds out a degree of promise. Urban society is economically much more efficient, so it's possible that the coming years' booming population of working-age Africans could unleash a new business dynamic. But it could also create the conditions for misery, social unrest, and political explosion.

Much will depend, needless to say, on education. If African governments can raise the skills levels of their people, then Mo Ibrahim's mooted challenge to China's manufacturing pre-eminence makes sense. New technologies such as 3D printing could, if Africa has enough trained people, mean that comparatively remote African communities would become manufacturing centres.

That demands much better communications and transport links, but truly determined infrastructural drives could do much to stimulate growth and act as a flywheel to industrialization. It's an area where China has already won respect and even admiration for its approach to Africa's development, and Europe, too, should be redoubling its efforts to encourage better infrastructure there.

The EU has the tools and, to a degree, the ambition, but has often failed to focus and coordinate its member states' national programmes. Perhaps that message is beginning to register in Brussels, for mid-2014 saw a surprise announcement that over the three years to 2018 the EU plans to sink €28 billion into African countries' education, health, and job creation programmes.

It may also be that Europeans are waking up to the rise in competitive pressures; not just from China and other Asian countries but from the United States. Shortly after the EU's announcement, president Obama welcomed fifty African government leaders to the White House to learn about Washington's $33 billion 'trade Africa initiative'. As well as increased US government infrastructure support, it will involve over ninety big American companies in an investment drive that groups together names such as Wal-Mart, Morgan Stanley, IBM, Marriott, GE, Lockheed Martin, and Ford. It's the sort of headline-grabbing, high-impact initiative that Europe, with its plodding EU bureaucracy and its national rivalries, can only envy.

## Africa Could Feed a Hungry World

The immediate challenge being created by Africa's population explosion is food. Feeding a hungry world of nine billion people or more, say bodies such as the UN's Food and Agriculture Organization (FAO), is going to demand at least a seventy per cent increase in food production, and quite possibly a doubling. That's going to be a tall order.

There are still about 2.5 billion people around the world whose livelihoods depend on agriculture, but productivity improvements in agricultural output have been lagging well behind population growth. And it seems increasingly unrealistic to look to India or China to deliver increases in food production that could be exported because both suffer from water shortages now being aggravated by climate change. By mid-century water scarcities could see their wheat and rice harvests cut by anywhere between thirty and fifty per cent, roughly the volume by which their own domestic demand is expected to rise.

Africa holds the key to just how hungry the twenty-first century world will be. Getting on for two-thirds of the planet's yet uncultivated arable land is in Africa, and Africa also has more than half of all the unused potential farmland that could be readily exploited without endangering the ecosystem. Growing enough food for Africans themselves and for export elsewhere is going to be an uphill struggle. Africa today produces less food per head of population than back in 1960. It's not like a famine that makes the TV news schedules, but there is already a slow-burning global food crisis that's forcing prices beyond the means of poor people, and Africa is at its centre.

The scale of the problem became fully apparent just as the world was plunged into financial and economic crisis in 2008. Food reserves are still at their lowest level in thirty years, and the price of many staples has doubled. It is a crisis that's largely man-made, created by European and American agricultural and trade policies as well as by the shortcomings of African governments. It's also a lesson in the law of unintended consequences, for the US switch to biofuels urged by environmentalists and supported by subsidies saw almost a third of America's maize crop redirected to the production of ethanol, with enormous knock-on effects on cereal prices around the world.

Europe's farm support measures have, like those of the US, long had the effect of dumping subsidized EU food exports on African markets at artificially low prices with which Africa's smallholders could not compete. Of late, though, Europe has in the eyes of Africans, compounded this effect with new trade policies. The deadlock over the

Doha Development Round—the World Trade Organization's unsuccessful multilateral trade liberalization negotiations—has produced a flurry of bilateral or regional deals that are imposing new burdens on African farmers.

The EU, as the world's largest and most powerful trading bloc, has been in the forefront; it has negotiated what it calls Economic Partnership Agreements (EPAs) to replace the non-reciprocal deals under which some categories of African commodities had preferential access to EU markets. Africans are instead being asked to end tariffs on at least eighty per cent of their imports from the EU, but without compensating concessions from Europe. 'It is not clear what benefits Africa's poorest countries will receive', Nigeria's former central bank chief, Charles Chukwuma Soludo, has complained. 'Europe's approach is harmful and unnecessary'. He even says that the EPAs are the modern-day equivalent of the notorious Berlin conference of 1885 at which much of Africa was divided up between the great European powers.

Not all of Africa's present ills can be laid at the door of others; many are rooted in Africa's long standing development problems. Former Romanian agriculture minister Dacian Ciolos, who is a trained agronomist and served as the EU agriculture commissioner from 2010 to 1014, says the chief problem to overcome is wastage: 'Africa's difficulty is the lack of agricultural investment and poor storage and transport'.

Between a third and a half of Africa's harvests are wasted—spoiled by disease, pests, and moisture. Raising farmers' productivity with advanced seeds and new techniques will be of fairly limited value until storage and transport are greatly improved. Africans need modern storage facilities for their crops to tide them over droughts and other ravages of nature, and they also need better road and rail links to get their crops to both local and international markets. Until they can earn foreign currencies from food exports, they cannot afford to pay for the massive infrastructural developments they so badly need.

A thoughtful analysis of this problem has been carried out by Roger Thurow of the Chicago Council on Global Affairs, who looked into the reasons for the disastrous Ethiopian famine of 2003, when thirteen million people, a fifth of the population, went hungry and tens of thousands died. Thurow, an American journalist and co-author of a 2009 book entitled *Enough: Why the World's Poorest Starve in an Age of Plenty*, points out that the years 2001 and 2002 had seen two of the richest harvests ever recorded in Ethiopia, yet a year later people were dying. Storage and transportation had been seen by the country's policymakers as lower priorities than the improvement of agricultural output, with disastrous results.

With nowhere to store the bumper crops of those two fat years, and few means of exporting the extra food, Ethiopia's markets were unable to absorb the food bonanza.

The result was that local prices collapsed, with farmers earning only a fifth of their usual income. Meanwhile, poor storage meant an estimated 300,000 tonnes of grain spoiled. Then, when the planting season came, the low prices forced Ethiopian farmers to limit investment in seeds and fertilizers. At that point came drought.

During that famine, the United States alone spent more than $500 million on food aid for fourteen million starving Ethiopians. But it also devoted less than $5 million to agricultural development that could help to head off future famines. Roger Thurow bitterly summed up the situation; 'Soon', he wrote, 'the drought that had struck Ethiopia spread from the Horn of Africa down the continent's east coast and into its southern savannahs, where the HIV/AIDS epidemic was already wreaking havoc on agriculture by killing millions of farmers. A few years into the 21st century, Africa was hungrier than ever before'.

Almost half a century earlier, the idea of creating a 'green revolution' to banish hunger in what was then called the Third World was being championed by the pioneering plant geneticist Norman Borlaug. His development of new hybrid strains of rice and cereals transformed much of Asia's agriculture and turned India into a wheat exporter, but largely passed Africa by. Less than five per cent of African land is irrigated, and on average African farmers use less than a tenth of the fertilizers employed in Asia and Latin America.

The International Maize and Wheat Improvement Center, which was the late Norman Borlaug's base, says hybrid seeds still account for less than thirty per cent of corn grown in Africa, yet could easily double yields and in some cases increase them four-fold.

The McKinsey Global Institute, a research outfit belonging to the international management consultancy, believes that if a green revolution were to take root in Africa the value of the continent's food output could triple, rising from about $280 billion a year at present to an estimated $880 billion yearly by 2030. To do so, say the McKinsey experts, Africa has only to raise the yield of key crops to just four-fifths of the global average.

The importance of improving Africa's agricultural infrastructure has been underlined by the man who from 2010 to 2014 was the top EU official in Brussels holding the purse strings for the European Union's €9 billion yearly development aid budget. Andris Piebalgs was for ten years Latvia's member of the European Commission and his development policy job was to direct and oversee the management of what has become the world's largest aid budget. Piebalgs is in no doubt that transportation and storage hold the key to Africa's farm policies, but he's less sure about the idea that genetically modified organisms (GMOs) hold out the promise of miraculous change.

'The problem with GMOs', explains Piebalgs, whose role as Europe's 'Mr Development' took him to the world's poorest and least privileged countries, 'is that smallholders and even quite substantial farmers don't think they can afford GMO seeds'. He points out that the royalties that have to be paid to the developers of the new 'miracle' seeds—giant multinational corporations like Monsanto—make unsophisticated smallholders very reluctant to commit themselves to a financial relationship they mistrust. The situation surrounding GMOs and other new technology farm inputs of today, comment veterans of Borlaug's green revolution of the 1970s, is that peasant farmers in those days were supplied with cheap, no-strings seeds without any sense of being trapped into an irreversible commitment that potentially could bankrupt them.

Piebalgs is not alone in believing the introduction of new products and techniques needs to be handled carefully. India's rural development minister back in 2010, Jairam Ramesh, nailed his colours to the mast when he delayed the introduction of a new pest-resistant transgenic aubergine, saying 'there is no hurry to introduce Bt brinjal'. The major reason for his reluctance, and that of other influential figures in India, is that they understand poor farmers don't want to become too dependent on multinational corporations for buying expensive GM seeds. Indian environmentalist Vandana Shiva says GM cotton has hit some farmers hard, and that Monsanto's policy of takeover bids to acquire control of its major competitors in India is forcing farmers to buy its more expensive seeds rather than subsidized government seeds.

The politics surrounding food aid and development policies in Africa have long been fiercely fought, and never less so than in the past decade. When Kofi Annan was UN secretary-general, he led the calls for an 'African Green Revolution'. At about the same time, vociferous lobbying forced the World Bank to retreat from its dogma of imposing structural adjustment on poor countries seeking assistance, and the 2008 *World Development Report* recognized the crucial importance of state investment in the agricultural development of poor countries, and acknowledged the need for a degree of subsidization for small farmers.

It's not just the developing world, of course, that's wrestling with the ethical and commercial dilemma of new seed technologies. European public opinion has done much to reject GM crops, so much so that German chemicals giant BASF is transferring all its biotechnology research to the United States and is abandoning all its GMO-related businesses in Europe, and Monsanto has ditched its plans to sell insect-resistant maize in France.

The proponents of plant breeding and genetic manipulation are nevertheless making progress. Their campaign to boost food production around the world is beginning to show some impressive results. GM crops are enjoying an eight per cent yearly rise in their use globally. Because tolerance of drought conditions and resistance to disease are the key aims of GM crop developers, 2017 is targeted as the year we can expect the widespread introduction of GM wheat along with drought-tolerant maize. On the non-GM side, India has improved a number of seed varieties, so much so that estimates of the boost to crop yields range from twenty-one per cent to forty-three per cent.

However much Africa's farmers improve their yields, there still remains the vexed question of whether they can sell their produce to the world's richest consumers in Europe and America. Farmers' votes in the EU and the US are courted by politicians and political parties, and although their stranglehold on international trade in farm exports is weaker than in the past, there remain protective barriers to be overcome.

Former EU agriculture commissioner Dacian Ciolos says that although the EU's Common Agricultural Policy, or CAP, is still too complicated and expensive, it is no longer the protectionist instrument of twenty years ago. He argues that there are no border controls, and that export subsidies encouraging Europe's farmers to unload food at prices undercutting local producers are increasingly rare. Ciolos acknowledges there was indeed a time when forty per cent of the hugely expensive CAP was devoted to trade distorting instruments of this sort, but says that's no longer the case. He points out that on the contrary, the EU is now a big importer of ACP (African, Caribbean, and Pacific) countries' farm exports—and takes more than the combined food imports of the US, Canada, Australia, New Zealand, and Japan.

Even so, is Europe, along with the other heavy hitters of the world economy, really doing enough to get African agriculture onto a sustainable growth path? Most signs suggest it isn't, and that the dangers to global stability and therefore Europe's own security, are under-rated. The thirty-four countries that make up the 'rich man's club' of the OECD spend about $250 billion a year on financial support of one sort or another to their own farmers.

Without a green revolution in Africa of some sort, warns the US Department of Agriculture, the 'food insecure' population there—meaning people whose diet is less than 2,100 calories daily—will exceed half a billion by 2020, around half the total population. Sub-Saharan Africa will be the hardest hit of all by this looming food shortage, for those countries make up almost a third of the people in the world's seventy least-developed nations, but almost sixty per cent of those afflicted by food insecurity.

These dry statistics do little to convey the brake that Africa's farming and food problems place on its overall development. They stand in the way of the revolution in education and training that African governments must undertake if Mo Ibrahim's prediction of industrial strength is ever to come true. The irony is that in the closing decades of the twentieth century, policymakers in Europe, America, and the major international agencies had thought the problems of feeding poorer people in Africa, Asia, and Latin America were solved. Between 1975 and 1985 global production of wheat, maize, and rice grew more than twice as fast as increases in the global population. Although a good deal of this agricultural productivity was down to seed breeding advances in the United States and Europe, international funding for agricultural development in poorer countries suffered deep cuts.

World Bank studies show that the sum total of development aid aimed at agriculture had by 2004 dropped to less than half the figure twenty years before—only $3.4 billion (in 1984 dollars) instead of $8 billion. In terms of overall aid spending, the retreat from helping dirt poor farmers in Africa and elsewhere was even more alarming; in the mid-1980s almost a fifth of all development aid went to boosting farm output, and by 2004 it was less than four per cent. American aid to sub-Saharan Africa's farmers nosedived to $60 million in 2006 from $400 million two decades earlier.

It's not just the politicians and the international civil servants who were to blame for this abrupt *volte face*; environmentalists had put heavy pressure on the aid-giving community and particularly the leading NGOs whose aid workers handle development assistance on the ground. They have said their concern was that the first stirrings of an African green revolution were creating a new type of pollution from fertilizer and pesticides. They had a valid point, because reducing fresh water supplies and souring the soil can only compound Africa's problems, but the policy response should instead have been to devote more attention to African agriculture, not less.

The scale of Africa's food insecurity is sounding alarms in a number of quarters. The head of the giant Unilever food products corporation, Paul Polman, was handed the tough job of reinvigorating international action when the G20 heads of government appointed him to chair the Food Security Working Group. His answer has been to call for an 'aid transfusion' of $70–80 billion to compensate for years of declining investment in food storage and transport. The chances of achieving that are not encouraging; spending on development aid by donor countries peaked in 2010, having risen by sixty-three per cent since the new century began, but has since been axed by austerity cutbacks. Oxfam spoke for many in the development aid community when it described such cuts as pointless, saying 'it's like cutting your hair to lose weight'.

The debate about the value of development aid is more confusing than ever. Some experts say there is increasing evidence that the aid poured into Africa since the 1970s and 1980s has had far less impact on people's living standards than was hoped. Controversy rages around a number of 'test beds' designed to show what works best. American economist Jeffrey Sachs, who made his name advising central and eastern European governments after the fall of the Berlin Wall, has been involved in a $150 million 'millennium village project' where half a million people in fourteen different sites in rural Africa were asked to introduce various improvements aimed at developing the local economy. The value of this ambitious project backed by billionaire philanthropist George Soros and involving Kenya, Malawi, and Ghana is as yet unclear. It has chalked up major improvements in access to safe water and primary schooling, and even in agricultural productivity, but an independent Dutch analyst reported that it has had no discernible effect on the local economy.

## Helping Africa to Help Itself

It's unlikely to be such projects that will help Africa confront its deep-seated problems, but policies. What must Africans do to help themselves and what must others do to help Africa?

The first thing African countries can do is learn the lessons of their own post-colonial history. It is half a century since the launch by thirty-two of them of the Organization of African States (OAS), the forerunner of today's fifty-four-nation African Union (AU). The aim was to create economic and political links between its members that would lead to booming trade and a new era of prosperity. For a while it seemed to be working; within a few years the governments of Tanzania, Kenya, Zambia, and Uganda had created a jointly run East African shipping line as part of the East African Community (EAC) that boasted a customs union and a common external tariff as well as close cooperation in areas ranging from communications to education.

It wasn't to last. Within a few years many of the African leaders who participated so proudly in the OAS launch ceremony in Addis Ababa had been toppled by military coups. There's a famous photograph at that event of Ghana's Kwame Nkrumah and Ethiopia's Haile Selassie inspecting an honour guard of troops; both were overthrown not long after, as have been so many others. Worse, the security role of the OAS was soon in tatters, with civil wars breaking out across the continent.

African governments know that regional cooperation is vital to their economic future. So much so that there are now eight regional economic communities. Of these, the Economic Community of West Africa (ECOWAS), the EAC (which had collapsed in 1977 but has since been revived), and the Southern African Development Community (SADC) also share human rights responsibilities and are trying to bring other groupings into an overall free trade arrangement for Africa.

It is far from clear where Europe fits into this renewed drive for African unity. Many African states seem increasingly resentful of the EU's approach to promoting more trade between Europe and Africa. Brussels is negotiating a network of Economic Partnership Agreements (EPAs) with individual states, saying that these 'tailor-made' agreements are better suited to their specific needs. But Africans themselves see the EPAs as a divide-and-rule tactic, pointing out that when it comes to the European Union itself, the EU has always strongly resisted attempts by others to fragment it with bilateral trade deals.

The EU commissioner who masterminded these negotiations while he held the trade portfolio from 2010 to 2014 was Belgium's Karel De Gucht. He says of the EPA negotiations that 'they're on the right track', but he also sees the need for a much more strategic EU approach to Africa. 'Some EU countries still have privileged relations with their former colonies', he says, 'and that might seem an advantage. But not really'. He believes the European External Action Service (EEAS)—the EU's fairly new diplomatic arm—should focus much more than it does on developing a strategic plan for Africa.

Convincing European public opinion of this isn't going to be easy. The widespread prejudice is that African governments are hotbeds of corruption, and that Europe's development aid is tantamount to pouring money down a black hole when it could be better spent at home. The task of convincing people in Europe of their self-interest in Africa's future and the enticing economic opportunities it offers is a real challenge. Africa's government and business leaders would do well to spend more time on a charm offensive in Europe and around the world. Their European counterparts, meanwhile, need to think far more carefully about Africa's potential and its importance to the EU.

# 6

# The Human Factor

*Not Enough Jobs, but also Not Enough Workers*

*Ageing, shrinking workforces in many countries, and the discouragement of women from working are all threatening Europe's economic structures. Drastic reforms are needed if European society is not to be pulled apart by the conflicting strains of slow growth, labour shortages, and increasingly unaffordable social protection for the unemployed and underprivileged. Europeans must wake up to the reality that workforce shortages will demand more immigration, not less.*

I s Europe big or small, united or divided, rich or poor? It's all of those things, which is why the choices that Europeans must make in the next few years are going to be so important. The path they choose will determine whether future generations can go on enjoying comfortable living standards and a hand in shaping the answers to global problems, or whether their children and grandchildren will suffer gentle decline and growing impotence in world affairs.

There are lots of questions hanging over Europe, not the least being whether its diminished size in both absolute and relative terms means that the age of European influence on all manner of things is coming to a close. It's hard to believe that from German cars to French or Italian fashions we are living on borrowed time, and that it'll be Chinese fashions or Brazilian cars that will soon be setting the pace. But it's all too possible, and Europeans need to start thinking about how to respond.

The first question people must confront is the one that for many is the most difficult: Are they 'European' or are they, as their forebears have been, French, Spanish, German, and so on? Is it possible that in the space of a generation Europeans will view their nationality in the same way they now define their regional origins, and so give being British or Belgian the same weight as hailing from Brittany or Bavaria?

This may sound like the ravings of a 'euro loony'—one of those true believers in the fantasy of a Europe whose national frontiers have magically vanished and who probably promotes Esperanto or some other 'globish' language. It's not, because the questions are practical ones about more effective political institutions, stronger security and defence capabilities, and economic policies that can address our business weaknesses and ensure that Europe's social model remains intact.

There are few signs that people in Europe have these questions at the front of their minds. On the contrary, public opinion in most EU countries seems to be heading away from closer union and the submerging of national identities. Either politicians don't know the basic facts and figures of Europe's position in the world, or they prefer to ignore them so as to get elected.

Yet the data are there, readily available, and profoundly unsettling. Europe is economically stagnant, its population is shrinking, and its national cultures will need to adapt to far larger waves of immigration to keep their economies turning. And if Europe wants to make its voice heard in the world, political leaders across the EU will have to haul down their national flags and be mandated by a European electorate, with all the turmoil that implies.

Staunch advocates of a more federal union—jovially nicknamed 'federasts' in Brussels circles—have been saying this for years; and theirs have been voices crying in the wilderness. Although EU institutions such as the European Commission and the European Parliament may look stronger than, say, twenty-five years ago, the reality is that the European Union is increasingly run by national governments that in their different ways are bent on resisting greater European federalism.

For much of the European project's half-century or so of existence, the federalists' aspirations were ideological, not to say visionary. The 'no more war' argument that fuelled economic integration in the early years was strengthened by the common-sense message of the single market that would give companies a continental scale marketplace comparable to that of the United States. And that in turn led, by seemingly inexorable logic, to the creation of the euro as a single currency to bind Europe's national economies into one.

The upshot has been an unhappy paradox. The eurozone crisis and people's misgivings about 'Europe' have come at a point when the case for genuine political integration has become as real as it is urgent. It's no longer a theoretical goal but a practical necessity. The figures tell their own story.

It makes most sense to use the figures for the fifteen western European (EU-15) countries that made up the EU until 2004 so as to avoid distorting the picture with the EU's eastward enlargements to poorer, formerly communist countries. Economic growth in western Europe shows a long-term slide, and contrasts starkly with America's much more stable performance. Even the wealthier EU-15 countries have an average GDP per head that is twenty-five per cent lower than in the US.

During the 1970s, the average growth rate for the EU-15 was a very respectable 3.2 per cent. In the 1980s that dropped quite sharply to 2.5 per cent, and slipped further to 2.2 per cent throughout the 1990s. For the first decade of the new century it plunged again to 1.2 per cent. All this can perhaps be explained away as symptomatic of 'saturated' economies that have satisfied so many of their people's needs that they quite naturally don't grow at the same rate as those of poorer countries.

But that doesn't explain the comparison between the EU-15 and the United States. In 1970, America's share of the world economy was twenty-six per cent, and that has held steady for two generations at a time of spectacular worldwide growth. The European picture is very different; now the share of the EU-15 in the global GDP is also twenty-six per cent, a vertiginous drop from almost thirty-five per cent in 1970.

## There's No Going Back to the Good Times

Many politicians in Europe like to give the impression that with the right policy mix Europe can regain the ground lost since the financial crisis of 2008 and the ensuing slowdown. Few analysts really believe that, for there is a growing consensus that the crisis has brought to the surface Europe's long standing structural shortcomings. The message has to be that the good times won't be coming back.

The IMF has forecast for the ten-year period following the 2008 crisis that eurozone countries' nominal GDP will rise so slowly that by 2017 it will be sixteen per cent lower than if the 1999–2008 trend-line had continued. Commentators at the London-based weekly magazine *The Economist* have devised what they call the 'Proust Index' (À *la recherche du temps perdu*) to measure the ground European economies have lost as a result of the crisis. Greece's economic clock has been turned back twelve years, they say, so it's now only just entering the twenty-first century, and the other hard-hit eurozone periphery countries have lost an average of seven years. The UK, for all its 'independence' of the euro, was reckoned to have gone backwards by eight years, and even Germany is said to have lost three years.

The implications of these slippages of Europe's economic power are disquieting, even though some people may prefer to dismiss them as consequences of the global crisis that will prove to be only temporary reverses. The truth is that Europe's debt problems are caused by Europeans living above their means, as are the Americans too. The IMF traces a graph of accelerating debt for all the advanced Western economies that shows how difficult it will be to escape from indebtedness. In 2007, just before the crisis broke, their net debt stood at forty-five per cent of their GDPs. By 2012 it had shot up to seventy-three per cent and is expected to reach seventy-eight per cent in 2016.

The EU's governments need to develop coherent common policies on a wide range of economic and social issues to stop the rot. The political narrative in Europe's national capitals and in Brussels is that the EU's fortunes can be restored by a determined competitiveness strategy that will give European companies a sharper edge in the global marketplace. If only it were that simple. Faster innovation and lower costs would certainly give Europe a welcome fillip, but they won't resolve the biggest problem of all, which is the demographic outlook.

Felipe González, the charismatic Spanish social democrat who as prime minister for fourteen years until 1996 saw his country emerge so confidently from its Franco era time warp, published a report in May 2010 that hasn't received nearly as much attention as it deserves. It estimated that over the forty years until mid-century the European Union's countries will need to absorb about a hundred million new immigrants.

They won't all be working-age people, he warned, because they'll bring family dependents with them. He saw little choice, though, because this new wave of immigration will be needed to keep Europe's potential labour force at its present level. Without immigration, the number of people in Europe who are available for work will have shrunk by sixty eight million people by 2050, roughly the present population of the British Isles (the UK and Ireland combined).

Another influential study by demographers Sheena Mcloughlin and Rainer Münz underlines the González message. They calculate that from 2015 onwards, the working-age population of the EU starts to shrink steadily from its present 240 million people. If immigration continues at its current rate, then by 2050 the workforce will be down by about thirty-three million to 207 million. And if immigration into EU countries were somehow to be halted, the mid-century workforce would number only 169 million.

The emigration of people leaving EU countries has, incidentally, been growing so fast that it's beginning to counterbalance immigration. The figures produced for 2008 by the EU's statisticians at

Eurostat put the number of legal, and therefore measurable, immigrants for that year at 3.8 million, a six per cent fall from 2007, and their lowest estimate for emigration, which obviously is harder to be sure of, was that it increased by thirteen per cent on the year before to 2.3 million Europeans or others seeking a better life beyond Europe. One of the most striking examples of this has been the exodus of Portuguese, often young professionals, to jobs in Maputo, capital of Portugal's former colony of Mozambique where economic growth is running at 7.5 per cent a year.

## Xenophobic Europe and the Global Competition for Talented Immigrants

There is going to be increasingly tough international competition for skilled workers, so employers in Europe will find themselves vying with one another, and with companies elsewhere, for people with high-tech qualifications, The McKinsey Global Institute projects that by 2020 there will be a worldwide shortage of forty million highly skilled workers, with China as desperate to attract them as Western countries.

None of this seems likely to alter Europeans' doubts about bringing more people into EU countries. Opinion polls show widespread and rising opposition to immigration throughout the European Union, even though most people are probably aware that Europe needs new blood, or at any rate young blood, to counter the ageing problem. Resentment of immigrants is often fuelled by competition for affordable housing and for jobs too, even though there's substantial research to show that immigrants don't take away job opportunities from the native population.

The need for more people in the workforce is driven home by the fact that there are at present four working-age people for every retired person in Europe, and by mid-century it is predicted there will be just two workers per pensioner. The costs of supporting such a dramatic change in the structure of European society clearly dwarf the costs of bringing in more immigrants and integrating them.

There are other pressing reasons for stepping up the pace of immigration, whatever the social and political strains may be. We don't only need more young people of whatever colour or creed to help pay the rising pensions bill; without a bigger working population more steam than ever will go out of the European economy. A decade ago, German economist Klaus Regling, now head of the eurozone's bail-out mechanism, warned of the brake the EU's dwindling work-force was placing on growth. He calculated that the 2.3 per cent potential GDP growth rate of the rich EU-15 western European countries would fall appreciably from 2010 onwards because of labour shortages. For the two decades up to 2030, Regling said, there would be a 'ceiling' to their average growth of 1.8 per cent, and from 2030 to mid-century that would drop to a maximum potential growth rate of only 1.3 per cent.

That warning was made before the worldwide economic crisis and the eurozone's serious difficulties. But that doesn't mean Europeans can forget about the looming demographic problem. America, too, worries about ageing and the way people are discouraged from being part of the active labour force, but the big difference is that by mid-century the US population is forecast to have surged from 300 million or so to around 400 million. That of Europe will drop, but by how much is the subject of dispute and confusion. A rough but widely used projection based on falling birth rates and rising longevity suggests a dizzying population decrease of as much as ten per cent, falling from around 500 million people in Europe today to only 450 million by mid-century.

That assumes a continuation of the fairly modest levels of immigration in past years. What the future volume of newcomers will be no one can tell, but it is precisely the rate at which economic migrants and refugees are to be admitted into European countries that will determine the size of the EU's population and available labour force.

As this is unknowable—depending as it does on political developments within the European Union and in its neighbourhood stretching from Ukraine to Syria and across North Africa—it is unsurprising that the demographic forecasts for Europe vary wildly.

The authoritative Berlin Institute for Population and Development, for example, sees an 8.3 per cent contraction by 2050, with the population of Europe rather than that of the European Union, falling from 591 million to 542 million. The European Commission, on the other hand, sees an increase in the EU's population by 2060. Alluding somewhat vaguely to migration rates, it expects the 507 million people recorded in 2013 as living in the European Union to rise by four per cent to a mid-century peak of 526 million, declining gently to 523 million people by 2060. The key point here is that it isn't the overall population figure that matters, but rather the make up of the immigrant community and the likely impact on the labour market and on the economy as a whole. So far, the picture is generally positive, despite the widespread prejudice that migrants are a costly burden.

Right now, almost four-fifths of the thirty-four million non-EU citizens living in the European Union are of working age. A further fifteen per cent are under the age of fifteen, and only seven per cent are over sixty-four. They are in precisely the age range that Europe needs to prevent its active workforce from dwindling to the point where a shortage of labour seriously depresses the economy.

As to the charge that immigrants are benefit scroungers, the vast majority are economically active, usually but not always holding down a regular job; that goes for sixty-nine per cent of non-EU nationals, rising to eighty per cent in Spain and Portugal and the Baltic states, and dropping to sixty per cent in France and the Netherlands. Indeed, the most significant finding of a 2015 analysis co-authored by the European Commission and the Organization for Economic Cooperation and Development was that those immigrants who had failed to find work were often the ones with the highest qualifications. Because red tape and question marks over non-European diplomas create difficulties in placing the best-educated people, Europe is depriving itself of those workers it most needs.

It is a lesson that the relevant authorities in European countries should take to heart. As the ranks of would-be immigrants swell, better methods must be developed for matching their skills and know-how to the jobs market. By much the same token, European governments should take immediate steps to end the irrelevant distinction between refugees seeking asylum and the economic migrants who are seen as so undesirable that they should be sent back to their country of origin. It's a false distinction, and attempting to enforce it is disrupting and delaying the integration of newcomers.

To return to the numbers game of population and labour market projections, it's clear that generalizations and EU-wide predictions are tricky and potentially misleading. Perhaps it makes more sense to look at the most successful of all the big European economies, Germany. Looked to as a locomotive for the EU economy as a whole, Germany has both a big immigrant population and also a daunting demographic outlook.

On the plus side, thanks to tough labour market reforms in 2003, Germany has Europe's lowest youth unemployment rate at around five per cent, and despite the crisis years since 2008 has almost halved the number of long-term unemployed to around a million. That's the good news. The bad news is that Germany is to be among those countries that will be the hardest hit by ageing and shrinking; its population of around eighty-two million will be only sixty-five million or so by 2060, and the pensioners of sixty-five years and more who at present account for a fifth of the population will have grown to a third.

Although Germany is clearly going to need an influx of new immigrants, this has become political dynamite, with overt resistance hardening. The country's Muslim community numbers over four million people, and because so many Turkish guest workers settled there from the 1960s onwards, about a fifth of Germany's total population is reckoned either to be people who have been born abroad, or whose parents or grandparents were.

The frictions generated by this became apparent when a former board member of Germany's Bundesbank, the central bank, published a bestselling book entitled *Deutschland schafft sich ab* (*Germany is doing away with itself*). An opinion poll suggested that well over a third of Germans agree with its thesis that the country is 'overrun' by immigrants, and getting on for two-thirds wanted to see Muslim religious practices 'significantly curbed'.

The liberal-minded establishment in Germany was horrified that an ex-Bundesbank boss should express such views. But the controversy sparked by Thilo Sarazin's 2010 outburst may have had the positive effect of prompting closer examination of the lifestyles and achievements of the large immigrant community. It emerged that Germany's efforts to integrate newcomers from outside Europe have been unsatisfactory from all points of view. Many immigrants have not been contributing as much as they might to the German economy because of shortcomings in the educational system.

Only ten per cent of young people of Turkish origin graduate from high school with the prized Abitur qualification, the passport to university, as against twenty per cent of 'pure' Germans. And when Turkish or other foreign-born youngsters achieve a university degree, they are often found to be working below their educational level because of hiring prejudices. That has created a pool of about 300,000 such people whose abilities and skills are not being properly harnessed.

Germany has tried harder than most to attract talent from abroad. Since 2005 it has been spending about ten times as much as the United States on special educational programmes for immigrants. German universities have been at pains to attract foreign students, but of the 60,000 foreigners enrolled, only one in ten stays on to work there. That's not at all what the authorities had planned, as their policies were in large part designed to help German employers who are increasingly worried by labour shortages.

Seven in ten German companies have told pollsters of their difficulty in finding craftspeople, especially for precision engineering and information technology jobs. Germany's Institute for Economic Research, the Berlin-based DIW, says the worsening skills shortage is already costing the economy €15 billion a year. The ageing of the workforce is threatening the future of German industry, so much so that the Stuttgart-based Daimler group, the makers of Mercedes cars, has warned that by 2020 more than half of its workforce will be upwards of fifty years old.

Recognizing the need for a much more ambitious immigration strategy, and a genuinely determined and expensive approach to housing, educating, and integrating non-European newcomers, is far from just a German concern. The problem is Europe-wide and getting public opinion to understand that is made all the more difficult because unemployment makes headlines when skills shortages don't. The mismatch problem of people who have the right skills but are in the wrong place regionally is aggravated in most EU countries by restrictive labour laws coupled with housing shortages. It's a structural handicap that is contributing substantially to the jobs crisis.

Europe's skills mismatch and overall labour shortage means that at any moment there are something like four million unfilled job vacancies in the EU. Some of these are seasonal, as jobs in hotels and restaurants fluctuate. The really worrying shortage is in the information technology sector, ranging from the merely computer literate to the writers of software code. The overall shortage in the EU of these ICT specialist workers hit three-quarters of a million in 2015, with warnings from would-be employers that this lack is crippling Europe's economic future.

In Brussels, the EU commission has created what it calls a 'Skills Panorama' to identify industrial sectors with the most unfilled job vacancies, and so encourage better training and education of young people. It reckons that by 2020 a third of all jobs will require a graduate qualification of some sort, whether from a university or technical college. That's far above Europe's present output of highly qualified youngsters.

Convincing public opinion of this is tough when the focus is on unemployment. The slow-growth, no-growth picture in so many European economies makes it harder than ever to shine the spotlight on the invisible challenge of a shrinking and under-skilled workforce.

It's a problem of such enormous dimensions that it needs a much higher Europe-wide profile, and here the EU's ability to seize the public imagination is sadly lacking. The commission has been in the forefront of those issuing warnings, but they've sounded more like bleatings than alarm bells and have attracted little attention. As so often with Brussels' attempts to communicate, their warnings tend to be couched in economists' jargon instead of the plain terms that attract media attention.

## Sense and Nonsense About the Jobs Crisis

Brussels' hunger for popularity leads it to back EU-level job creation strategies, and to claim that its emphasis on 'green jobs' will create twenty million of these by 2020. Rather than that, EU officials should be using their expertise and their budgets to drive home the message that governments in most of the EU's member countries must remove restrictive practices and job protection devices if they are to make their labour markets work more efficiently.

The Brussels commission has been reluctant to emphasize this because it fears accusations of interfering in national politics. But the plain fact is that there's a widening jobs gap between the northern eurozone countries, where labour market reforms before the 2008 crisis encouraged hiring by employers, so unemployment has held steady at around five per cent, and southern countries where jobless-ness can be as high as twenty-three per cent.

The jobs picture looks grim in many European countries, and the possibility of a 'lost generation' of young people who may never have a decent job and a useful role in society is alarming. But it is also fair to say that the hysteria being whipped up over their plight can be exaggerated and clouds the task of selecting the right policies. It took an American commentator to point out what a good many economists and officials knew, but were reluctant to say on the record; the youth unemployment figures most often used by journalists are misleading.

Steven Hill, from the Washington-based New American Foundation think tank, is the author of a 2010 book entitled *Europe's Promise* and an articulate advocate in the US of the more caring European style of capitalism. He has explained that youth unemployment rates of almost fifty per cent in Greece and Spain, and thirty per cent in Italy and Ireland are grossly exaggerated because they are calculated as a percentage of unemployed people divided into the total number of workers in a country's or a region's labour force. In this way, twenty people without a job in a labour force of, say, 200 equals an unemployment rate of ten per cent.

That sounds reasonable, but there's a better way of calculating unemployment and getting a realistic picture of the jobs crisis among the young. It is to work out the ratio of under-twenty-four-year-olds without a job in relation to the total youth population. Using 2012 figures, he reckoned that method would cut Spain's headline youth unemployment rate from 48.9 per cent to nineteen per cent, Greece's from 49.3 per cent to thirteen per cent, and the 30.5 per cent attributed to both Ireland and Italy to 11.7 per cent and eight per cent respectively. The overall figure for young people in the eurozone would drop from 20.8 per cent to 8.7 per cent, making the challenge of getting school leavers into work far more manageable.

The EU's own statisticians at the Eurostat agency in Luxembourg, which gathers together national data on just about everything, in fact use both methods of calculation and releases unemployment ratios as well as rates. Unsurprisingly, journalists usually ignore the less dramatic figures. Steven Hill has also made the point that the difficulty of finding a job is encouraging young people to stay in education, and that discouragement from entering the workforce can severely distort the true picture. He cites France, which at one point was reporting a youth unemployment rate of twenty-two per cent, but once its large university-level student population was subtracted, France really had a 7.8 per cent rate, roughly the same as the UK, Germany, and, indeed, the United States.

These confusions about how best to measure unemployment don't mean that there is no jobs crisis in Europe, or that it is negligible. It's serious, but best tackled at national or even local level, leaving the much more structural problems of streamlining and modernizing European industry to EU-level cooperation and concerted action. There are, though, several ways that EU governments can address the structural difficulties that make finding and keeping a job harder than in the past. The first is to stop taxing employment so heavily, and the second is to encourage more women to work. And for many of them there's a third, which is to do what Germany did a decade ago and Thatcherite Britain in the 1980s, and that is to sweep away the many job protection devices that make labour markets rigid and inefficient.

Laszlo Andor, the Hungarian economist who as an EU commissioner held the employment and social affairs portfolio from 2010 to 2014, says that Europe needs new models for more flexible employment, and that a more inventive approach should be taken. 'We need a reset, not gradual improvement. We must think greenfield'.

This is an approach that should strike a chord with an industrialist like Harry Van Dorenmalen, chairman of IBM Europe. He is advocating a thorough shake-up in the hiring practices of big corporations such as IBM. Rather than take people on for the usual employment span of around twenty-five years, he suggests that companies like his own should consider guaranteeing fifteen to twenty years of employment, but not all of them necessarily with the same company. 'They could also be seconded elsewhere, or could even spend a year working on some project of their own. In return, the employer would expect to pay them less, let's say four-fifths of a full salary'.

Radical changes take time, and that's something young jobseekers don't have. The most immediate way to get more people into work is to overhaul the tax burden on employing and on being employed. Europe as a whole taxes labour much more heavily than most other parts of the world. The EU's *Taxation Trends Report* says that nearly half of member states' total tax receipts came from labour, with taxes on consumption contributing about a third, and those on capital less than a fifth.

The Brussels commission's report acknowledges that the EU has to be seen as a 'high tax area' with tax and social security contributions now more than forty per cent greater in terms of the overall GDP than in the US or Japan. The average tax rate on people's incomes across the OECD countries is thirty-five per cent, and in the EU the average rises to forty-five per cent. Taking the eurozone alone, the commission believes that a strong shift to taxing consumption rather than labour could over ten years add €65 billion in terms of output and create 1.4 million jobs.

Tax is a touchy issue because it's all about national sovereignty, and in general EU officials run scared of highlighting it. Brussels nevertheless needs to make a more determined and courageous effort to explain the benefits of an EU-wide rebalancing of taxation. That's easier said than done. Tax codes, with the huge body of law that builds up around them, are very difficult to reform. Governments speak constantly of doing so, but in reality they tend to add more layers of taxation instead of reducing them. The issue of how tax can help Europeans resolve their problems instead of compounding them is of crucial importance, and one where the refusal of so many EU governments to talk of a more collective approach needs to be challenged publicly by Brussels and debated openly by civil society organizations.

Going back to jobs, the second area where the European economy could be given a major boost is to raise the level of women's participation in the labour market.

In southern European countries, an average of only one woman in two of working age has a paid job, while in northern EU countries, and especially the Nordic ones, the figure is seventy per cent. It is a terrible waste of talent and energy, especially when looked at in relation to the shrinking of the European workforce and the threat it poses to long-term prosperity.

The first step that EU governments should take is to heavily subsidize child-minding facilities. A UK study has found that the costs of pre-school daytime child care that couples pay out of taxed income is greater than average mortgage repayments. In other words, it costs more to be a working mother than it does to keep a roof over the family's heads. Small wonder that women are discouraged from working, and that birth rates in Europe are too low to halt population shrinkage.

Another step towards fixing the problem of gender inequality would be to tackle the pay gap and increase the number of women in top jobs. Some governments—again, it's the Scandinavians who are in the lead—have been trying to do so through quotas and other means, but it's an uphill struggle. In Germany and the UK about sixteen per cent of company boardroom seats are occupied by women, rising to a quarter in Sweden, and slumping to a miserable one per cent in Portugal.

The pressures of child-rearing are well known, as are the cultural barriers that women have to contend with. But women are often better educated than men—in the richer countries a third now have a degree, against a bit more than a quarter of men—and are therefore a valuable resource. Getting more women into high-flying careers and ensuring that they are paid the same salaries as men would blunt the impact of Europe's demographic shrinkage, and would also have a fairly immediate effect in economic terms.

Econometricians at investment bank Goldman Sachs reckon that if the pay gap between men and women were to be eliminated, the eurozone economy would overnight get a strong boost, eventually becoming thirteen per cent larger. That's not an overly optimistic figure, because when their opposite numbers at the McKinsey management consultancy looked at the US over the last forty years they found an even more remarkable effect; they believe the additional women entering America's labour force over that period pushed the GDP twenty-five per cent higher than it would otherwise have been.

As discussed earlier, one of the key factors determining a labour market's efficiency, or lack of it, is mismatch, when the available workers and available jobs don't match up either geographically or in skills. Europe's mismatch problem is on a giant scale, with the economic crisis that began in 2008 underlining the way rising youth unemployment not only co-exists with but mirrors the growing number of unfilled job vacancies.

Mismatch in Europe would to some extent be reduced by the resumption of growth and improved economic activity in the most depressed cities and regions. That still leaves the more deep-rooted problem of needing more immigrant workers when Europe feels the impact of its ageing and shrinking. It may turn out that persuading public opinion of this will eventually prove a lesser problem than integrating newcomers of different ethnicities and religions into the European social fabric. Immigrant communities in many parts of the EU are already strikingly underprivileged, and often their young people are disaffected. In social terms that is shameful and potentially very dangerous, and in economic terms it is wasteful and costly. European society must make a far more determined effort to integrate immigrants and equip them with the necessary skills.

# 7

# Europe's Stuttering Efforts to Catch Up with the Digital Revolution

*The widespread failure of many European governments and businesses to keep up in the digital age has developed into a profound structural weakness. Productivity in the US that twenty years ago lagged behind the EU has leapt ahead, thanks to Americans' speedier introduction of new technologies. Europe's industrial shortcomings increasingly reflect underfunded research and sluggish innovation.*

Europe's industrial performance will largely determine its future, and contrary to what many believe, manufacturing in Europe is far from dead. It is growing and there's a school of thought that with the right choices industrial Europe should enjoy excellent prospects.

The widespread perception is, of course, that factories are closing down throughout the EU. This owes much to the way companies in China, India, and South Korea have grabbed larger shares of global manufacturing output, but that shouldn't blind Europeans to the importance of their own industrial base. The point is perhaps best illustrated by Germany, which has won universal admiration for its booming high-tech and engineering exports yet is slipping significantly in the global manufacturing league. It is currently in fourth place although in the 1980s it was number two, right behind the US. The point, needless to say, is that relative decline can be deceptive;

Germany's expensive added-value goods are far more desirable and profitable than China's more humdrum products.

Analysts at the McKinsey Global Institute see a healthy future for manufacturing in Europe 'as long as companies and countries understand the evolving nature of manufacturing and act on the powerful trends shaping the global competitive environment'. They underline the continuing importance of manufacturing around the world by pointing out that a huge proportion of service industry jobs are in fact services to manufacturers, and that nine-tenths of the money that funds R&D projects comes out of the pockets of manufacturing industry.

Europe is threatened by three serious structural problems. The first is that industry in the EU is no longer as innovative as before. It is a dangerous illusion to think that engineers and designers in European companies come up with novel ideas, and that Asian competitors only copy them and so are always one step behind. The KPMG accounting and consultancy group's *Global Manufacturing Survey* has painted a very different picture.

Its research into the operations of several hundred leading companies around the world saw a reversal of the long standing domination of the advanced industrial nations in research and development and new technological innovations. Warning that 'the next wave of transformational innovation' has already started, KPMG found that over sixty per cent of manufacturing companies in the emerging economies are now pouring their resources into fundamental research with the aim of coming up with their own world-beating products and technical breakthroughs.

The second big drawback is the structure of manufacturing industries in most EU countries. They have shrunk so much that they may no longer be able to grow. Britain is a case in point; the birthplace of the Industrial Revolution today accounts for a tiny 2.4 per cent of global factory output and ranks behind such newcomers as Brazil and South Korea as a manufacturing nation. Thirty years ago, over six million people worked in British manufacturing, but that's down to 2.5 million and is still falling, with such formerly powerful names as motor manufacturer British Leyland, the ICI chemicals group, and engineering giant GEC either dismembered or having disappeared altogether.

Manufacturing used to account for a quarter of Britain's GDP, and now it's just over ten per cent, which is the same as the contribution made by the City of London and the UK's financial services sector. The archetypal British manufacturing company today employs fifty people and the only really big engineering groups left are the defence contractor BAe Systems, whose chief customer is the UK government, and the Rolls-Royce aerospace and jet engines group.

Britain's manufacturing sector lags far behind Germany, and also behind France and Italy, but that doesn't mean the industrial outlook in those and other European countries is much rosier. The problem they all have in common is that there are no longer enough big companies to generate more start-up ventures and so boost overall manufacturing activity. Germany's famous *Mittelstand* of medium-sized engineering companies—the often family-owned specialist outfits that are its export backbone—are pulled along by their business with really big groups like Daimler, Siemens, Bosch, VW, and BMW, which also see trouble ahead.

Germany's exporters have become so successful that German manufacturers' profits in 2013 amounted to three quarters of the total profitability of all Europe's manufacturing companies in Europe. The implications of that for future investment and growth in the EU are discouraging. Nor is it entirely good news for Germany itself because it has come to rely heavily on three sectors—precision engineering and machine tools, chemicals, and motor vehicles—that are all vulnerable to change. The engineering economy risks being reshaped by such advances as 3D printing, and in chemicals there's North America's shale energy challenge and the accelerating trend in oil-producing regions such as the Gulf to start producing their own petrochemical feedstock.

The most immediate challenge is to the future of Germany's highly successful car industry. It's far from certain that its leading companies can stay ahead without shifting more and more of their manufacturing outside Germany. Almost half of German-badged cars are now manufactured abroad, and its biggest volume producer VW makes a third of its cars in Asia. For the European automotive industry as a whole, the outlook is grimmer still; twelve million European workers rely on an industry whose factories are running at only two-thirds capacity even though the minimum profit-making level is fourth-fifths.

The third question mark over European manufacturing is productivity, where EU countries lag well behind the US. The early lead taken by American companies in moving to the 'knowledge economy' has served them well, because in both goods and services they are able to produce more with fewer people. In manufacturing, the US and China are now more or less neck-and-neck in terms of output, measured by value of the goods being produced, but America does so with just a tenth of the Chinese workforce.

## How Europe Lost Its Productivity Advantage

Productivity is one of those fundamental forces in determining economic performance that are very hard to get to grips with, and harder still to explain to the general public. The way the US caught up with Europe in terms of productivity and then overtook it is of overriding importance, yet hardly figures in European debates over politics and policies.

During the last quarter of the twentieth century, the EU-15 western European countries chalked up productivity performances that easily outstripped those of the US. Their average yearly improvement was 2.7 per cent when America's was stuck at 1.3 per cent. The turn of the new century saw a sudden and dramatic reversal, with Europe's slowdown and America's acceleration a reflection of their very different approaches to the knowledge economy.

American companies' productivity now improves by a little more than two per cent every year, while Europe flounders with annual productivity growth rates that at 1.5 per cent at most are getting on for half their own late twentieth century performances. The slower pace in Europe of computerization and digitization of industrial processes is the obvious explanation, and it's not at all clear that Europe can ever catch up with the US or with new competitors in Asia whose industries are starting from scratch and don't have to wrestle with the complications of streamlining old-style factories.

Productivity improvements hold the key to Europe's collective future. The importance of concentrating on that rather than on expensive public spending schemes has been emphasized by Philippe Maystadt, a former deputy prime minister of Belgium who for more than a decade until 2011 ran the European Investment Bank, the EU's funding arm in Luxembourg. In a hard-hitting article in the Brussels-based policy journal *Europe's World* entitled 'The myths that Europe's policymakers must forget', Maystadt wrote:

> Many people conclude that for their country to prosper it needs to outperform other countries. Not surprisingly, the competitiveness of countries understood in this way continues to motivate a wide range of policy initiatives, including industrial policies to create and defend national champions and support for a variety of so-called strategic industries.

He went on to demolish the myth that countries compete with one another in the same way as rival companies. His point was that competitiveness should not be based on the company–country analogy but on productivity, arguing that:

> Budgetary support for R&D policies and competition rules that keep companies on their toes while granting successful innovators appropriate patent protection, should be combined to spur innovation. Europe has not moved as rapidly and vigorously on these fronts as one would wish, but it is clearly not too late to quicken the pace. The scope for unleashing productivity growth seems to be particularly great in the services sector.

Another factor contributing to the loss of market share of Europe's key industrial sectors is the high cost of labour. Political pressures have been making it hard for European companies to reduce their unit labour costs, and it takes an unusual degree of political courage by a national government to cut workers' wages. When Germany did so in 2003—the move that famously cost Social-Democrat Chancellor Gerhard Schroeder the 2005 general election—the country's runaway wage inflation was abruptly halted. Unit labour costs there were soon lower than those of the eurozone average, and also of the UK and the US.

It doesn't always take a political initiative to confront wage cost and productivity problems. The revival of the UK's car industry has been among the few bright spots in Britain's otherwise gloomy manufacturing picture, and it's been down to the determination of foreign owners and their managers to achieve great productivity improvements. When Japan's Nissan first invested in a greenfield plant in north-east England, its output was acceptable but hardly spectacular. The Sunderland factory employed 4,600 workers in 1999, and they produced 270,000 cars in that year. Since then the workforce has grown by another 800 people to 5,400, and production has shot up to 480,000 cars a year.

Nissan's decision to invest in the UK, and later in northern France and in Spain, was largely determined by its need to manufacture inside the EU's single market. Its success in achieving steady productivity gains at Sunderland did much to attract other foreign investors, with the result that the once-moribund British motor industry now produces 1.5 million cars yearly and is heading back to its 1972 record output of almost two million vehicles when the British Leyland group was at its zenith. The Indian conglomerate Tata bought up Jaguar Land-Rover in 2008 and introduced much the same flexible working practices as Nissan, transforming production and profitability at its two West Midlands factories.

Europeans cannot, however, look to foreign investors to save their industrial base. What is needed are policies that will address the structural weaknesses of EU countries' economies, and one of the greatest of these weaknesses is Europe's high energy costs and its vulnerable dependence on imported oil and gas. The Ukraine crisis, Russia's annexation of Crimea, and the confrontation over Moscow's backing for Russian-speaking separatist militias in eastern Ukraine have highlighted Europe's failure to tackle its long standing energy problems. Over a quarter of Europe's gas comes from Russia, and rising tensions over the Kremlin's assertiveness and the EU's sanctions are driving home the message that European governments have badly mishandled their energy policies.

Europe now finds itself in an impossible position on energy; its energy-dependent industries are paying such high prices that they can't compete internationally, yet subsidized prices to Europe's consumers are too low to end the present alarming standstill on investment in new power stations. To keep the lights on in the years ahead, EU governments will need to cut through the tangle of competing subsidies and fragmented national energy markets and tackle political sensitivities they have long avoided.

American companies are riding high on their country's shale energy boom, while their competitors in Europe are having to pay three to four times more for gas, and double for their electricity. Yet electricity prices in Europe need to rise by at least twenty per cent to tempt energy utilities to invest the $2 trillion that's needed over the two decades up to 2035 to replace old or loss-making power plants. EU governments are to some extent the victims of their own laudable efforts to lead the world in the struggle against climate change.

Subsidies to encourage renewable energy sources such as wind and solar power have distorted Europe's energy markets and discouraged investment by removing the long-term certainty that's needed to attract funding. Less forgivable is the muddle and petty rivalry the same governments created through their national energy policies. Brussels is again trying to promote a pan-European energy policy and is calling for an 'Energy Union', but is uncertain of success. Talk of a European electricity grid that could balance power surges in one part of the EU with shortages elsewhere risks remaining just talk.

Energy is crucial to Europe's future. Soon after taking office, the new European Commission led by Jean-Claude Juncker declared it would champion its predecessor's 'energy blueprint' containing ambitious targets for 2030, and if anything it is redoubling the EU's drive to create a single energy market and kick-start investment in new power stations. Just as important is the need for the commission to redouble its promotion of an EU industrial policy that will address the structural weakness of Europe's industries and place more emphasis on developing services like software. Its first goal must be to help put an end to what some people call 'the European paradox', meaning Europe's enviable track record in scientific breakthroughs coupled with its abysmal performance on turning them into industrial innovations and cutting-edge products.

## 'Captains of Industry' Aboard a Rudderless Ship

The heads of some of Europe's most powerful industrial companies have a yearly lunch meeting with the president of the European Commission. It's not a formal affair, but it gives them a chance to get their worries off their chests.

And that's about all; neither the hosts nor their guest seem able to make much headway on tackling the policy inertia that holds back Europe's business corporations. From the lack of employable people with high-tech skills to cripplingly high energy costs, and from sluggish public investment in basic research to the many areas where the EU's single market is still non-existent, the big bosses who belong to the European Roundtable of Industrialists have plenty to complain about.

The Brussels commission has been doing its best. In the two decades since the EU's single market was supposedly completed in 1992, it has been urging member governments to scrap the remaining barriers in such vital areas as energy, banking, and public contracts. But domestic political pressures still exert the power to protect those barriers, with the result that Europe's big companies don't have the same continental-sized economy as America, and small companies don't have the same room to grow.

The Roundtable group comprises about fifty corporate chieftains and was started in the early 1980s to put some business backbone into Brussels' renewed effort to turn the long standing ambition of a European single market into reality. It supplied the sort of expertise on trade barriers and unfair practices that the commission lacked, and so contributed substantially to the project's achievements. Since then, its efforts to see EU governments' remaining protective devices swept away have been a good deal less successful.

Its president until stepping down in late 2014 was Leif Johanssen, head of Sweden's huge Ericsson telecoms group. He complains of the long way Europe has to go in most key areas if it is to be globally competitive. 'The information technology and telecommunications sectors are very fragmented', he says, 'there's no European transport system as such, and when it comes to energy there's absolutely no single market.'

Johansson acknowledges that the problem goes deeper than national dodges to protect local companies, or a failure by the EU to fix shortcomings in the digital economy. 'It's impossible to have people retire at sixty, especially if they've been in education until the age of twenty-eight or so. We need much greater flexibility in our work practices.'

The British secretary-general of the European Roundtable Brian Ager has been instrumental in putting together a prescriptive report entitled 'What EU policymakers should do, and what they should not do'. Ager points to the growing shortage of engineers in Europe, saying that by 2020 there will be a deficit of 400,000 of them. That training gap will take longer than a few years to fix, and the industrialists are deeply concerned at the way Europe's governments are failing to put money into basic pre-competitive scientific research in universities.

In the US, they point out, public authorities of one sort or another spend about twenty times more than in Europe on funding research and buying goods and services related to it. The Roundtable report's authors want to see much more of the €2 trillion-plus spent yearly by EU governments on procurement programmes earmarked to help close Europe's R&D gap with the US and with all the Asian countries now coming up fast.

Among the report's detailed demands for improvements to trade policy and the rules governing fair competition, there is the wider charge that Europe suffers from the absence of an integrated industrial policy. Dismissing the Lisbon Agenda adopted in 2000 as ineffective, and doubting that its Europe 2020 successor is backed by an adequate 'implementation mechanism'—meaning national governments won't meet their commitments—the report calls for a 'comprehensive and pro-active European industrial policy strategy'.

A good many political leaders past and present agree. Joaquin Almunia, who was Spain's EU commissioner for a decade, says: 'We knew Europe needed new dynamism as we entered the Information Age, but the Lisbon Agenda was a delusion. France's President Jacques Chirac prevented the 'naming and shaming' of countries that failed to deliver on their promises to meet the Lisbon Agenda's goals, so it was a major lost opportunity. Also, we didn't explain to citizens where the EU was meant to go; the political messages didn't match the scale of the problems'.

Those problems have grown in the intervening years, with only a handful of countries defying the trend. Germany, Austria, Finland, and Sweden have been living up to their Lisbon commitments to raise spending on R&D to three per cent of their GDPs, but for the rest it still averages around the two per cent it stood at in 2000, and in some cases not even that. With less money in real terms being spent on research by so many European companies and governments, what Europe's industrialists used to call the sharp cutting edge of technological innovation is getting blunter by the year.

Across the Atlantic, the total figure for investment in research is appreciably higher. R&D gets 2.5 per cent of America's GDP, in Japan it's over three per cent, and in Asia's tiger economies it's higher still. The result is that their products and services are making inroads into the market shares that European companies once considered impregnable, and European jobs and living standards on which they so heavily depend. Maire Geoghegan-Quinn, who was Ireland's EU commissioner responsible for research, innovation, and science policies, says: 'It is true that Europe has been missing out on some cutting-edge technologies, which is why the EU has fewer fast-growing innovative enterprises than the US. It is also true that in a worst-case scenario the EU's share in the global economy could halve by 2050.'

Warnings from Brussels of the consequences of neglecting research and innovation run counter to the rhetoric of European governments trying to persuade voters that austerity and the axing of public spending is essential, and that a return to economic growth is just around the corner. No one doubts that the financial markets will sooner or later punish countries that fail to tackle their debt problem, but Brussels' message is that the EU's long-term outlook depends on keeping ahead on science and technology, and that's best done by pulling together, not separately.

The commission has been rebranding its efforts to promote cross-border research projects linking universities and companies in different countries in the hopes of creating a Europe-wide innovation policy. The EU's long standing 'framework programmes' are being repackaged as a successor initiative called Horizon 2020 which is investing €80 billion in research by 2020. As well as trying to talent-spot promising new technologies, this approach will attempt to shake up the emphasis on 'pre-competitive' research that has been the *leitmotif* of the framework programmes.

This sounds good, but there is widespread unhappiness with the way the EU manages its R&D efforts. 'The way we fund collaborative research', says Danish scientist Jens Rostrup-Nielsen, who was one of the founders of the European Research Council, 'results in nice reports and networking, but fails to stimulate actual innovation. Precompetitive research becomes non-competitive research. Projects should instead be given to competing groups working in parallel and feeling the heat.'

Areas where the commission hopes to stimulate innovation include a new approach to protecting intellectual property and improved financing for small and entrepreneurial companies. A single European-level patent that could cut the cost of protecting an invention by four-fifths is in the pipeline, though Spain and Italy have refused to go along with it because it has restricted its three working languages to English, French, and German. To help smaller companies get access to funding, the commission has proposed the creation of an EU-wide market for venture capital. It's far from certain that anything will come of this as venture capital has never really taken off in Europe; only two per cent of small company funding comes from the private financiers reviled as 'vulture capitalists', whereas in the US it's fourteen per cent and rising.

The commission dangles before European governments the promise of handsome rewards if only they would implement all the ideas they've agreed to. It says that as many as four million new jobs could be created by 2020 if innovation policies start to bite, adding a possible €800 billion to the European economy. Michel Barnier was the French member of the 2010 to 2014 commission handling single market policies, and he waxes lyrical about the benefits for the twenty-two million large and small companies that do business in the EU if the fifty proposed measures being advanced for fully completing the internal market were to be put into force.

To mark the twentieth anniversary of the single market's notional completion in 1992, Brussels unveiled a slew of further ideas that ranged from making online buying safer to improving air and rail travel. Intended as a rallying call for public opinion across Europe, it was greeted with polite scepticism by the media, many of whose reporters had heard it all before, and had also observed the absence of results.

Barnier's career has seen him shuttling between Brussels and Paris, arriving first at the commission in 1999 to take charge of the EU's regional policy, then back to France in the sensitive role of agriculture minister, and back to Brussels again to handle internal trade barriers. He knows all about the sensitivities that discourage national governments from seeing sense on EU-level policies. Talking about ways to overcome the weaknesses in the single market, he says: 'It's not a question of protecting different European industries; it's about investing in them'. He has been particularly anxious to breathe more life into the services sector, where Europe is so much slower than America to embrace the digital economy. 'Just by applying the EU's Services Directive', he says, 'we could by 2020 add up to 2.6 points to the overall GDP'.

Research by a host of independent analysts shows a good many other fairly straightforward steps that European governments could take to boost economic performance. Opening up the public contracts awarded by central, regional, and local authorities to competitive tendering from across the EU would cut costs and deliver savings to taxpayers. EU member governments have agreed to that in theory, but it is a pledge likely to be measured more in the breach than the observance. Public authorities may claim they award contracts on purely objective criteria, but somehow their business still seems to go overwhelmingly to national bidders.

## The EU's Stuttering Industrial Policies

Drawing up and implementing Europe-wide policies is a tricky business. Governments and big businesses insist they want a level playing field, but they don't want new rules that might rob them of advantages they already possess, and they certainly don't want Brussels to have intrusive new powers.

The upshot is that although the EU has been doing its best to create a concerted industrial strategy, it hasn't met with much success. European governments entered the twenty-first century with the Lisbon strategy's well-intentioned but vainglorious declaration that by 2010 the EU would be 'the most competitive and dynamic knowledge-based economy in the world'. The combination of determined reform and streamlining needed to turn that ambition into reality eludes them to this day.

The European Commission had drawn up a detailed and workmanlike approach to improving productivity and stimulating growth and innovation in its Lisbon agenda, but it has been unable to arm itself with the power to make EU governments honour their commitments. The waning of Brussels executive authority began well before then, and the chances of securing even some sort of 'naming-and-shaming' procedure whenever national governments fell behind on their Lisbon Agenda goals were probably non-existent. In any case, the commission never attempted to do so, and by as early as 2005 it was clear that the Lisbon strategy was doomed to fail.

It has been succeeded by a new attempt called Europe 2020, whose prospects seem little better. To start with, EU governments have included job creation in it, which in many ways risks running counter to the aim of improving productivity. The new strategy is also a confusing mixed bag of unconnected policies; they range from reducing the level of secondary school drop-outs to raising to almost a third the proportion of renewables in the EU's energy mix. The commission then tacked on in mid-2012 a couple of further initiatives called European Innovation Partnerships that are designed to encourage innovation by boosting cross-border investment and reducing the legal and other inconsistencies that make the EU marketplace more of a Gruyere cheese than a homogeneous whole.

The single market continues to be the cornerstone of EU-level policy efforts to overcome Europe's structural disadvantages. Without a continental-scale economy equivalent to the US, say its protagonists, there will be little chance of turning the tide on Europe's problems of a shrinking and insufficiently skilled population and low productivity together with high unemployment and social costs that are outstripping Europeans' ability to pay for them. Michel Barnier insists that completing the unfinished single market project therefore has to remain Europe's top priority. 'The failure of the Lisbon Agenda is a very real alarm bell', he says. 'We must decide on the key technologies we want, and how to save them. We need a twenty-first century industrial policy, and that's why the commission identified seven or so sectors. It's not a question of protecting European industry, but investing in it.'

Yet even when Barnier held high office in the EU, he knew that the odds are stacked against a truly unfettered single market. He and a special task force of officials prepared an impressive range of programmes, but were nevertheless uncomfortably aware that these did not add up to a radical assault on European countries' backwardness and were still far from the 'large-scale labour, product, market, and pension reforms' the IMF was saying could 'boost output by 4.5 per cent over the next five years' if implemented with determination.

In Paris, a leading economic think tank, the Centre d'études prospectives et d'informations internationales (CEPII), has published its own report on the value that European economies are still failing to derive from the EU's single market. Removing the hidden barriers that continue to discourage intra-European trade could by 2020 increase those EU members' national incomes by an average of over fourteen per cent, and would substantially add value in manufacturing, services, and agribusiness.

'The complete elimination of obstacles to trade across the Single Market,' commented the authors of the CEPII report, 'is indeed a stylized and unrealistic assumption. However, the magnitude of the potential gains is such that the study confirms undoubtedly the potential of the Single Market as one avenue to boost EU growth in the years to come and to escape from a vicious circle of recession'.

There's really no shortage of expert analyses of what ails Europe, and what to do about it. Not far away from CEPII's Paris offices, at another French think tank, 'Confrontations Europe', former MEP Philippe Herzog has developed a detailed twenty-five-point strategy for creating a pan-European industrial cooperation pact and for fundamentally reforming the rules governing EU markets. Herzog's ideas are visionary to the point of impracticality, ranging from the creation of an all-powerful EU finance ministry to having a common legal identity for all companies in Europe, great or small. His is, though, the sort of thinking that's needed to spark genuine debate on where Europe should be heading.

## Back to the 1930s: Pump-Priming the Economy with Infrastructure Projects

A very immediate and practical approach to the slow-growth, no-growth tentacles wrapped around so many of Europe's national economies is being championed by one of Germany's most successful management consultants. Roland Berger, who was an influential adviser on economic affairs to Chancellor Gerhard Schroeder, believes that a concerted strategy for modernizing Europe's crumbling infrastructures would be a powerful stimulus.

Europe is far from the only region of the world where a massive effort to build new infrastructure and modernize old is seen as the way to revive or create sustainable growth. In a report called 'Infrastructure productivity: The $1 trillion a year opportunity' the McKinsey Global Institute reckons that $57 trillion should be spent worldwide by 2030, and compares that to the $50 trillion value of existing infrastructure. Its report calls on EU governments to raise their infrastructural investments from an average of 2.6 per cent of GDP over the last twenty years to 3.1 per cent over the next two decades.

Roland Berger estimates the cost of an infrastructural overhaul at a trillion euros, breaking that down to €180 billion at very least on roads, €200 billion on water and waste disposal, €220 billion on energy, and €270 billion on telecommunications. As well as priming the pump of the European economy, that spending would also give a huge boost to the competitiveness of European companies. But how to pay for it? Public–Private Partnerships (PPPs), which have been looked to by the European Commission amongst others as the way forward for funding public services and infrastructure projects, are nowadays dwindling as private sector interest fades. At less than €12 billion in 2012, they have dropped back to the same level as 2003.

Perhaps the answer to where the money will come from is that put forward by French economics guru Jacques de Larosière, whose career saw him heading by turns the IMF, the Banque de France, and the European Bank for Reconstruction and Development. He is urging a strategy for using securitized loans, in which national governments would package and guarantee private sector debt to attract investors. His proposal aims particularly at revitalizing investment in smaller companies, and also seems appropriate for financing an ambitious European infrastructure strategy. As Roland Berger points out, there's an estimated €170 trillion in private capital sloshing around in the world's capital markets and looking for safe but profitable projects to invest in.

'We have to give up the idea that it is up to governments to supply infrastructure', insists Berger, who points to the attractive business opportunities that could be unleashed if private sector investors were encouraged to renew infrastructures like water, sewage, and railways that often date back to the nineteenth century. 'These are local decisions', he comments, 'but the EU's contribution would be to make the case for privatized infrastructure'. He says national governments should create investment-friendly conditions for private entrepreneurs to tackle problem sectors such as utilities and transport. 'It could have the same impact as the European single market or the "Open Skies" policy that opened the way to cheaper air travel', Roland Berger adds.

At the European Commission, Jean-Claude Juncker has set himself up as champion of a determined infrastructure investment strategy he believes could get the EU economy back into high gear. Even before taking over at the head of the commission he announced a €315 billion investment package as a central feature of his five-year term. Poland's then finance minister Mateus Szczurek then suggested that the stakes should be raised higher still and called for the European Investment Bank to launch a €700 billion infrastructure drive.

The shape and scale of the EU's infrastructure remains to be seen, but it's definitely not going to be a European version of the 'New Deal' launched by president Franklin D. Roosevelt when the Great Depression of the early 1930s reduced many Americans to abject misery. It will be much more modest, and it won't have the authority of federal initiatives grappling with the desperate situation the United States found itself in in the aftermath of the 1929 Wall Street crash.

There has been much resistance in Germany and other parts of northern Europe to the idea of using public works for a huge Keynesian pump-priming exercise. There are also doubts on a technical level about the criteria and management methods to be employed. Just as important, more than ninety per cent of the money envisaged must come from private sector investors, and not only is that going to take time but also it will require guarantees that EU governments are slow to give.

'Financial engineers' who put together ambitious infrastructural projects say, meanwhile, that Europe's problem is not so much money as a lack of projects. Discouraged by their own governments' insistence on austerity cutbacks, public authorities across the EU have been soft-pedalling on the preparation of infrastructure programmes and the bidding procedures they involve. Much of Europe lacks adequate housing and efficient transport links, and is burdened by outdated energy systems and nineteenth century water and sanitation arrangements. Yet no EU strategy exists to address these shortcomings, or even identify them.

The rights and wrongs of austerity designed to address many European countries' debt problems look set to go on dominating discussion of recovery measures and the rethinking of industrial policies. Of course they're important, but they are also eclipsing the more fundamental issue that Europe is slipping steadily behind its global competitors. The overriding priority for EU countries must be to modernize their industries, their education and training methods, and their work practices. Productivity is the key to competitiveness, and competitiveness is the key to employment. It's not a message that politicians with short-term electoral goals care to spell out, for they prefer to talk comfortingly about job creation schemes, but what we Europeans need most is knowledge creation.

# 8

# Why 'Brussels' Lacks Legitimacy, Credibility, and Even Genuine Power

*Never loveable, the European Union is nowadays downright unpopular. Brussels is scapegoated for rising unemployment and falling living standards, and also for strangling Europe with red tape. The benefits of European integration seem quickly forgotten and now doubts about the EU's democratic legitimacy are coming to the fore. EU decision-making was always ramshackle, and the eurozone crisis is underlining the need for a clear-sighted rethink of the European Union's basic structures.*

The opaque and unfathomable politics of the European Union have entered a new era, even if to the naked eye they look much the same. To outsiders nothing has changed, so national ministers go on meeting in more or less secret conclaves, MEPs in the European Parliament still enjoy power without responsibility, and the pampered high-priesthood of unelected and unaccountable EU civil servants continue to dream up cumbersome new regulations.

It's a distorted picture, even though it is widely shared by Europe's voters. The more accurate one is that the elections to the European Parliament that took place in mid-2014 mark a new departure, with the destination still unknown. Insiders knew that the EU-wide voting would herald a political storm of some sort, but were uncertain what sort of tempest it might be. In the event, it turned out to consist of two linked but different weather systems.

The less significant of these is that approaching a third of MEPs are now, to a greater or lesser degree, Eurosceptics. They are mostly a ragbag of nationalists and single-issue malcontents, so their disruptive power is likely to be limited. It's not impossible that they will make common cause on one or two policy questions, but their arrival seems unlikely to add up to much more than that.

Far more important is the power struggle that took place soon after the elections between EU member governments and the leaders of the biggest voting blocs in the parliament. These leaders insisted that the head of the grouping that had won the most seats should be made president of the incoming European Commission, and after some bitter and very public wrangling they won.

The distribution of top EU jobs had always been a cosy arrangement between the chancelleries of national leaders, involving secret, behind-closed-doors negotiations and a good deal of opaque horse-trading. The EU governments' decision to accept the European parliamentarians' nomination of Jean-Claude Juncker, leader of the centre-right European People's Party (EPP) grouping marks an important new development in the EU's governance.

At first glance, not much has changed; Juncker is a classic example of someone who EU government leaders could well have chosen themselves. Until 2013 he had been Luxembourg's prime minister for almost two decades, and so fitted neatly into the profile of commission presidents who for more than twenty-five years have all been former premiers. Described by UK prime minister David Cameron in what were obviously intended to be unflattering terms as 'a classic Brussels insider', Juncker has been among the architects of EU policies since the early 1990s.

Take a closer look, though, and his appointment as a 'democratically elected' commission chief can be seen to mark a new departure for the EU. Whether he likes it or not, Juncker has become the symbol of a much more assertive European Parliament. Although criticized even before he formally took office for not being the sort of reform-minded figure that widespread anti-EU voting clearly called for, the commission's new president will be answerable to MEPs in a way that none of his predecessors have been.

It would be wrong to believe that the European elections of late May 2014 were in any way a ringing endorsement of the European Parliament. It's more realistic to see the results as a massive rejection of the EU as such than as a sign that Europe's voters have started to take a closer interest in its institutional balance. Juncker's EPP lost about a fifth of the seats it had held in the previous parliament, the slightly smaller centre-left Socialists and Democrats (S&D) grouping also lost a little ground, while the mainly liberal ALDE (Alliance of Liberals and Democrats for Europe) coalition lost around a quarter of its seats. The winners, needless to say, were the Europhobes in all their various guises.

Nor was the process that led to Juncker's appointment any triumph of democracy; the three so-called *spitzenkandituten* (leading party candidates)—Juncker for the EPP, the S&D's Martin Schulz, and ALDE's Guy Verhofstadt—were chosen by just a few people within their own parties, leaving voters at the polls largely unaware of their existence. None of them won an impressive pan-European popular mandate, but at least the national governments' armlock on top EU jobs was broken. The long standing assertion by Europe's national governments that they bring democratic legitimacy to the EU because they were themselves elected has been countered, even if the parliamentarians' own claim is equally tenuous.

In the minds of many journalists, and so in terms of public opinion, the European Parliament gained a new level of authority. That may help counterbalance the widespread perception that the EU is run by faceless and unelected officials of the European Commission whose tentacles reach out into every level of business and government. In the eyes of many Europeans, and not just Eurosceptics, the sheer scale of the EU's rulebook—the *acquis communautaire* that runs to 140,000 pages—symbolizes the democratic deficit that enables EU officialdom to dominate their lives.

It is a complaint voiced across Europe, yet it is a misleadingly over-simplified view of the political muddle that is the European Union.

The EU's decision-making arrangements have tangled into a Gordian knot of enormous complexity, with competing ideas for unravelling it or cutting right through it. So it is worth sorting fact from fiction about how the EU works, along with who calls the shots and on what. The reality bears little resemblance to a 'super state'.

To begin with, the European Commission is no longer the same as the institution launched in the early 1960s, when Euratom and the European Coal and Steel Community's 'high authority' were merged with the infant Common Market's executive to form a single body. Then, and for a good many years to come, as well as being the guardian of the treaties, honest broker, and neutral referee between national governments, the European Commission could claim to be the world's biggest think tank.

As soon as the executive body of the new European Economic Community (EEC)—the EU as such wasn't born until 1992—was up and running and beginning to struggle with trade and other economic issues, it became a magnet for youthful idealists from its six founding countries. The challenge of creating a supranational authority attracted a new breed of imaginative young officials, most of them lawyers or economists by training, eager to invent new ways of breaking down the barriers that separated Europe's nations. Armed with the 'monopoly of proposal' awarded in its founding treaty, the commission broke new ground.

As it grew, the commission found itself overseeing and administering the snowballing body of European laws, policies, and funds, and that has turned it into a very different animal. Since its heyday in the 1980s, the commission's policymaking role has been steadily sapped by the biggest of the member governments, while its culture has undergone unattractive changes from within. Bruised by various minor scandals over the misuse of funds, it has become a bureaucracy that favours bean counters over adventurous problem solvers. The 'can-do' spirit of years past has been replaced by a concern to observe the commission's myriad rules that is often obtuse and at times verges on a perverse delight in its own rigidity.

'Eurocrats' who were once the enthusiastic advocates of European unity have become the heavy-handed administrators of budgetary programmes that seem designed to confuse and frustrate. And it's no longer certain that new recruits to the commission are motivated by idealism rather than by its generous pay scales. In Brussels and beyond, there's a widespread perception that EU civil servants are overpaid and arrogant. The commission has a lot of ground to make up on its public image. Its spokespersons are legion, but are so hampered by internal constraints that their communications skills are as dismal as ever.

There's one respect, though, in which the commission hasn't changed a lot. It is surprisingly small. Far from being the huge administrative octopus that so many of its critics charge, it has grown fairly slowly. Its payroll of some 17,000 people in the 1990s has risen to about 25,000 today, more or less in line with the increase in the EU's population through successive enlargements. As a British study of the Brussels executive noted not long ago, 'that should be compared with the 160,000 civil servants employed by just the Ministry of Defence'.

A bit bigger, then, but quite a lot weaker. The drawing away of power from the commission to the two other main EU institutions, the European Parliament and the Council of Ministers, the member governments' decision-making body, has led to a rise in the number of inessential and sometimes pettifogging initiatives the commission takes. As its former president, Jacques Delors, commented not long ago: 'Technocratic excesses do exist; the fewer powers the commission has, the more civil servants tend to overreach, going beyond their duty to propose and to execute. It is the duty of the commission—as a college—to be vigilant.'

## Democratic Legitimacy: The EU's Elusive 'Holy Grail'

The European Parliament can't hatch policy proposals in the same way as the commission, but its powers are far greater than before. Its members increasingly shape or modify EU legislation, it has oversight of EU spending in a good many areas, and it has to give its approval before new commissioners can be appointed. It has the 'nuclear weapon' of being able to dismiss the whole College of Commissioners, although not individual ones. In 1999 it threatened just that, but never actually did so because the commissioners themselves resigned en masse to avoid being ignominiously sacked over a petty financial scandal involving one of their number.

For all that, it isn't a real parliament; it can't raise taxes, it can't declare war, and it doesn't provide the EU executive with any sort of democratic legitimacy. That's the nub of the EU's problem; when things go wrong, there's no mechanism for ousting those who have been responsible for taking far-reaching political decisions on behalf of the people of Europe.

At official level, they are the diplomats and senior civil servants appointed by national leaders to run the intergovernmental mechanism that is the Council of Ministers. Its decision-making powers make it the EU's true legislative body, but the process for taking council decisions is to say the least opaque. Business is conducted in large part behind closed doors and the council has sometimes been described as a secret legislature, sharing that dubious distinction with Pyongyang.

The Council of Ministers should more accurately be known as the councils, for it groups together a number of specialist councils composed of different ministers, be they justice ministers, environment ministers, or finance ministers. Above them there's the supreme decision-making body of the European Council, composed of prime ministers and in France's case its president. The European Council's presidency used to revolve every six months between the member governments, but nowadays as part of a typical EU fudge, although they still hand the baton on to each other, genuine authority is in the hands of a council president with a five-year term, currently former Polish premier Donald Tusk who took over from Belgium's Herman Van Rompuy.

That makes it no less secretive. As Joachim Fritz-Vannahme, a think tanker at Germany's Bertelsmann Stiftung, puts it: 'The European

Council now has a permanent president, however it is neither fish nor fowl. It is a European assembly of national executives which performs a legislative function, and behind closed doors at that. A chamber of this kind would not be tolerated in any of the democratic systems of the member states.'

It's also a system that makes it easy for national governments to blame 'Brussels' for unpopular decisions they themselves had a hand in. Philippe Legrain, a British academic turned journalist, asks in his book *European Spring* on the future of the euro: 'Which other democratic legislature debates and takes decisions in secret, without a public record of who said what and how they voted?'.

The ministers who come to Brussels to deliberate and vote at the various specialist council meetings have either been elected themselves at national level, or at least are part of an elected government. They are not answerable to any EU interlocutors, nor are they subject to public scrutiny. That's perhaps understandable because intergovernmental decision-making is all about member states being able to protect their perceived national interests, but it makes the council's democratic pretensions unconvincing.

In the world of EU policymaking no one is accountable, and no one has to set out before electors their thinking on European-level policy options. In the commission, a culture of *omertà* protects officials from outside scrutiny, and at times even lawsuits have been threatened to discourage the media from publishing Eurocrats' names. Such discretion is true of most civil services, of course, but the difference between Brussels and national administrations is that government ministers can be called to account for their actions. In the EU system, there is no procedure and no forum for commissioners to be forced to justify what their officials have, or have not, done.

The complexity of European decision-making makes transparency difficult. Ideas for new rules or policies in theory have to come from the commission, and only the commission. In practice, they quite often come from EU governments instructing the commission. On top of that, there are the consultative procedures that enable companies' lobbyists along with civil society representatives to input their thinking and exert influence, and then there's the often lengthy process of getting the European Parliament's approval.

The parliament's members are sometimes dismissed as lesser politicians who are either on the way up or the way down. In fact, sitting on the parliament's specialist committees they frequently demonstrate remarkable expertise and technical knowledge. That and their elected status makes them an increasingly effective backstop against muddled or wrong-headed projects advanced by the other EU institutions. That still doesn't make them a real parliament.

If it's axiomatic that all politics are local, it's equally true that they are theatre. The European Parliament is neither. Its members' constituencies averagely number half a million people, and the nature of the parliament's work rarely sparks local interest anywhere. Its democratic credentials have even been challenged on the grounds that the constituencies of its 751 members are so unevenly distributed. Germany's constitutional court at Karlsruhe has expressed doubts about the European Parliament's legitimacy because of the huge disparity in the ratio of voters to members between some countries, notably between Germany (sixty-four million voters: ninety-six seats) and Luxembourg (260,000 voters: six seats).

As to theatre, the proceedings of its plenary meetings, whether in Strasbourg or Brussels, are generally dull and incomprehensible. Members of the European Parliament have the right to speak in any of the EU's twenty-four official languages, so the dedramatizing effects of simultaneous interpretation coupled with the sheer size of the 'hemicycle' and its tiers of often empty seats mean that parliamentary sessions are hardly a spectator sport.

When MEPs have the floor they all too often read out a statement rather than engage in debate. In 2008, the European Parliament decided to raise its profile by launching its own television channel called EuroparlTV. It's a brave attempt to foster greater interest, but the heavy hand of EU officialdom prevents it from being the sort of lively and controversy-provoking television that is needed. Its diet of 'talking heads' and coverage of MEPs making worthy points in Strasbourg at plenary sessions is far from the cut-and-thrust of political debate that viewers of national TV stations tune in to.

Where the European Parliament falls down most of all is in its lack of true left–right disagreement, argument, rivalry, and conflict. A pie-chart of MEPs' affiliations shows centre-right members grouped in the European People's Party, centre-left ones in the Socialists and Democrats group, and liberals belonging to the ALDE coalition, but instead of tooth-and-nail opposition to each other, they are models of cooperation. Until the shake-up of the latest European elections, they colluded in alternating the post of president of the parliament between them.

The technicalities of EU legislation often eclipse left–right considerations. It's hard to take an ideological stance on the regulation of food labelling or the properties of solar panels. The most common division among MEPs tends to be their views on the EU itself, meaning the balance of power between its institutions and its authority *vis-à-vis* national governments; in crude terms, the degree to which they are pro- or anti-Europe.

## The Reform Roller Coaster

The three main European institutions are thus all flawed in one way or another, and there is growing pressure for change. But to what? We've been here before in various ways and at different times, most recently with the Lisbon Treaty of 2007 and before that the European Convention in 2003 that arguably made matters worse.

Back in December 2001, EU leaders announced a new commitment to 'greater democracy, transparency, and efficiency'. Their Brussels summit at the Belgian monarchy's royal palace of Laeken set in motion a reform process that however well-intentioned was to prove divisive and confrontational. At that time, the EU was riding the crest of a wave following the successful launch of the euro in January 1999 as Europe's new single currency, and with its ambitious 'big bang' eastward expansion of 2004 already coming into sight.

There was a palpable sense of the European Union's gathering strength. The eight-year single market project was deemed to have met its 1992 deadline with only a few loose ends to be tied up. The fall of the Berlin Wall in the autumn of 1989 had led not just to German reunification but also to the EU's ambitious strategy of enlargement that would bring in formerly communist eastern and central Europe. And now the euro would bind Europeans together into a single continent-wide economy. It was clear to all that the time had come to turn a new page in the EU's political development.

The upshot of the Laeken summit was that a European Convention would be called so a cross-section of political representatives could hammer out ways of adapting the EU's decision-taking machinery to its changing circumstances. Under the leadership of the seventy-six-year-old former French president, Valéry Giscard d'Estaing, a body of 105 convention members drawn from national governments, parliaments, and the European institutions would look at ways of streamlining the EU's hybrid structure into a more democratic, transparent, and efficient mechanism.

Formally called the Constitutional Convention, its aim was above all to agree on how much power EU member states should retain and how much would be handed to a central—that's to say federal—authority. It was vaguely modelled on the Philadelphia Convention of 1787 that gave birth to the constitution of the United States, and whenever Giscard d'Estaing's age was called into question he happily pointed out that Benjamin Franklin had been eighty-one when he played a leading role in Philadelphia. America's founding fathers are frequently cited by European federalists, especially Alexander Hamilton and his model for federal government.

Despite the upbeat rhetoric, the European Convention inflicted wounds that are not yet healed, with participants still at odds over where it all went wrong. Some believe that in retrospect it was too soon to raise the federal issue, others that highlighting the idea of an overriding European constitution sank the whole initiative. It certainly divided public opinion. In countries such as Britain and France it was a red rag to a bull, and in others it was warmly welcomed. In Germany, the idea of a new 'basic law' common to all Europeans was hailed as an excellent initiative.

The text of the Constitutional Treaty that emerged from the convention in mid-2003 was a barely readable fudge, and was duly signed in late 2004 by all of the EU's then twenty-five governments, the eastern enlargement having brought in ten newcomers. But it was never ratified because referenda in the Netherlands and France saw voters reject it. That torpedoed the whole project because of the need for EU countries to accept it unanimously.

A hasty rethink bound together those elements that could be rescued into the 2007 Lisbon Treaty, whose unlovely formal name is the Treaty on the Functioning of the European Union. It created the EU's new diplomatic voice and addressed the thorny question of decision-making by abolishing the need for unanimous agreement on almost all matters through the introduction of what is known as double majority voting. To take account of the generally smaller countries joining the union, a majority now has to be at least seventy-two per cent of EU governments instead of fifty-five per cent previously, representing sixty-five per cent or more of the European population.

The Lisbon Treaty's changes were only significant to the few diplomats, officials, and business people who specialize in EU affairs. For the mass of public opinion in Europe they were eclipsed by the financial crisis of 2008 and the ensuing economic malaise.

The eurozone crisis has wreaked havoc in more than the financial markets. It has highlighted the north–south divide in Europe, even though bridging that wealth gap had been among the original aims of creating the euro as a single currency. Opinion divides sharply amongst economists, politicians, and journalists over the euro's likely future health, and over the way its existential crisis was managed. But perhaps the greatest cost has been to the EU itself; the credibility of the whole European project has been badly shaken, and the disagreements between northern and southern eurozone countries over the austerity and bailout terms imposed on the latter have badly soured mutual confidence.

With living standards under attack and the outlook so gloomy for Europe's younger citizens, people's faith in the EU has undergone a serious setback. Rising doubts about the value of European integration and its ability to deliver positive results aren't only about the EU's diminishing returns but also about trust in its institutions, with the European Parliament no less under fire than other parts of the EU machinery.

Criticism of the EU from outside Europe is particularly painful. The US-based Pew Research Center sent shockwaves through EU officialdom in 2013 with a survey entitled 'The New Sick Man of Europe: the European Union'. This reported that support for the EU had slumped to forty-five per cent from sixty per cent the year before. It saw favourable opinion of the EU as greater in Germany, where it slid from sixty-eight per cent to sixty per cent, than in hard-hit eurozone bail-out countries such as Greece, where it stood at only a third. A year later, on the eve of the European elections, Pew revealed that Europeans' positive views of the EU had dropped to only thirty-six per cent, with almost two-thirds seeing the EU as 'remote' and seventy per cent complaining that 'their voices went unheard'.

Pew's analysts said the economic crisis in Europe has 'created centrifugal forces' that are undermining popular support for the EU. Its polls made headlines around the world and caused much soul-searching in Brussels, yet they can have come as little surprise to anyone who had been tracking the increasingly negative opinion surveys being conducted around Europe.

The EU's own Eurobarometer pollsters have for some years been reporting disastrous increases in negative opinion of the European Parliament along with a stubborn majority of people who say they are indifferent to it. In 2008, over a third of people interviewed had a positive view of the parliament, and in the years since then that support dropped to around a quarter. The same proportion of people, twenty-six per cent, expressed a negative opinion of it, although five years earlier its critics stood at only seventeen per cent.

Those figures need to be seen in a wider context of economic crisis and discontent with politicians generally. Eurobarometer reported in mid-2013 similarly gloomy views when people were asked whether they were satisfied with the way their own national democracy works. Only twenty-three per cent of the people interviewed in Spain said they were, rising to thirty per cent in Italy, and fifty-five per cent in the UK.

## Addressing the EU's Credibility Gap

European politicians of all stripes are increasingly concerned that steps must be taken to address the EU's waning support and credibility. In Madrid, the EU's former top diplomat, Javier Solana, insists that a radically different approach is needed. He argues that 'the Brussels bureaucracy hasn't legitimated change... The EU has so far been top down, and now we need to create a more bottom up approach'.

A first step, he thinks, would be to introduce an annual EU-wide referendum on a topic of real interest to people, whether it be the need for a common European tax on financial transactions, green taxes, or anything else. 'The present generation of European leaders is finished', says Solana. 'We need a new generation of leaders, and they should meet once a month so as to create teams of national civil servants who would be working on the same problems.'

The views of a life-long socialist like Solana on the need for radical change are partially shared by his former political adversary José Maria Aznar, who was Spain's right-wing Partido Popular prime minister from 1996 to 2004. 'We should give no more powers to the European Parliament', says Aznar, 'while the commission has become irrelevant and the European Council is weak. We must organize European decision-making better'.

Aznar is far from being the only former national leader who wants to see real change. Wolfgang Schüssel was Austria's centre-right chancellor from 2000 to 2007 and sees the decision-making question in starkly practical terms. 'One of the very real problems', he says, 'is that foreign ministers have lost influence. Heads of government meeting in the European Council are "late deciders" so we need earlier decision-making to keep policies moving'. He thinks that what the EU really needs is fully-fledged 'Europe ministers' whose seniority would ensure that they have the authority to make the intergovernmental mechanism work more effectively.

Schüssel adds that when looking at ways to improve the EU's present political arrangements it is important to improve 'subsidiarity', the jargon term for leaving decision-making at the appropriate national, regional, and even local levels. 'The European Parliament and the EU as a whole are always seeking more, and often unnecessary, powers. We should instead be taking subsidiarity more seriously'.

At the other end of the political spectrum, one-time communist Massimo d'Alema, who as leader of Italy's Democratic Party of the Left has been both prime minister and foreign minister, is impatient with what he sees as a still theoretical debate about overhauling EU decision-making. 'What we don't need now is an abstract discussion about legitimacy', he commented to a group of experts in Brussels in early 2013, adding: 'The EU is hidden behind a veil of technocracy. The commission's president should be chosen by voters in the European elections'.

Politicians who were EU commissioners in the outgoing team headed by former Portuguese prime minister José Manuel Barroso generally share this gloomy view of the situation. 'I always hoped a big crisis in Europe would help', says Spanish socialist Joaquin Almunia, 'but to resolve this one requires new political institutions—you need to convince voters you've got a way out. The question now is whether the institutional architecture that dates back to Jean Monnet and the 1950s is still valid. An unelected commission weakens its own credibility, but how can it be given the authority needed to tackle EU-level issues that include structural reforms on pensions and social welfare?'.

Almunia is a former Spanish employment minister who went on to serve two five-year terms as a commissioner. He had a ringside seat for the tug of war between the champions of the 'community method' of EU decision-making and those who insist that intergovernmental power must be supreme. 'During the first Barroso commission', he recalls, 'there was little or no debate on EU versus national authority. The commission was reduced to a more technocratic role. But if citizens are seen to prefer intergovernmental methods, then it's hard for the commission to resist'.

Much the same concerns exist amongst commissioners from the EU's newcomer countries. 'The European Convention was a golden opportunity, and we missed it', says Andris Piebalgs, who until late 2014 was the Latvian commissioner whose two stints in the executive saw him handle development aid and before that energy policy. 'The EU's unpopularity is not just about its communications—it is about its democratic accountability, and it is therefore very serious'.

Piebalgs puts his finger on Europe's fundamental political problem when he says: 'I believe we need to build a federal Europe, but we nevertheless have to remember that the centre of life in the EU is national sovereignty. The changes that are needed may be too deep to be championed by the commission. And if they are too sensitive for the EU, the lead needs to come from Europe's political parties. And not just within the European Parliament with the European People's Party, the centre-right coalition there, or the Socialist Group, but Europe-wide'.

Janez Potocnik, who was Slovenia's member of the commission for the ten years after his country joined the EU in 2004, sees the future in similarly sombre terms: 'The structural and cultural problem facing Europe is that our democracies and economic systems are very short-term, while our twenty-first-century problems have to be addressed long-term. The checks and balances of EU decision-making may prevent us from taking wrong decisions, but they also prevent quick reactions to new developments'.

Stefan Füle, who was the Czech Republic's member of the second Barroso commission, agrees: 'We don't need more firemen to put out the flames of the crisis in Europe. What we need most of all is strategists to avoid "the big one"—the major crisis that lies ahead'.

## What is the Way Ahead?

So where does the EU go from here? Its structures and its culture now appear to be no less criticized by political leaders who have had a hand in running its affairs than by ordinary people. In large parts of Europe the EU seems reviled rather than merely criticized. The signposts to Europe's future point away from unity and towards a strengthening of the go-it-alone mood in all European countries.

In France, the anti-EU, anti-immigration Front National was able to win twenty-five per cent of the votes in the European elections, more than the twenty-one per cent of France's centre-right UMP, or the governing socialists' fourteen per cent. In Britain. UKIP's supporters gave it twenty-seven per cent of the vote, beating the Labour party with twenty-five per cent into second place. Similar Eurosceptic triumphs made headline news in Denmark, Austria, Belgium, and Greece, and are prompting political reassessments in many other countries.

The results of European elections are often dismissed by incumbent governments as 'protest votes', and that's surely the point. Europeans are protesting about the way the EU is run and its failure to deliver on its promises. That leaves the unresolved question of whether those voters genuinely believe that their own national politicians and decision-makers are capable of confronting global challenges more effectively than the EU, or whether they could be wooed back to the EU fold by more persuasive advocates of a much more united and effective Europe.

There's a strong consensus amongst the more hard-headed analysts that individual European states are so small in global terms that they'll be hard put to defend their interests against the pressures exerted by the rising economic powers of the twenty-first century. That's a macro-vision that isn't very evident in national political debates, and EU officialdom's inability to hammer home this message is a major shortcoming. The excuse senior Eurocrats often trot out is that stressing the EU's geopolitical role would be 'to interfere in the domestic affairs of member states'.

Jean-Claude Juncker has an opportunity to try and change that, and should use the muscle and resources of the European Commission to engage public opinion in a much wider discussion of the the value of European unity. That means greatly enlarging the agenda for EU reform. During the run-up to the last European elections, the focus of those urging reform was chiefly on internal matters such as cutting red tape or strengthening subsidiarity rules to 'repatriate' the EU's powers back to national authorities. There was scant emphasis on Europe's international role.

Europeans need to have a much more global vision of their place in the world and the influence they can exert, and that means clearly defining Europe's aims. The EU has to fashion more effective political machinery, and it requires the new leaders of its other institutions— Donald Tusk at the European Council and the present EU top diplomat Federica Mogherini—to rank strategic thinking above the purely tactical. If they can begin to identify longer-term ambitions for Europe on the world stage, that would mark a very welcome new phase. Brussels has long been satisfied with the largely tactical approach that sufficed for creating EU standards, but has proved incapable of addressing global challenges. Europeans must wake up to the fact that the EU and its mid-twentieth century ramshackle institutional compromises are no longer fit for purpose in the twenty-first century.

# 9

# Searching for an Exit from the EU's Political Labyrinth

*Europe's half-century of wider and deeper integration has seen EU institutions originally designed for one function now required to serve quite another. New structures are needed, but what? Adapting political mechanisms that suited six broadly similar economies to serve twenty-eight very different ones is urgent but divisive. To tackle its global challenges, the EU needs some form of political streamlining. That'll be tough, so a first step is a more honest Europe-wide public debate on the issues.*

The European Union lacks the political institutions for efficient and transparent decision-making. There's a good measure of agreement on that from Eurosceptics and Euro enthusiasts alike. So what sort of changes could fix the worsening political problems coming down the road at the EU, and how can the ramshackle structures of a European project that has evolved in fits and starts from a free trade area of six economically similar countries be adapted to today's twenty-eight-nation hybrid whose members' needs and priorities are so varied?

Whatever the solutions may look like, in the longer term they all need to resolve the eurozone crisis by finding new governance mechanisms for the single currency. And whether a country is in the eurozone or outside, all the EU's member governments agree that the sustainability of the euro is in their own vital national interest. That means creating a new political dimension to the economic and monetary union.

The origins of the eurozone crisis are generally accepted; its southern members had been using the cheap credit it offered to live far beyond their means. 'The euro's crisis was always going to come', remarked Latvia's Andris Piebalgs towards the end of his ten-year stint as an EU commissioner, 'the question was when'. His country, incidentally, somewhat counter-intuitively joined the eurozone in January 2014 and was followed by neighbouring Lithuania a year later.

Joaquin Almunia, who became the EU commissioner for economic and monetary affairs when the euro's good times were roaring ahead in 2004, says much the same. He believes that Europe's structural problems long predate the eurozone crisis. 'The euro was presented', he recalls, 'as a magic solution that would remove the economic and political obstacles to closer integration. The talk was of the "powerful dynamics" of the single currency, but meanwhile EU countries were losing their competitiveness, and that in turn was hitting their ability to observe the Maastricht criteria conceived in the early 1990s to encourage convergence of their economies and to limit debt levels.'

Pedro Solbes, another Spanish socialist who was Almunia's predecessor in that post when the euro was launched in 1999, believes that to safeguard the single currency it is essential to tackle debt levels. 'We need to go back to the stability pact, but with tougher sanctions', he says, referring to the Stability and Growth Pact that eurozone countries signed up to when the euro was born, and which limited governments' deficits to three per cent of GDP and of debt to sixty per cent. But in 2005, for short-term reasons that turned out to be disastrously short-sighted, Germany and France insisted on 'greater flexibility'. By relaxing the pact's disciplines they opened the door for spendthrift countries that have since had to be bailed out.

In the wake of those nations' sovereign debt crises there has been a flurry of policies aimed at enforcing greater discipline in the eurozone. There is nevertheless widespread agreement among both analysts and policymakers that these are only sticking plasters when what's needed is major surgery.

For the eurozone to be genuinely stabilized there must be a new political structure embracing not only the nineteen EU countries in the eurozone but also the nine outside it. The twin challenges facing Europe are, first, to find an acceptable way of making the EU more democratic; and, second, to introduce new rules and procedures that strengthen the economies of countries both inside and outside the eurozone. Some call for 'political union' as the way ahead, but to others this is anathema.

## No Consensus on What 'Political Union' Would Mean

German thinking on political union was mapped out by Chancellor Angela Merkel when she seized the occasion of the Maastricht Treaty's twentieth anniversary in 2012 to set out her aims. In a widely reported speech at Berlin's Humboldt University she said:

> Without doubt, we need more and not less Europe. That's why it is necessary to create a political union, something that wasn't done when the euro was launched...We believe we will stand better together if we are ready to transfer competences step by step to Europe.

Merkel saw three phases in this process. The first was the Fiscal Compact that was signed just a few weeks after her Humboldt speech by all EU governments except those of the UK and the Czech Republic. She explained that the compact's introduction of tough new budget disciplines was an essential first step because it demanded a constitutional commitment. The second phase would be a more intrusive approach to the coordination and even harmonization of taxes, with national budgets supervised by the European Commission and eurozone finance ministers collectively. This would involve an insistence on meeting competitiveness and growth targets, and on funding key areas like education.

That second phase is now well under way. It began at the end of 2011 with the 'six-pack' measures for strengthening the old stability pact disciplines, followed soon after by the 'two-pack' initiative for giving the European Commission surveillance and enforcement powers. If it continues along the lines spelled out by Merkel it would eventually mean a substantial transfer of sovereignty away from national governments and their parliaments.

Merkel's third phase would see the commission becoming what she termed 'an EU economic government'. In this vision, the European Council grouping the EU's national leaders—heads of government, and in the case of France the head of state—would become the second legislative chamber in a new bi-cameral European Parliament that would be at the heart of a federal Europe.

It is often said these days that what Germany wants Germany gets. But Merkel's vision certainly isn't shared by all the other EU governments. In the UK it has support on neither the right nor the left. At about the same time Chancellor Merkel was making her milestone Berlin speech, in London an influential Labour Party figure was saying the opposite. Jack Straw, who was Britain's foreign secretary from 2001 to 2006, was calling for the European Parliament to be junked and replaced by a new assembly of national parliaments. He was responding in part to an opinion poll showing that only eight per cent of Britons thought their voice counted in European decision-making, with seventy-eight per cent saying it doesn't.

Straw may be among the yesterday's men of British politics, but he spoke for more than a few disaffected Britons when he told an audience at the left-leaning Institute for Public Policy Research that 'the mechanism established thirty years ago to fill the gap of the democratic deficit, the directly elected European Parliament, has not worked, and in my judgement cannot work in its present form'.

That's not just a British view, of course. Few in the EU would deny that the European Parliament has its shortcomings, but there's little agreement on how to address them. It's obviously unrealistic to think that it could be scrapped and replaced overnight by something more efficient and as, if not more, democratic. Sad to say, the European Parliament has become something of a whipping boy for the EU in general, and for its perceived failure to head off the economic slow-down hitting living standards.

Rather than abolish the European Parliament, most of the practicable suggestions for overhauling the EU and addressing its political shortcomings seek to build on its democratic legitimacy. One innovation that is expected to strengthen the parliament's role and that may eventually alter the character of the commission was the way the 2014 European elections decided who would be the EU's new chief executive. Thanks to what seemed at first glance just a throwaway paragraph in the Lisbon Treaty, Jean-Claude Juncker received a democratic mandate of sorts to become president of the European Commission.

Although not directly elected by European voters, he was indirectly elected as a consequence of the votes awarded to the major political groups in the European Parliament. That's because of a few ambiguous lines hidden away in the acres of text of the Lisbon Treaty that EU leaders signed in December 2007. A brief passage says the commission's future presidents would be chosen by the European Council 'taking into account' the result of European elections.

## Bringing Democracy to the European Commission... and the Parliament

The head of the EU executive had until then been chosen by national leaders in far from transparent fashion; much secret horse-trading between prime ministerial aides would result in a papal-style announcement that lacked only the puffs of white smoke. For the two decades after Jacques Delors stepped down in early 1995, national leaders' choices were made on the basis of two criteria, one openly acknowledged and the other strenuously denied.

The first criterion to be eligible for the commission's top job was that a candidate should be a former prime minister. The other, the hidden one, is that no troublemakers need apply. Delors satisfied neither of these conditions, especially not the second; his widely acknowledged success in breathing new life into the European project during his ten years in Brussels owed much to his being a thorn in the side of member governments. When he thought it necessary, he defied objections based on national rather than European considerations. Without his grit, the single market project would never have progressed from unattainable dream to reality. It spoke volumes of their attitudes to the European project that EU member governments never again saddled themselves with another Delors.

Under the new system, the 2014 European elections decided whether the commission would be headed by someone from the political left or the right, with what that implies for its leanings during the president's five-year term. The coalition of centre-right parties making up the European People's Party, to which the UK's Conservative Party no longer belongs, selected Juncker as its candidate, just as the centre-left Socialists and Democrats chose the German MEP Martin Schulz, who then as now held the presidency of the European Parliament, while the ALDE liberals' candidate was former Belgian prime minister Guy Verhofstadt.

Europe's national governments tried hard to contest the Lisbon Treaty's meaning, arguing that 'taking into account' was not the same as deciding. The outcome of the wrangle was probably determined by UK prime minister David Cameron's ill-judged public objection to Juncker as 'an arch-federalist', as this demonstration of British Europhobia quickly swung the argument in Juncker's favour. It is now hoped that the choice of even just a semi-elected commission president will help answer criticisms that the EU's main institution is without any democratic legitimacy. It may also be that in future the triumph of the *spitzenkanditaten* process ('top candidates' from political groupings) will make European elections more relevant and interesting because the political groups will lay competing policy platforms before Europe's voters.

It is an innovation that some experts have been working towards. Sir Julian Priestley, a British Eurocrat who for many years headed the European Parliament's administrative machinery as secretary-general, put forward detailed proposals along these lines in a report for the

Paris-based think tank 'Notre Europe', whose titular head is none other than Jacques Delors.

Priestley had some harsh words to say about the European Parliament's electoral system. 'When is an election not an election?' he asked in an article shortly before the parliament itself backed the idea of indirectly electing the commission's president. His answer was:

> When there is no campaigning worthy of the name, when there are few perceptible differences between candidates, when the candidates themselves are kept in the shadows, when political parties do not compete and seem almost indifferent to the outcome, when the electors have no clear idea about the role of the body to be elected, and when campaign topics appear to have nothing whatsoever to do with its functions.

He added that 'this is, of course, a caricature, but as a description of past elections to the European Parliament it contains more than a grain of truth'.

The present administrative head of the parliament, the German CDU Christian Democrat Klaus Welle, shares Priestley's view that there's much to be done to improve matters. In a brainstorming report called 'EP 2025' he foresaw a heightened role for it as a eurozone parliamentary body with full powers of scrutiny over budgetary decisions and their implementation. His vision of a much more muscular parliament includes the right to assess the impact of draft EU legislation 'as an equal to the commission' and to monitor member governments' implementation of EU rules.

The European Parliament in any case gained considerable new powers through the Lisbon Treaty. The *Financial Times* summed up its progress neatly: 'Once derided as a powerless talking shop, the parliament has through perseverance and some low cunning grabbed hold of almost all EU policy; financial reform, banker pay, trade pacts, data protection rules and a trillion-euro budget.'

Greater power in the hands of elected MEPs has done little to allay popular mistrust of the EU. The mood across Europe is that the EU has to change. Increased parliamentary power and the indirect election of the commission's president will probably not be enough to silence criticisms of the EU's democratic shortcomings. Many voices continue to argue strongly for direct elections to the commission's top post that would give the holder an unassailable mandate, while others advance compelling reasons for not doing so.

When Germany's finance minister Wolfgang Schäuble accepted the city of Aachen's prestigious annual Charlemagne Prize in 2012, awarded to people considered to have most advanced European integration and understanding, he suggested that the European Parliament should be sidestepped and that there should be direct elections to choose the European Commission president. Not long after that, two experts with hands-on experience of how the EU works coauthored a paper setting out the case against direct elections.

In an analysis published in Brussels by the Centre for European Policy Studies think tank, former Belgian ambassador to the EU, Philippe de Schoutheete, and a former commission director-general for industry, Italian economist Stefano Micossi, wrote: 'The direct election of the commission president does not seem a very good idea... As an alternative, one may have to consider mechanisms to strengthen the democratic legitimacy of the presidency of the European Council.' Among their conclusions they included a stronger role for national parliaments in EU decision-making and the introduction of 'some form of direct accountability of the European Council to the European Parliament'.

It may be a reflection of Britain's increasingly Eurosceptic mood, but political scientists in the UK seem in the vanguard of those advancing ideas for reforming the way the EU works. Charles Grant, founder of one of the few pro-European think tanks in Britain, the Centre for European Reform, thinks that even the indirect election of the commission chief is fraught with danger, arguing that politicization of the traditionally neutral and apolitical EU executive could backfire. *The Economist*, where Grant was once a journalist, took a similar view when its Brussels correspondent worried that 'a more overtly political president would damage the non-partisan role of the commission, which claims to act on behalf of large and small states alike'.

Another expert on European politics, Vernon Bogdanor at King's College, London, has taken the idea of submitting the president of the commission to election an ambitious step forward by suggesting that the president's twenty-seven colleagues in the College of Commissioners should also be directly elected. At present they are nominated by their own governments in consultation with the incoming commission president, and must then be confirmed by the European Parliament. Electing them could ensure they are household names, and that would automatically raise the commission's profile and improve its standing.

The sad truth about the EU's commissioners is that for fifty years they've been a very mixed bag in terms both of ability and political clout. Appointment to the Brussels executive can be a government's recognition of someone's virtues, and it can also be a useful way of sidelining an embarrassing rival or thanking a has-been with a salary and pension on a scale rarely matched in national politics. Germany should be singled out as having sent not a single front rank politician to Brussels since Walter Hallstein, the distinguished and very able first president of the commission whose undying legacy is that he based its structure on Chancellor Otto von Bismarck's nineteenth century model for regional government.

Still with the history books, a suggestion from Larry Siedentop, a UK-based American political philosopher and author of a much-discussed book entitled *Democracy in Europe*, is for the creation of a European senate comparable to the nineteenth century US Senate with members appointed from the ranks of Europe's national parliaments.

That's an embellishment on the various ideas put forward for bringing national parliamentarians back into European decision-making. Before direct elections began in 1979, MEPs were delegated, with many of them holding a double mandate with a seat in their national parliament as well as in the European assembly. Looking back, that wasn't such a bad idea as it created expertise on European affairs now so lacking in national capitals.

One of the most common suggestions has been to concentrate on tightening the connection between nationally elected MPs and MEPs through the mechanism of COSAC. It's the acronym for the awkwardly named Conference of Parliamentary Committees for EU Affairs created in 1989 to coordinate national parliaments' scrutiny committees and promote contacts between MEPs and national parliamentarians. Weak and neglected, it has long been among the living dead in the EU system. But it could yet be the means to strengthen democratic oversight of EU decision-making. COSAC was among the beneficiaries of the Lisbon Treaty's recognition that national parliaments should have some sort of EU role. It introduced a system of yellow and orange cards that enable national parliaments to contest commission proposals, although unlike the cards that referees show to football players, there's no red card.

A yellow card requires a demand by at least a third of them that the Brussels executive should reconsider a proposal, and an orange one that has to be backed by two-thirds forces its abandonment. By mid-2014 two yellow cards had been played, with the commission backing down on one—EU-wide rules on the right to strike—and sticking to its guns on the other, the creation of an EU 'public prosecutor'. An idea for introducing a green card to let national parliaments review EU laws or propose new ones has been tabled by Dutch MPs and the UK's House of Lords, and may yet pick up more support.

The snag with a good many of the reforms being advocated is that they would need treaty change, and even if the EU's member governments agree, that must also be ratified by the European Parliament. One suggestion that looks helpful and sidesteps treaty change has come from another British academic, Simon Hix at the London School of Economics, who argues that changing the proportional representation method used to elect MEPs would do much to revitalize European elections and halt the steady slide in voter turnout.

Hix points out that the two methods of proportional representation most used to elect MEPs are the closed and open systems, with larger EU countries generally opting for the closed version in which voters choose a party, and party bosses decide who should head their list and thus be assured of a seat. He reckons that a switch to the open system in which voters can choose both party and candidate would do much to reverse the slide in voter turnout. As a bonus, in Britain it would probably be bad news for the Eurosceptic UK Independence Party, UKIP, with support moving back to the Conservatives.

These are just a few of the myriad proposals from throughout Europe in print and broadcast media as well as in specialist academic and party political publications. They aren't necessarily a representative cross-section of the suggestions being advanced, but they reflect the view among people familiar with the EU that its democratic deficit continues to be a major problem requiring a radical solution.

## The Eurozone Crisis and Governance of a Two-Speed Europe

Discussions of the EU's future usually zero-in on its legitimacy. Opinion surveys show ebbing public enthusiasm for the EU institutions that contrasts with buoyant support for achievements such as the single market and the euro. Even when fears about the collapse of the single currency were at a peak in 2010, Eurobarometer found that although only forty-two per cent of those polled had respect for the EU's institutions, three-quarters wanted to see closer economic policy coordination in the wake of the eurozone crisis as well as more EU-level supervision of banks.

Confidence in the EU continues to wane. When Eurobarometer put much the same questions two years later, the situation had worsened. Faith in the EU had suffered such a vertiginous fall that in Spain almost three-quarters of people polled said they mistrust it, worse than the UK figure of sixty-nine per cent, and with comparable figures of fifty-nine per cent in Germany, fifty-six per cent in France, Italy fifty-three per cent, and Poland forty-two per cent. In other words, people may want 'more Europe', but not from the EU.

Before the eurozone crisis, much of the debate over improving the EU's democratic accountability appeared theoretical and certainly lacked urgency. Instead of worrying about its own unelected status, the Brussels commission was wont to congratulate itself on the size of its accredited international press corps—'second only to Washington'—and the expertise of those journalists on even the most arcane aspects of policy. This ignored the reality that journalists' coverage of ideas for tinkering with the EU's decision-making arrangements excites little interest among the European public.

It isn't so much that the general public find it too distant and theoretical; it's also that opinion-formers in national media and politics have a limited interest in encouraging any shifting of the spotlight of public attention elsewhere. Journalists covering national politics don't really want to focus on supra-national policymaking shaped far from home. The same goes for national politicians who strive to maintain the fiction that they still control the levers of power.

That's beginning to change. The focus for democratic reform of the EU is moving from people's rights to the rights of countries. The unending crisis over the euro's sustainability is pitting debtor nations against creditor nations and creating an urgent need for new governance mechanisms. The bail-outs and austerity measures that have been forced on Cyprus and Greece, and to varying degrees on Ireland, Portugal, Italy, and Spain, have done great damage to the notion of fairness and democracy inside Europe, and thus have fuelled the rise of extremist and usually Eurosceptic political parties.

It's not only the debtor nations that feel hard done by and are demanding more democratic ways of handling matters. German voters resent being forced to contribute to rescue funding that from 2010 to 2012 amounted to €400 billion, and rally round the familiar slogan of 'no taxation without representation'. There are similar resentments in Finland, the Netherlands, Austria, and even France. Some of the braver politicians in those countries have tried to explain that, far from suffering loss, their economies have gained substantial advantage from lower borrowing costs and inflows of capital previously held in southern eurozone countries, but no one's really listening.

This in no way diminishes the need for more satisfactory democratic mechanisms to make the euro manageable in the long term. Consensus is growing that for the common currency to survive, radical changes must be made. That demands much stronger disciplines to bind together the very different economies and political cultures inside the eurozone, for it was the lack of a common discipline that allowed the southern countries' indebtedness to get out of hand. Public opinion in the northern EU countries has therefore to be convinced that the sharing of the southerners' debt—'mutualization' in the jargon—is essential, that national economic policies must be scrutinized by a powerful central authority, and that there should even be a common eurozone budgetary policy.

The eurozone's shortcomings have been neatly summed up by UK prime minister David Cameron, who clearly was never a great fan. He told a House of Commons debate that the vital features of any successful currency union must be that there is a lender of last resort, economic integration, and the flexibility needed to deal with shocks, fiscal transfers, and collective debt. 'Currently,' he said, 'it's not that the eurozone doesn't have all of these; it's that it doesn't have any of these.'

He was speaking before the European Central Bank's (ECB) president Mario Draghi took a much tougher stance on eurozone rules. In mid-2012, Draghi's blunt statement that the ECB would do 'whatever it takes' to defend the euro calmed financial markets overnight. He backed that up by declaring that the ECB would be the euro's lender of last resort through its 'outright monetary transactions' mechanism. This commitment to unlimited purchasing of any troubled eurozone government's bonds effectively ended the sovereign debt crisis, but of course doesn't tackle the root problem of a monetary union that is pushing its members apart instead of bringing them closer together.

Europe's North–South gap is going to remain a serious threat to the integrity of the EU for the foreseeable future. The origins of the eurozone crisis can be traced back to the fact that, once part of the eurozone, southern Europeans were able to take on far greater amounts of debt than would have been possible had they still been using their own national currencies; and when the system's creditor countries imposed austere bail-out terms their economies suffered terribly. The big question now is how to fashion an economic strategy and a political mechanism that can reconcile the interests of the southern debtors and their northern creditors.

The London-based Belgian economist Paul De Grauwe has suggested that the key will be a more symmetrical approach to eurozone countries' macroeconomic policies. To avoid placing an unsustainable burden of austerity on the debtor countries, he proposes that creditors, especially Germany, should give a powerful stimulus to the whole eurozone by allowing governments' budget deficits to rise, arguing that even if they reach three per cent of GDP their own economies will be growing fast enough to keep the debt to GDP ratio constant.

Germany's political leaders are increasingly aware that their vital national interest is to preserve the euro, but convincing voters of that is another matter. The history of the euro is unlikely to sway opinion, but the hard fact is that when the deutschmark was replaced by the euro at the start of 1999, Germany's exporters gained a huge advantage overnight. Their goods were suddenly much cheaper to buy because they were denominated in a substantially cheaper currency. Had that occurred in any other circumstances than the birth of the euro, Germany would have been accused of an unfair competitive devaluation and would doubtless have been sanctioned by other major trading nations.

If the past is unpersuasive, perhaps future threats are more convincing. Researchers at the Bertelsmann Stiftung think tank in Germany reported in mid-2013 that a return to the deutschmark would very badly affect the German economy. They looked ahead to 2025 and calculated that each year it would lop 0.5 per cent off the annual GDP, probably amounting to a one-third cut in potential German economic growth. The Bertelsmann report reckoned that the cumulative cost would be €1.2 trillion, about half the present annual value of the whole German economy.

Germany more or less ties with the US as the second biggest exporter after China. Its exports account for around a third of national output, yet reports of this sort make few headlines in the popular press. Persuading public opinion in Germany and in the other more successful northern eurozone countries of the concessions they must make to keep the single currency intact isn't easy. The idea of 'eurobonds' that would capitalize on creditor countries' creditworthiness to enable debtor ones to borrow at reasonable rates of interest makes good sense, but meets with unwavering opposition.

People in the troubled southern eurozone countries—unsettlingly referred to as 'peripheral'—are equally suspicious of a tough new centralized authority for governing the euro. Athens and Nicosia bitterly resent the high-handedness with which the 'Troika' of officials from the European Commission, the International Monetary Fund, and the European Central Bank imposed punitive bail-out terms on them. They have suffered at first hand a combination of loss of their own sovereignty and a lack of the solidarity between member states that was among the EU's most attractive features.

It's impossible to tell when and if the eurozone countries will stop their bickering over new governance mechanisms. The 'six-pack' and 'two-pack' measures that arm the Brussels commission with greater powers are a step in that direction, but anything tougher demands a new treaty, and treaty change risks rejection by voters in those countries where a referendum is either mandatory or impossible to avoid.

It also opens a Pandora's box on the future of the EU as a political arrangement. How should the eurozone be governed when the EU is so deeply split between countries in the eurozone and those outside it? The arrival of Latvia in the eurozone in 2014 and Lithuania in 2015 raised its membership to nineteen countries, leaving nine EU states unrepresented in the 'Eurogroup' of eurozone finance or economy ministers whose policy decisions inevitably affect Europe as a whole. The introduction in November 2014 of a 'double majority' amendment to the EU Council of Ministers' system of qualified majority voting means that while at least sixty-five per cent of the EU's population still has to be represented in a majority, the proportion of member states needed drops from seventy-two per cent to fifty-five per cent. Eurozone countries have a permanent in-built majority, should they wish to exercise it.

If the euro is to be underpinned by new rules and more solid institutional mechanisms, where would that leave the outsiders? There has already been ill-tempered wrangling in which the UK and the Czech Republic refused to allow eurozone countries to use the framework of EU law to implement their agreement on fiscal cooperation, and that's likely to be just the first of such stand-offs. If the European Commission is to be given more responsibility for managing closer cooperation between eurozone governments, how does that square with its duty to the EU as a whole?

The short answer is that it doesn't, and it can't. That's the message being conveyed by those who say that a 'two-tier' Europe is the only answer to these problems. The case has been very clearly articulated by French constitutional lawyer Jean-Claude Piris, who for many years headed the legal services in Brussels of the Council of Ministers. In an influential book entitled *The Future of Europe: Towards a two-speed EU?*, Piris rejected the notion of the EU eventually becoming some sort of federation. Instead, he set out various options for reconciling the closer integration of countries inside the eurozone with the running of the wider EU.

Piris's sharp legal mind helped draft a good deal of EU legislation, and he believes a *de facto* move towards a two-speed EU could be achieved by harnessing the Lisbon Treaty's provisions covering closer eurozone cooperation within the framework of EU law. A *de jure* option would be for those countries to conclude an international agreement between themselves that would allow them to establish a genuine economic union in parallel with the existing EU treaties.

He has sketched out ways the EU institutions could be tweaked to accommodate parallel eurozone decision-making, emphasizing that the eurozone members' additional treaty would need to underline the obligations of the EU to all its members. All of this would rest on the idea, Piris explained in an article for the *Europe's World* policy journal in 2012 that 'the eurozone must not become the first class of a permanent two-class EU, but should remain the temporary vanguard of the whole Union, playing the role of a locomotive and showing the way to all other member states willing to be part of it'.

That may sound acceptable, but it's not how public opinion in much of Europe sees the prospect of a two-speed arrangement in which some countries could press ahead with closer integration without waiting for the EU as a whole. Eurobarometer has found that in Greece no more than a quarter of people accept the idea, and misgivings are much the same in Portugal, Malta, Spain, Ireland, and Italy. Even in Germany and Austria only fifty-seven per cent think a two-speed Europe is a good idea.

The strains created by lengthy and persistent recession in much of Europe and by the tough austerity measures introduced to counter sovereign debt crises make it hard to believe that for the foreseeable future European voters will be in the mood to accept any radical changes to the EU. John Maynard Keynes's well-known dictum that austerity should only be applied at times of boom but not bust applies equally to all policies requiring popular support. Any EU government that even implicitly acknowledges the difficulties of economic recovery by advancing political change risks punishment by its electorate.

## An Impossible Maze of Unacceptable Choices

So where is the exit from this impossible maze of unacceptable choices? The outlook for EU-level politics seems increasingly grim, with the greater representation of Eurosceptic parties in the European and national parliaments and the possibility that 2017 may see the departure of the UK from the EU. Optimists in London think that the referendum promised by David Cameron would strongly resemble the 1975 vote that confirmed British membership by a two-thirds majority. They argue that despite all the Eurosceptic rhetoric, the three major UK parties will all campaign for a Yes vote.

If they are wrong and the British were to withdraw from the EU, that could well be the catalyst for overwhelming change and even the end of the European Union in its present form. Whether or not that's what the future holds in store, the overall picture isn't encouraging. There seems unbreakable deadlock between those who believe the EU cannot advance without some form of political union and those determined to resist it.

Europe's economic doldrums look set to bar the way to even a minor redrawing of its political institutions. The EU is locked into a vicious circle. All the warnings that without a political breakthrough there will be no long-term economic improvement have fallen on deaf ears. These include the forebodings of prominent financier and philanthropist George Soros, who has said that Europe faces a long period of economic stagnation comparable to that which beset most Latin American countries throughout the 1980s and has been suffered by Japan for more than a quarter of a century. 'They survived', he comments, 'but the EU is not a country and it is unlikely to survive ... The deflationary debt trap threatens to destroy a still incomplete political union'.

Soros's prescription for nursing Europe back to economic health contains elements that not a few governments would reject as medicine too bitter to take. He sees the fiscal compact that London and Prague refused to sign, and that has still to prove itself, as no more than a starting point. He wants much tougher debt reductions to be policed by a new EU-level body, and he urges that commercial debt be counted along with financial debt when assessing indebtedness. He wants EU countries' budgets to distinguish between current spending and public investments that pay some sort of dividend. These might sound like the airy thoughts of someone who isn't saddled with political constraints, but they are also the suggestions of a financial expert who knows what's needed to reassure the bond markets.

Rejigging eurozone governance and the roles of EU institutions may well be essential, but it looks impossible. European governments' paralysis is best illustrated by the stand-off between Paris and Berlin over economic policy. At its heart is German policymakers' abiding fear of anything that might stoke inflation—they cannot forget Weimar Germany's hyper-inflation in the wake of First World War, when workers collected their wages in wheelbarrows and a five pfennig postage stamp in 1920 cost ten billion marks by the end of 1923. Berlin will never accept any scheme to save the euro that doesn't also offer cast-iron guarantees of price stability.

That fear of runaway inflation is why Germany insists on some form of political union in return for any new 'solidarity' arrangements amounting to a long-term and perhaps permanent transfer of its resources to the weaker eurozone countries. Chancellor Angela Merkel's aides have reportedly shown her a balance sheet weighing the effects of EU-level and national policies that shows how some member governments' spendthrift ways plunged the eurozone into crisis. For Berlin, the no-brainer answer is political union that would entail more rigid rules and searching oversight powers.

In France, the view on both sides of the left–right divide is very different. The Franco-German partnership forged in the 1980s by François Mitterrand and Helmut Kohl bridged many differences and has done much to drive the EU forward, but it does not extend to a shared view of European political union. The sweeping powers vested in the president and his Elysée Palace officials by Charles de Gaulle's Fifth Republic would be severely weakened by the co-decision demands of a political union. To accept that would be tantamount to declaring a Sixth Republic, and in Paris that's not a topic for discussion, let alone negotiation.

Without a joint Paris–Berlin approach, there's little chance of political union in any shape or form. That harsh reality leaves the European Union unable to advance or retreat. It cannot go back without shredding the bonds of treaty law and EU regulation, and if it were to do that the whole edifice of free trade and the free movement of people and money could quickly collapse. It's equally hard to see it going forward without some significant shifts in Europe's political landscape.

The EU is criticized from all sides for poking its nose into areas that have long been of purely national concern. It usually does so because many of the laws that protect citizens' safety and well-being can easily be turned into protectionist trade barriers unless they are the same throughout Europe. It is also why somewhere between three-quarters and four-fifths of all the really important legislation affecting people's lives, and especially the way they do business and earn their living, is now decided consensually at EU level.

Europe's governments have all been complicit in those decisions and all enjoy democratic legitimacy. But that hasn't been enough to take the EU forward into the new era that irresistible external and internal pressures are demanding. Europe is in the notoriously uncomfortable position of being between a rock and a hard place.

# 10

# Putting some Muscle into Europe's 'Soft Power'

*Politicians and diplomats speak of Europe's need 'to speak with one voice', but still the EU doesn't walk the talk. That's largely because bigger countries such as France, Germany, and the UK see foreign policy as their preserve. At the heart of the EU's lack of clout lie its weakening military capabilities; to contribute more to international security Europe must develop global outreach and reverse its crippling defence cuts. The vaunted 'soft power' of the EU is really no power at all.*

The building that houses the European Union's new diplomatic service stands out against the dullness of the neighbouring office blocks inhabited by the Brussels bureaucrats. It is light and airy, and is built in a circular form that provides a mini-campus in which its new breed of officials can stroll and converse. If architecture is any guide, it holds out the promise of change.

This handsome addition to the EU landscape was designed for the European External Action Service that it is hoped will see the twenty-eight-member governments speaking with one voice on foreign affairs and global issues. Now it is up to its occupants to prove that this is possible despite those governments' lamentable track record of disagreement on many of the major shifts taking place around the world. If they can't, their spanking new building risks becoming a monument to EU muddle and waste.

About two kilometres away as the crow flies there is another office block that also represents the EU's ambitions to be much more than the economic giant but political pygmy it's characterized as. This second building is down a side street close to one of Brussels' main cinema and shopping areas, and is significantly more modest. Home to the European Defence Agency, it's probably no accident that it is located so far from the heart of the 'European quarter' where the EU's commission, council, and parliament buildings are clustered together.

No accident because although security and defence is the most recent addition to the family of EU policies it is also a neglected orphan; the agency is undervalued, underfunded, and underemployed. Set up in mid-2004 after European governments led by Britain and France had awoken to the need for a common foreign and security policy, its ups and downs have since 2008 been chiefly downs. A variety of factors have seen the ambition of creating a muscular European defence identity and credible security arm reduced to a fading dream.

Awareness of the need to strengthen Europe's military capabilities through closer cooperation has been a feature of EU governments' thinking for a good many years. With the 1989 fall of the Berlin Wall, the collapse of communist Europe, and the end of the Cold War, it became obvious throughout the 1990s that Europe needed to review its security thinking. EU countries' humiliating weakness as they failed to prevent genocide in Bosnia drove the lesson home.

Their inability to quell by either diplomatic or military means the conflicts that broke out in the western Balkans between the countries of former Yugoslavia contrasted embarrassingly with the determining role played by the United States. Europe's impotence was somewhat disguised, though, by the eagerness of the ex-Warsaw Pact countries of central and eastern Europe to join NATO. For more far-sighted observers, the most important lesson of all was that the removal of the threat shared with the United States of Soviet-led conflict meant that the long standing North Atlantic security partnership was certain to change.

Two decades on, Russia's renewed assertiveness may prove a blessing in disguise for NATO and for Europe's neglected defence arrangements. The Ukraine crisis following Ukrainian president Viktor Yanukovych's ousting in February 2014 has been a sharp reminder that peace and security in Europe must not be taken for granted. Leaving aside the rights and wrongs of Russia's annexation of Russian-speaking Crimea and Moscow's support for separatist militias in eastern Ukraine, the clear message has been that Europe has ignored at its own peril Russian nationalism and the Kremlin's strategy for rebuilding its outdated Soviet-era armed forces.

The saga of the European Union's security policies has been an unhappy one. It began with high hopes in late 1998 when a Franco-British declaration outlined the two countries' plans for greatly heightened defence cooperation. Britain's prime minister Tony Blair travelled to the Brittany seaport of St Malo to stand alongside France's President Jacques Chirac and emphasize that Europe's two most militarily effective powers would be working together on joint projects, and that these cooperative arrangements would be open to others. Their formal agreement was signed on board the visiting British destroyer HMS *Birmingham*, and a year later almost to the day EU leaders at their Helsinki summit meeting in December 1999 set out fresh thinking on Europe's security goals.

Momentum was building fast for a radical overhaul of Europe's defence capabilities. In Brussels, Javier Solana, the veteran Spanish foreign affairs specialist, had moved across town in autumn 1999 from NATO's headquarters where he had been the alliance's secretary-general to a newly created post as 'high representative' for the EU's fledgling common foreign and security policy. The importance of the job was underlined by its being combined with the secretary-generalship of the EU Council of Ministers, emphasizing that Solana had behind him the full authority of all the member governments.

By December 2003, Solana's energetic promotion of defence cooperation saw the publication of a European Security Strategy which set out principles rather than policies for addressing the security threats of the post-Cold War world. It made clear that Europe's goal was to be an international player with its own agreed and consistent approach to foreign affairs. 'Europe should be ready to share in the responsibility for global security', it said, adding: 'We need to develop a strategic culture that fosters, early, rapid and, when necessary, robust intervention'.

Preparation of the document was paralleled by the creation of an EU Military Committee headed by a four-star general and made up of national military representatives of two- or three-star rank. Occupying quarters that had previously belonged to the commission, its uniformed permanent staff quickly became a familiar sight around Brussels' European quarter. Its job was to start on operational and contingency planning, and within two years a civil–military planning cell was added to coordinate the EU's humanitarian assistance with its future military outreach.

Solana's determined lobbying saw the birth the following summer of the European Defence Agency as a new player on the EU political scene, headed significantly by a Briton, Nick Witney, a top civil servant from the UK's Ministry of Defence. Its first priority was to use research partnerships and closer technological collaboration to strengthen Europe's large but steadily weakening national defence industries. It aimed to do so chiefly by persuading member states to scrap the protectionist devices that favour their national suppliers and instead save money through common procurement programmes. A study by McKinsey consultants has since estimated that by doing so EU countries could lop thirty per cent off their defence equipment budgets at a total yearly saving of €13 billion.

In 2000, the outgoing US President Bill Clinton had said that Europe at last had in Solana the single telephone number that Henry Kissinger had so famously if apocryphally called for. As well as creating a more coherent EU foreign policy, it began to look as if Europe's sprawling military forces numbering over two million people in uniform would be turned into an effective and mobile force capable of reacting quickly to distant conflicts. There was even talk amongst the most optimistic of a 'Pax Europa' eventually to be comparable to 'Pax Americana'.

The future looked bright. A follow-up Franco-British summit in London in November 2003 launched the creation of European 'battle groups'. First mooted at Helsinki four years earlier but not followed up on, the original idea was for EU nations to create multinational groups of roughly 1,500 troops capable of being deployed at very short notice. This at last took concrete form when a UN-backed European peacekeeping force was sent in June of 2003 to the Democratic Republic of the Congo. 'Operation Artemis' was a modest French-led force of 1,800 soldiers with a squadron of British engineer troops, and a tiny eighty-strong Swedish contingent, but it drove home the message that multinational European operations were feasible.

Governments and their military top brass leapt at the idea. Within a remarkably short space of time they had signed up to the creation of fifteen battle groups with a six-month roster system to ensure that two would always be on standby for immediate deployment. The Nordic, Baltic, and Balkan battle groups were flanked by Benelux, Franco-German, and various other national ones. It seemed an important advance towards the goal of interoperable European forces that would be able to communicate with each other on the battlefield, work under a unified command, and in the fullness of time would even use the same weaponry and ammunition.

But it was a paper army. In the years since the battle groups were declared fully operational at the beginning of 2007, not a single one was ever sent into action. EU governments' failure to exploit the achievement of creating them has been symptomatic of their overall neglect of the military. The battle groups were not deployed during the EU-led Libyan intervention in 2011 to oust Muammar Gaddafi, and there is a growing debate over their future. Germany's unwillingness to send its soldiers into combat, together with the political considerations that led it to stand aside from the Libyan operation, is putting the survival of the battle groups concept in doubt. They should either be abolished or their scope should be widened, say protagonists in this debate, and their fate has become more uncertain still following

NATO's creation of 'Spearhead' rapid-deployment troop formations in response to Russia's behaviour in the Ukraine crisis.

## Strong on Promises, Weak on Deliverables

Their uncertain future is in any case no more than a reflection of Europe's inability to get its act together on either diplomatic or defence questions. The promise of a much more muscular EU stance on foreign and security issues has turned in the space of a decade into a series of embarrassing failures. Europe's military capabilities— including those of France and the UK—are diminishing fast, and the EU's diplomatic ambitions have yet to produce measurable results. The jury is still out on the value of the European External Action Service. Starting a multinational diplomatic arm from scratch obviously takes time, but the signals on EU governments' willingness to adopt common foreign policies are discouraging.

The economic crisis that began in 2008 has wreaked havoc with the military. Deep cuts in defence spending have weakened EU countries' already neglected armed forces, raising doubts that they can ever again be made deployable. The worst example is the British army, long the most effective force in Europe and for many years capable of sustaining a divisional strength expeditionary force when France could field only a brigade. The UK government's austerity-driven eight per cent cutbacks in defence spending for 2011 to 2014 reduce the regular army to 82,000 troops, the smallest since the Napoleonic Wars two centuries ago. The head of Britain's armed forces, General Sir Nick Houghton, warned publicly that the emphasis on supporting defence companies at the expense of military personnel risked creating a 'hollow force', with sophisticated equipment but no one to operate it.

Right across the board, EU governments have seized on defence budgets as natural candidates for the axe. Putting a figure on it isn't easy because different monitoring agencies use different definitions, but for 2012 the European Defence Agency assesses defence spending in the EU at €189 billion, noting that it had dropped by over a billion euros from the year before, and was more than ten per cent down on the the level of six years earlier. And at an average of only 1.5 per cent of their GDPs, European governments were spending far less on defence than the two per cent level they have long committed to.

Sweden's respected Defence Research Agency had a particularly scathing comment on the neglect by NATO's European members. Looking at Russia's defence modernization efforts, which it said were 'plagued by corruption and bad planning', the Swedish experts went on to say that even if truly modern weapons systems comprise only thirty to forty per cent of Russia's inventory, 'a larger part of Russian systems will be newer than similar systems in NATO countries'.

The picture is not entirely black; EU-badged troops have been deployed around the world in a variety of missions, and since its launch in December 2010 the EU's diplomatic service has modestly begun to make its mark in a number of ways. From policing and training operations, to peacekeeping and border security missions, getting on for twenty EU interventions have made a useful contribution. In the Balkans, in support of the Palestinian Authority, in Georgia and Moldova, in Indonesia's Aceh province, and a growing number of African flashpoints, EU forces have been doing the work that Kofi Annan looked for in 2004 when as the UN secretary-general he welcomed the help the EU's growing military outreach could bring to the world's trouble spots.

Operation Atalanta against Somali pirates is seen as a pointer to what European countries can achieve when they wish. Some twenty-three EU members have at some point contributed their ships to the force of up to seven naval vessels patrolling the waters around the Horn of Africa where vulnerable merchant ships enter or leave the narrow Red Sea. Commanded from a bunker at the British Admiralty's Northwood operational headquarters near London, the Atalanta task force is seen as a model for international and interservice cooperation.

If only it were not just a model, but rather an example among many other collaborative missions. The reality is less encouraging. The reluctance of governments to relinquish sovereign control of their armed forces, however worthy the cause, coupled with a generalized failure across Europe to modernize, has seen a fading of the vision of the EU as a powerful new global security player.

On paper, when Europe's armed forces are lumped together they're impressive. Their total payroll of about two million (if ancillary paramilitary forces such as gendarmeries are counted) compares well with China's 2.28 million and US military personnel of 1.56 million. And although Europe's defence spending is roughly half that of the US, it is double that of China. These reassuring figures are misleading. The vast majority of uniformed Europeans are support staff of one sort or another, with only a tenth able to perform any sort of combat role, and that's an optimistic figure. The rough rule of thumb is that no more than two per cent of the two million could ever be dispatched overseas on a military operation.

Modern armies need substantial and sophisticated support ranging from communications to transport, as well as administrative and welfare services. The problem created by this huge army of what British generals might term 'cooks and bottlewashers' is that Europe's political leaders have apparently come to believe that these uniformed civil servants represent military muscle. Half of Europe's defence budgets go straight into paying wages, whereas in America it is less than a quarter.

Rather than cut the payrolls of their forces, with all the political furore that risks provoking, a good many EU governments have preferred to cut their equipment programmes, creating the opposite problem to that facing the UK. It's equally short-sighted, as eventually the job losses will surface downstream in defence industry lay-offs, and Europe's defence industry workforce is already forty per cent smaller than at the turn of the century. It still employs around 700,000 people if half a million aerospace jobs are included in the count, and indirectly something like two million other jobs depend on it.

The mood of European public opinion has not been conducive to a strengthening of the military or of the defence industry for some time. Pacifism is marked in Germany but echoed elsewhere. Governments have done little to explain that Europeans' own security is being threatened in new ways in the volatile post-9/11 era, and defence equipment companies have not highlighted the high-tech spin-offs from their R&D that are so important to Europe's competitiveness. These are communications failures, but they are dwarfed by the effects of indiscriminate cutbacks to the armed forces and by unnecessarily cut-throat competition between Europe's national defence champions.

The European Defence Agency has worked hard to promote cross-border projects and the sharing of research costs, but national procurement systems have proved stubbornly resistant to the creation of a single market in which EU governments buy each others' military equipment. They have also missed attractive opportunities to create world-beating new defence giants, the prime example being the German government's decision to block the proposed merger between the military arm of Airbus, the Franco-German-Spanish EADS group, and the UK's BAe Systems which would have brought with it a healthy and expanding US operation.

Europeans' nationalism is likely to cost them dear. EU countries have much to lose in the face of rising competition from defence companies in Asia and Latin America. Europe currently produces almost a third of all defence equipment in the world, and three of the top ten defence companies are European. But China and Brazil are hard on their heels, and with advanced electronics such a vital part of the avionics that drive new developments in aerospace, alarm bells are ringing in the boardrooms of EU defence companies.

Industrial competition is easy to understand. Defence and aerospace companies such as Italy's Finmeccanica, Sweden's Saab, or France's Dassault are all rivals for business in world markets. Creating alliances between them isn't straightforward, but it is essential. For Europe to hang on to its position as the global number two behind America's defence sector it has to consolidate its strengths. That means more mergers, and above all joint purchasing by EU governments. The Airbus 400M military heavy airlift project is a good example of what needs to be done, and of the pitfalls that threaten success.

The military in Europe have long suffered from a lack of heavy airlift, whether it be to move troops, weapons, or humanitarian aid. They have had to rely on renting American and even Russian aircraft that are expensive and not always available. More than thirty years ago, in 1982, a French-led group started work on what became the Airbus Military project, and the test flight of the giant A400M at its Seville assembly plant in southern Spain eventually took place in December 2009, with the first delivery made to the French air force in 2012.

This essential workhorse for military operations is already coming under tough commercial pressure, with three of its four main purchasers—the governments of Germany, the UK, and Spain—cutting back on their orders. Competition from across the Atlantic isn't just from Lockhed Martin and Boeing but from Brazil's Embraer aerospace company, whose competitively priced KC-390 military transport goes on sale in 2016, less than ten years after the first blueprints were drawn.

China and Russia too are going to be major rivals, and not just in the heavy airlift sector. Their defence industries are determined to seize market share around the world for the political leverage that gives as well as for the economic benefits. The technological lead enjoyed by the seven biggest US defence giants will make them hard to beat, and that leaves Europe's national champions as the new-comers' easiest prey.

On the industrial and military fronts, Europe's outreach is neglected and still shrinking. In contrast to all the brave talk about a greater role in world affairs, the EU's governments are failing to live up to their commitments and are even contributing to the decline. Worse still, they have no common view of what Europe's strategic interests should be. EU politicians and officials speak of having a single voice in world affairs, but can't agree on what that voice should say.

## The Muddled Definitions of Europe's Security Goals

There's no real consensus within the EU on what a common foreign and security policy ought to consist of. Its upgrading in 2009 was seen as a major achievement of the Lisbon Treaty, but today the Common Foreign and Security Policy (CFSP) remains more a reactive mechanism than a clearly defined set of objectives. The picture has long been fogged by the European Parliament's tendency to take moral positions that cannot be translated into concrete actions, but the chief drawback is that the EU's foreign and security policy lacks depth.

Foreign policies aren't so much about raw clout as about a positive involvement in other countries' development, and the EU has been slow to understand that its economic and trade policies could be the sinews of its security policies. Nor has much thought been given to developing EU cultural policies that would support education and promote artistic activities and values. In other words, there's little real focus on Europe's so-called 'soft power' at a time when its hard power is being allowed to wane fast.

A damning analysis of EU governments' very different security strategies was carried out in 2013 on behalf of the French defence ministry, and branded them 'a motley collection'. Published by the London-based European Council on Foreign Relations (ECFR), the report warned that 'most European governments are simply not serious about defence, or about doing more together'. It looked at the geopolitical threat assessment documents prepared by national authorities across the EU, and found them outdated and often very banal. The chief author of the ECFR study was none other than the European Defence Agency's former chief executive Nick Witney, and he argued that the 2003 European Security Strategy (ESS) should urgently be updated.

'Widely and rightly praised in its day', he said in his report, 'the ESS's day was a decade ago—a bygone era in which the West still ran the world, the Chinese economy was less than half the size it is today, liberal interventionism had not yet learned lessons from Iraq and Afghanistan, financial and economic crisis in Europe seemed not so much improbable as inconceivable, and the US had not yet "pivoted" to Asia.'

The report added that although the Lisbon Treaty which came into force in 2009 was intended to make the EU a more effective global player, 'Brussels continues to display a rooted aversion to formulating the strategy by which such a player might operate'. Decisive opposition to an updating of the ESS along the lines Paris wanted came from London and Berlin, the former because it would involve discussion of the UK's uncertain future in the EU, and the latter because it risked highlighting Germany's touchy relationship with Russia. Thanks to the Ukraine crisis, that is no longer a sensitivity, and the need for the EU to define a Russia policy along with an overall security strategy is plainer than ever.

A fresh look at Europe's strategic role, in light of Russian president Vladimir Putin's defiant support for Ukrainian separatists, is very much on the cards. Even before then, when EU heads of government held a long-awaited but all too brief defence summit in late 2013 they touched on a number of ways to patch up their countries' military vulnerabilities, some of which had been put forward in Witney's report.

He had suggested that EU governments might at least start informing one another of their defence spending plans. The long lead times on defence planning—'it takes a lot to change the direction of the ponderous defence juggernaut', he noted—are such that to collaborate EU countries need to share their thinking well in advance. A process of 'show and tell' could, he urged, easily be managed by the European Defence Agency.

Another idea that European governments are supposed to be pondering is to show the way forward on the integration of national forces by establishing a common approach to the policing of EU airspace. Witney's report argued that culling redundant military aircraft could save hundreds of millions of euros, and those savings could then be redeployed into a joint European Strike Force, creating 'the collective capability Europe should have had at its disposal two years ago to wage the Libyan air campaign without having to fall back on the Americans for air-tanking, reconnaissance, smart munitions, and so on'.

The Libyan operation had been proof that Europe's military strength has shrunk even faster and farther than feared. Although Gaddafi's forces were equipped with fairly modest and outdated weapons systems, the European forces were severely handicapped by their lack of naval support and the aircraft carriers needed for close-range air strikes, and most tellingly by their inability to share information, ammunition, and in some cases the same grades of aviation fuel. Their narrow victory, as the Duke of Wellington observed of his defeat of Napoleon at Waterloo in 1815, was a damned close-run thing.

## The Atlantic Dimension

European governments' ability to fall back on the US for support is central to the EU's thinking on most security issues, and on geopolitics in general. The attitude is that 'Uncle Sam' has always been there, so although the US may grumble from time to time at having to pay for Europe's defence shortcomings, Washington will always come good in the end. It's a dangerous idea because European and American interests have been diverging for some time.

Divergences across the Atlantic go much deeper than President Barack Obama's announcement in late 2011 of America's 'pivot' towards Asia. With the end of the Cold War it quickly became plain that US concerns were much more global than those of the Europeans. The EU has for a quarter of a century been preoccupied with developments on its own doorstep, beginning with the reunification of Germany, and extending further eastwards to the integration of the formerly communist countries of central and eastern Europe into a wider if lopsided European economy.

During the eight years that President Bill Clinton occupied the White House there was little surface change in the transatlantic relationship, chiefly because his multilateralist convictions ensured that on issues such as trade policy or on rising climate change concerns the US and the EU stayed more or less on the same page. They were also bound together by the web of investments in both directions across the Atlantic that are reckoned to be worth more than $5 trillion and have created fifteen million jobs. Europe accounts for three-quarters of all foreign investment in America, while almost two-thirds of US corporations' foreign investments are made in Europe.

The election to the White House of George W. Bush in 2000, and within a year the 9/11 attacks on New York and Washington, soon disrupted the transatlantic harmony. The new breed of 'neo-cons' in the upper echelons of the Bush administration who believed in a more assertive and unilateralist America, and who were urging a global 'war on terror', had few connections and little sympathy with Europe's political leaders. That frostier relationship became icily antagonistic when the largest EU countries split over the US decision in 2003 to invade Iraq. The UK, motivated by a desire to maintain its 'special relationship' with the US, and by Tony Blair's blind belief in Saddam Hussein's possession of 'weapons of mass destruction', took part in the invasion, backed politically by Italy and Spain.

But France and Germany opposed the action to depose Saddam as wholly illegal. They also made the point that if Washington's aim was to root out the al-Qaeda terrorists behind 9/11, as the US had been doing since late 2001 in its military action in Afghanistan, then it should be aware that Saddam was al-Qaeda's most determined foe. In any event, the invasion of Iraq was the catalyst for a profound shift in US–EU relations. Washington began to review the purpose and even the usefulness of NATO, and old tensions surfaced on a variety of economic issues. Instead of being quickly ironed out, minor trade frictions began to contribute to the deadlock over the World Trade Organization's (WTO) Doha Round of international trade liberalization negotiations. On rules governing banking and financial services, the US and continental Europe in effect agreed to disagree, contributing to the conditions that led to the global financial crisis of 2007–8.

The differences between America and Europe extend well beyond trade and financial regulation. Diplomats in the State Department and generals in the Pentagon across Washington's Potomac River had begun to see NATO as little more than useful political cover for any American actions whose unilateral character they wished to disguise. The inclusion of troops from some European allies in NATO's ISAF operations in Afghanistan against Taliban insurgents helped to internationalize a drawn-out war that has nevertheless been overwhelmingly American. But it does not mean that Europe and the United States still have a shared view of what to do about global security challenges that range from the Arab Spring of 2011 (and its aftermath of conflict throughout much of the Arab world) to intensifying resource competition in Africa or central Asia.

European governments are themselves at sixes and sevens over many of these issues, and the US is no longer as open to discussion as before. Two decades of being the only superpower in a unipolar world have eroded the multilateralist political culture in America that had been so strong when the United Nations was created at the San Francisco conference of 1945. As well as many of its politicians' hostility towards the UN, America's unilateralism hardened to such a degree that Washington contested the International Criminal Court's jurisdiction over American peacekeeping troops, at one point threatening to withdraw its forces from their bases in Germany unless its soldiers were exempted from the court's authority.

## Keeping Pace with Geopolitical Change

All these shifts in what for half a century seemed an unbreakable partnership have been neatly summed up by a leading American observer. 'Durable bonds across the Atlantic seem implausible', commented David Calleo in the *Europe's World* policy journal. 'As the world's two richest and most powerful economic spaces, the EU and

US are bound to be rivals.' Calleo is one of the foremost American experts on Europe, holding the senior chair at Johns Hopkins University's School for Advanced International Studies, and he fears the disagreements provoked by American actions in the wake of 9/11 have set the NATO allies on separate courses. 'Americans project their own continental model onto the world at large', he has written. 'They see the United States fated to be the globalizing world's federal centre. Europeans tend to reject this unipolar vision … they naturally think of their own post-war model.'

That may well be the case, but unfortunately it doesn't mean that Europeans share a coherent view of how global security can be guaranteed, or what EU countries' contribution should be. In France, François Godemont, who heads the independent Paris-based Asia Centre, puts forward the views of those who believe Europe needs to focus on conflict-prone Asia. Because Asian nations have so many unresolved territorial and ethnic disputes, they argue, there is a strong case for Europe to widen its Asian relations from being chiefly commercial and embrace security.

'There is a growing list of critical issues that demand greater action by Europe if it is to safeguard its own security by preventing conflict in Asia', wrote Godemont, also in *Europe's World*. 'The role that Europe should start to play is to provide security cooperation without any of the strategic implications that an increased US role would involve, while at the same time heading off the risk of greater military competition between Asian nations.'

President Obama implicitly echoed this when he said in the summer of 2014 that NATO countries should extend their security focus eastwards to Asia. Spending by Asian governments on their armed forces, particularly China and India, has roughly doubled in less than a decade, while Europe's profile in the region has been diminished by the ripple effects of the eurozone crisis. The EU's weight and authority has also been weakened by the efforts of countries such as Germany and the UK to establish advantageous bilateral links at the expense of a more collective European relationship.

Closer to home, the turmoil throughout the Middle East has also found the EU seriously wanting. Its efforts to establish a unified European approach to developments there have attracted little public interest and support, either in Europe or in Arab countries themselves. When EU governments other than in pacifist Germany reached consensus on intervening militarily in support of Libya's anti-Gaddafi rebels, that seemed to promise a greater common commitment to helping the Maghreb countries of North Africa and those along the eastern Mediterranean seaboard. But nothing that might be called an EU strategy in support of the Arab world has since emerged.

Long before the popular uprisings of the Arab Spring called into question European governments' unquestioning acceptance of autocratic Middle Eastern regimes, the EU had produced a number of what were claimed to be 'strategic approaches'. There was the 1995 Barcelona Process, championed in large part by Madrid, that led to the creation of a wheel-and-spoke arrangement of bilateral 'association' pacts between Brussels and various Arab governments. These contained little in the way of trade concessions other than guaranteeing very competitive Arab fruit and vegetable producers access to European markets, and even less in the way of financial assistance for their economies and embryo industries. The EU's attention and resources were fixed on extending its membership in eastern and central Europe, not on improving conditions for its southern Mediterranean neighbours.

When the shortcomings of that approach became inescapable, France's President Nicolas Sarkozy put his weight behind a 2008 successor plan called grandiloquently the Union for the Mediterranean to link the EU and fifteen Arab states. It was to have more funding and greater powers, and to demonstrate that it wouldn't be a purely European initiative, the new UfM appointed Arab representatives to high office, including that of secretary-general. It was equipped with headquarters in Barcelona at a handsome palace with extensive grounds, and has a busy schedule of meetings and projects.

Other than that, not much changed. Europe followed up with what's claimed to be an even more ambitious policy instrument called the European Neighbourhood Policy (ENP). But because it spans countries not only in the Middle East but in eastern Europe and the Caucasus, it has fallen between these various stools. It got off the ground in 2009, had its budget beefed-up to almost €7 billion in 2011, and looked at first as if it might establish the EU as a central and important player in all those regions. Events almost everywhere covered by the ENP have, though, shown otherwise, and often have highlighted Europe's weaknesses and disarray rather than its strength and good intentions. The ENP's days look to be numbered, with a thorough rethink widely expected.

Russia was given a rather woolly special status through the ENPs 'EU–Russia Common Spaces' arrangement, and the inclusion of Moldova, Georgia, Belarus, and Ukraine along with Armenia and Azerbaijan did little to allay Moscow's concerns over an EU 'encirclement' seen as encroaching on its own 'near-abroad'. As to the Arab world, the events of the Arab Spring and the subsequent conflicts that engulfed so many of its countries made a mockery of Europe's attempts to play both an economic and a security role.

On the economic front, there had been high hopes that in the wake of the Arab Spring's upsets in Tunisia, Libya, and Egypt, the EU would quickly deploy specialist advisors on privatization and financial services to galvanize those countries' sclerotic state-run economies. But even on straightforward problems such as giving temporary bail-outs to bankrupted governments and their central banks, the EU's own red tape and unimaginative approach hampered the efforts of the senior officials charged with offering emergency help.

The upshot is that Europe has done precious little to tackle the region's economic and social problems. Business between the neighbouring countries of the Maghreb remains stuck at only two per cent or so of their already very small foreign trade, even though improving relations between Arab countries should be an urgent priority for Brussels. The EU is proposing a new breed of trade deals—known in the jargon as Deep and Comprehensive Free Trade Agreements, or DCFTAs—to replace its Association Agreements, but already there are criticisms that these impose a heavy and unnecessary regulatory burden on struggling economies.

Disappointment over the EU's leadership on the economic front is widespread, but it is perhaps on security that its failings are most evident. European public opinion has been appalled at the violence throughout much of the Middle East, but the EU has stood by helplessly. Hand-wringing over renewed fighting in Iraq, Syria's ever-bloodier civil war, Israel's merciless retaliations in Gaza, and the deepening conflict between Egypt's military forces and the supporters of the Muslim Brotherhood reflects the fact that no one in Europe knows how to react in ways that won't exacerbate these situations. The emergence of al-Qaeda's successor, the Islamic State of Iraq and Syria, known variously as ISIS or just IS, which seeks to establish a new caliphate to give jihadists a home base, has further perplexed EU foreign ministers.

That's understandable, for the politics of Islamic jihad and the bitter Shia–Sunni schism are often baffling to outsiders. Where the EU has arguably been at fault, though, is in its failure to respond adequately to the Arab Spring. It is too soon to judge the true impact of the popular uprisings that began in Tunisia in early 2011, swept eastwards to Egypt and Libya, and then provoked unrest in many other Arab countries, but it's clear that it's a geopolitical game-changer.

The Arab world numbers 370 million people, more than ten times as many as a century ago, and is strikingly underdeveloped and backward in relation to its rich European neighbours. The scale of youth unemployment is hard to judge, but visibly the bulge of jobless and frustrated young people poses a very real threat to the stability of Arab countries themselves, and therefore to the security of European ones. That so many thousands of young Muslims born and raised in European countries have flocked to join the ranks of IS and other jihadist forces is creating mounting concern among EU governments over how to handle their eventual return.

Political grandstanding is not in Brussels' DNA, yet it's precisely what is needed. The EU should be designing a headline-catching strategy capable of reassuring Arab public opinion that Europe will henceforth be deeply involved in raising living standards in their countries. Because autocratic Arab regimes favoured state-owned enterprises, however inefficient they might be, the EU should be funnelling southwards the privatization expertise gained by its newer eastern member states in unscrambling the omelettes of state-run economies.

Most important of all, the EU should present a two-pronged strategy for helping Arab countries. On the economic side, assistance that doesn't consist of ponderous EU projects wrapped in red tap. It should instead feature financial incentives for private-sector European companies to play a hands-on role through joint ventures. Parallel to that, the EU should launch a high-profile initiative to bind Arab countries into a new security framework. The low levels of cross-border trade between Arab countries reflect the way their governments rarely speak to each other. Instability in the Middle East could be reduced if governments there were in much closer and more regular contact with one another.

Europe should be making it a condition of its economic assistance that Arab governments meet regularly with each other and with EU counterparts to review security-related and other political issues. Europe's experience of bringing nations together and forging positive relationships between them is a model for the increasingly divided and volatile Arab world.

The EU's complex policymaking machinery doesn't greatly encourage innovative thinking. Its efforts are also hindered by in-fighting between the various arms of the European Commission, and by their rivalries with the diplomats of the European External Action Service. Outside analysts of the EU's response have been almost unanimous in identifying officialdom's preference for imposing its existing methods and programmes on Arab countries instead of fashioning new ones more appropriate to their individual circumstances. No one contests the unsuitability of the European Neighbourhood Policy designed to extend EU help to poorer countries around its periphery, but for the time being it remains the basis of Europe's assistance.

## Why Brussels Doesn't Walk the Talk

Where do we Europeans go from here? The largest EU countries hold fundamentally different views on an alarming number of foreign policy issues—not just in the Middle East and Africa but on how to deal with Russia and with Asian countries. Energy is a highly divisive factor because import-dependent EU countries have separate bilateral relationships with those they rely on for their oil and gas supplies. Above all, it is the insistence of national governments and their public opinions that they themselves should be seen to handle foreign policy rather than 'have it dictated by Brussels'.

The EU's fledgling diplomatic service isn't yet muscular enough to dictate anything to anyone, just as the EU's military staff has no troops to deploy and, thanks to NATO-centric Britain's opposition, no 'command and control' capabilities to direct them. The EU's small diplomatic corps consists of about 1,600 people of diplomatic rank and a support staff of 3,700 people, and they are spread across 136 missions around the world, most of them in reality still the commercial delegations of the European Commission. Europe's national diplomatic services are far bigger—those of the UK, France, and Germany average 12,000 people each—and in all they cost taxpayers a total of €7.5 billion a year, or €16 per head, against the EU diplomats' yearly budget of less than €500 million, which works out at about a euro per head of population.

The problem with the EU's diplomats isn't just money, it's also their lack of imagination. Foreign ministries in the member states mostly have long traditions of analysing developments around the world and drawing up for their political masters detailed reports and contingency plans that suggest possible responses. The senior ranks of the new EU outfit are being bolstered by experienced former ambassadors from national services, but lower down the European External Action Service is largely manned by former commission officials whose backgrounds are in trade or aid rather than geopolitical analysis and policy planning. The result is a lack of clear-cut and well-informed foreign policy proposals from Brussels that combines with the conflicting demands and historical sympathies of the EU's member states to produce some very shaky stances on key issues.

The best answer to intra-European disagreement and muddle may lie in improving the EU's foreign policy cooperation with America. The US is aware that it, too, must face dwindling power and influence around the world. In Washington, the National Intelligence Council's 'Global Trends 2030' report warns that 'with the rapid rise of other countries, the "unipolar moment" is over and Pax Americana—the era of American ascendancy in international politics that began in 1945— is fast winding down.'

It is a concern widely shared among the coming generation of US policymakers; two who formerly worked for the CIA, David Kanin and Steven Meyer, underlined the point in an article in the influential journal *Current History*. 'Although America's bloated military establishment is almost impervious to change, and its hidebound foreign policy establishment acts as though the world has hardly evolved since 1989', they wrote, 'the US must begin crafting a useful approach to a world it can no longer dominate, instead of persisting with useless rhetoric about America as the indispensable leader.' Other experts who agree include Leslie Gelb; a diplomat-turned-journalist who until 2012 was for a decade head of the powerful New York-based Council on Foreign Relations. Now its president emeritus, Gelb readily acknowledges that 'the US is less and less able to translate its economic strength into influence'.

On the economic front, Brussels and Washington are engaged in high-risk, high-yield discussions on a new transatlantic trade and investment pact that could in effect create an EU-US. common market. To do so, both sides need to overcome their traditionally different approaches to such issues as banking regulation and farm subsidies. If successful, such a deal could also hold out the hope of a *rapprochement* on security issues, something that Russia's president Vladimir Putin seems perversely bent on encouraging.

It is to be hoped that the need for a measured Western response to the Ukraine's threatened integrity, but also to its Russian-speaking regions' right to some form of self-determination will produce a new Washington–Brussels security doctrine. In the US, Kurt Volker, who was ambassador to NATO from 2008 to 2009, is among those who believe in a stronger transatlantic approach to key questions like dealing with Russian assertiveness. At CSIS, the Center for Strategic and International Studies in Washington, Simon Serfaty's is another influential voice arguing for a renewed Euro–Atlantic security strategy to compensate for NATO's shortcomings.

Finding equally articulate opinion-formers in Europe is less easy. The EU has long lacked anything approaching a coherent agenda for shaping its geopolitical role and reinforcing its links with the US. One former head of government, Spain's José Maria Aznar, sees the need very plainly but acknowledges he no longer has any real impact on thinking in the European Council or at NATO. From his office as president of Madrid's conservative FAES think tank, Aznar stresses that 'defending the transatlantic relationship is more urgent than ever. We need an economic union of the US and EU that would create a common Atlantic area. The Atlantic basin will still be important in the Asian century'.

The idea that Europeans' security and economic interests can be defended effectively at national level by individual governments no longer seems credible, especially when so many of them pull in different directions. But national politics trump slow and uncertain EU policy-making every time. To counter this, Jacques Delors and a host of senior figures advanced the idea in a June 2014 letter to the *Financial Times* of an EU-level 'strategic comeback' spanning crisis management, a new definition of common positions, notably on Russia and the Middle East, and collective foreign policies on energy supplies and illegal immigration. 'No individual member state is able to address these issues alone', they emphasized, adding 'we therefore call on the European political authorities to commit to a strategic comeback'.

An important step towards waking Europeans up to the pressures of the twenty-first century would be to stop talking of Europe's soft power, the reassuring term coined some years ago by the distinguished American analyst Joseph S. Nye to describe EU countries' cultural influence. The idea of soft power has been bandied about in Brussels for more than a decade, and is often advanced as proof that to contribute to international security Europe need not resort to the 'crude militarism' of the US. More sceptical voices point out that examples of soft power are chiefly found in Brussels' influence on countries hoping to joint the EU.

Exasperation with the notion that soft power can be an instrument for Europe to advance its interests and meet its responsibilities boiled over when Anders Fogh Rasmussen, who was NATO's secretary-general from 2009 to 2014 and before that Danish prime minister, made his views clear to a meeting of European parliamentarians. 'We Europeans', he told the MEPs, 'must understand that soft power alone is really no power at all. Without hard capabilities to back up its diplomacy, Europe will lack credibility and influence'.

Such plain speaking is badly needed at a time when public opinion in most EU countries opposes more spending on defence, and when governments resist paying anything other than lip service to the 'pooling and sharing' goals they signed up to. Only by combining European nations' military strengths will the EU's attempts to create a common foreign policy have any muscle behind them. First. though, there has to be a much greater public awareness across the EU that national diplomacy risks weakening rather than strengthening Europe's ability to help stabilize an increasingly volatile and violent world.

# 11

# 'Juncker's Curse'—Why EU Leaders Don't Deliver on Their Promises

*There is little democratic accountability at European Union level, but it works well nationally. The upshot is that when national leaders espouse policies in the wider European interest they become vulnerable to domestic criticism and risk being punished by the voters. Yet it is EU rather than national policymaking that's needed to strengthen Europe's economies for the tougher global conditions ahead. With the alarm bells of the eurozone crisis apparently not loud enough for public opinion to accept the need for a new beginning, it's up to Europe's politicians to rise to the occasion.*

The scene is easy to imagine, whether in Berlin, Paris, London, or any other European capital. As your country's leader you are sitting in the blond wood and stainless steel glory of the German federal chancellery, the presidential grandeur of France's Elysée Palace, or the somewhat pokier prime ministerial premises of 10 Downing Street, and you've been listening to your advisers on EU affairs take you through their dossiers for the next European Council in Brussels. It's important stuff, and you resolve to play a positive role in pushing them forward on the EU agenda.

Then you welcome your next visitors, campaign managers and back-room analysts of your own party. They arrive armed with charts and statistics that immediately send shivers down your spine. Instead of the soporific dronings of the senior diplomats, the party workers have brought you instantly awake with warnings of trouble looming at the polls. Almost everything they have to say about strengthening your electoral support base runs counter to what a moment ago was being said by the advocates of a more European mindset.

The title of this chapter refers to the wry warning by Jean-Claude Juncker as Luxembourg's premier to his fellow heads of government when the eurozone crisis was at its nadir. 'We all know what do to. What we don't know is how to be re-elected when we've done it' has come to be known as 'Juncker's curse' because it neatly encapsulates the difficulties of reconciling European and national concerns. With Juncker himself until the end of this decade now in the EU's hot seat as president of its executive arm, the European Commission, much is riding on his ability to persuade national leaders to do the right thing.

But do Europe's political leaders really know what must be done to get Europe onto a path of healthier economic growth, and is it certain they would be punished by the voters for doing so? There are no easy answers to the questions that Europeans must begin to grapple with, but it's plain that so far we in Europe haven't begun to debate them seriously as political choices. Politics across the EU still focus chiefly on twentieth century issues—meaning largely national ones—rather than the European-level ones that the twenty-first century calls for. The Internet notwithstanding, there is sadly no shared political arena that could help Europeans determine their collective future.

Questions that should be aired include discussion of how painful reforms would be for streamlining Europe's different national economies, and how sure we can be that the economic benefits would outweigh the damage to our social fabric. In many EU countries, the austerity policies that were governments' responses to the eurozone and sovereign debt crises are increasingly seen as having made matters worse. Heavy debt burdens are set to remain a problem, and it's also far from certain that Europe's voters will accept tough reform packages on top of austerity unless they can be convinced of rewards in the foreseeable future.

Europeans will want to know how their relative decline in global terms is going to affect them and their children. Will the rise of other parts of the world inevitably mean a slump in living standards, with fears of a 'lost generation' of unemployed young people only a foretaste of worse to come? Rather than rely on the dry statistics and conflicting forecasts of economists, doesn't a 'looking out of the window' analysis of Europe's political economy show a prosperous and stable society with deep financial pockets that is resilient enough to adapt to change without being panicked into revolutionary upheavals?

And speaking of revolution, how persuasive is the case for radical change? Is it worth sacrificing tried and tested national democratic structures to create some sort of streamlined replacement of the present ramshackle EU arrangements? The advantages and disadvantages of more effective European mechanisms have to be spelled out far more clearly, with the arguments expressed in simple facts and figures instead of the technocratic jargon of the Brussels Eurocrats.

Public opinion in many European countries finds the EU wanting, with people almost everywhere blaming either the euro or the EU as a whole, and quite often both, for the hardships of what's being called 'the Great Recession'. The EU is accused of doing no more than muddling through since the economic crisis began in 2008, and of having failed to conceive and implement a recovery plan.

The scale of Europe's problems—not just the eurozone's viability but the tectonic shifts in the world economy—makes it hard to think in terms of a coherent plan, let alone a far-sighted strategy. Yet that's what Europe needs. Not a detailed plan of attack but a convincingly strategic approach that would awake Europeans to the uncertainties clouding the future and that would encourage them to accept change as the price for improving their collective outlook. It's a strategy that could embrace many of the good ideas and suggestions advanced at different times not only by business and political leaders but also by civil society organizations, which have individually gained little traction.

Europe faces two major obstacles. The first is to get the EU's governments to cooperate with each other and to accept a more centralized approach to economic management, whether by the commission or some such body as the European Central Bank. The second problem, more intractable still, is how to address Europeans' cultural mindsets and prejudices. The balance between economic efficiency and social entitlements has to be addressed, even if deep-rooted European cultural attitudes make that very difficult.

It's not just a question of stubborn workers and over-indulged social security beneficiaries. A key reason why it took thirty-five years from the signing of the Treaty of Rome for the European single market to become a reality, incomplete though it still is, was the resistance it met from national civil services. When in the mid-1980s the European Roundtable of Industrialists lent its weight to the commission's efforts, that opened the way for business expertise to come to the aid of the beleaguered Eurocrats whose efforts were being quietly blocked by national officials jealous of their own authority, as well as being stymied by protectionist national lobbying. That reluctance to surrender powers to Brussels or any other centralizing body still exists, and not only explains but to some extent even excuses the EU's shortcomings.

Government ministries across Europe resist handing over more decision-making, or even greater monitoring powers, and public opinion stands right behind them. Rightly or wrongly, polls show that getting on for six out of ten Europeans don't want to see any further transfers of economic and budgetary policymaking to the EU. Only in Germany does a majority favour that, with slightly over half welcoming more economic power for the EU. In the UK, an unsurprising four-fifths oppose that, and in Sweden three-quarters. In other words, however strong the economic arguments may be, any government agreeing to beef-up the EU's authority could well be committing electoral suicide.

It says much of the poor communications skills of officials in Brussels and at the European Central Bank in Frankfurt that they have so resoundingly lost the public relations battle in the wake of the eurozone's near-collapse. The EU has always been bad at getting its messages across, and faced with a chronic single currency problem that may yet threaten its existence, it has failed abysmally to present the case for economic and monetary union. Well over half of those surveyed in southern European countries, including France, blame the euro for their troubles, even though as a currency it gave them stability in the foreign exchange markets and an inflation rate that at two per cent was even lower than the three per cent Germany's deutschemark averaged over its fifty-year life.

The cultural resistance to becoming more innovation-friendly is equally daunting. Europeans pride themselves on being different to Americans, who they see as accepting market-driven policies that are brutally insensitive to people's economic security. On any measure of entrepreneurship, Europe lags well behind not just the US, but China and India too.

The Chinese top the charts on new start-up companies and the proportion of highly motivated self-employed people, while attitudes to launching one's own business show that young Europeans are becoming less interested than ever in being their own boss. Ten years ago, almost a third of those polled for Eurobarometer said they'd like to be self-employed within five years, but probably thanks to the recession that has since shrunk to around a quarter. In the US it's well over four in ten.

## The Innovation Gap That's Dividing Europe

People in Europe may say they want to modernize and fight back in the global marketplace, but they also want to have their cake and eat it. France has become the prime example of a society that understands the pressures that threaten it, but at the same time refuses to compromise the gains and privileges of its workforce. The contrast between France and Germany on unit labour costs is striking, and will have serious consequences for the rest of Europe because it undermines the concept of a Franco-German tandem that can drive the EU forward.

Over the decade since it introduced tough social security and labour market reforms in 2003–4, Germany's labour costs have risen by a fairly modest eighteen per cent while those of France are up by forty per cent. Germany's reforms, introduced by a centre-left government on the recommendations of former Volkswagen personnel director Peter Hartz, removed unemployment benefits for the jobless unless actively seeking work, and created a new breed of 'mini-job' that has made it much easier to find employment. They were also so controversial that they did much to cost Chancellor Gerhard Schroeder his job.

About a quarter of Germany's workforce is now reckoned to earn no more than the very modest minimum wage amounting to 1500 euros a month introduced in January 2015. On the other hand, youth unemployment there is the lowest in Europe, and the German economy has been powering ahead. Booming exports, which owe a good deal to being priced in euros, have combined with disciplined labour costs to create a virtuous circle. Because German companies are doing so well they can afford to invest heavily in research, and are now spending a record-breaking €50 billion a year on R&D.

From being labelled 'the sick man of Europe' in the late 1990s, when its economy was worryingly sluggish, Germany has been paving the way to ever-greater export successes. It's exactly the pattern that France's president Nicolas Sarkozy had hoped for, but failed to emulate. Now it's France that's sick, and around Europe there is rising concern that deteriorating conditions in France represent a threat to Europe as a whole.

Sarkozy came to power in mid-2007 promising modernization; his slogan was 'work more to earn more'. He raised the minimum legal retirement age from sixty to sixty-two years, and set sixty-seven as the age when full pension rights kick in. But he couldn't rally the necessary political support for determined wage restraint that would be accompanied by cutbacks in public spending. His major difficulty was that those cuts would hit the twenty-two per cent of the workforce that in one way or another are state employees, for the public payroll in France is almost twice as big as in Germany.

Rising labour costs in France without compensating productivity improvements have seen exports plummet and the economy stagnate. French industry's share of world exports was a fifth smaller in 2010 than five years earlier, and that trend is accelerating; between 2011 and 2012 France's share of the EU's total exports dropped from seventeen per cent to thirteen per cent. French companies' profit margins are at their lowest for twenty-five years, and the chief upward graph for many companies is their investments abroad. In the years since the global economic crisis began to bite, the big companies listed on the Paris Bourse's CAC-40 have cut their payrolls in France by four per cent but increased the number of people they employ abroad by five per cent.

A report by well-known top French businessman Louis Gallois who had been head of the Airbus aircraft group, laid out prescriptions in autumn 2012 for curing the country's malaise. It was a long list, beginning with the spending cuts and labour market flexibilities that Sarkozy had stopped short of, and going on to recommend greatly reducing taxation on both employees and employers, boosting VAT levels, and making it much easier to start a small company. François Hollande, Sarkozy's socialist successor, acknowledged the Gallois Report and then in the main quietly buried it.

The widening gap between the French and German economies is deeply troubling, for it calls into question the whole concept of European solidarity and economic cohesion. If the two countries that are the heart of the European project are set on opposite courses, the wider implications are serious. An end to the Franco-German partnership would compound the way the eurozone crisis is exacerbating the north–south divide between the backward but spendthrift 'Club Med' countries of sunny southern Europe and the hard-working northerners. The gap is graphically illustrated by the way that just one German company, Siemens, registers around 250 important patents a year, six times more than the forty or so recorded for the whole of Spain. When the EU's Eurostat statisticians graded Europe's 271 regions in an 'innovations scoreboard', Italy, Spain, and Greece were unable to contribute a single one of their regions to the forty-one designated as 'innovation leaders'.

France has long been the bridge connecting north and south, as well as the intellectual powerhouse generating fresh thinking on how to push Europe's integration forward. Now France appears much more the problem than the solution. The answer is not a reiteration of the Franco-German commitment to working together in fraternal peace and amity, although there was much of that in early 2013 when the two countries loudly celebrated the fiftieth anniversary of the 'treaty of friendship' signed between Charles de Gaulle and Konrad Adenauer. Champagne toasts and fireworks could not disguise the realities of their economic and political divergence.

A key to Europe's future is a dramatic turnaround by France comparable to that achieved by Germany. At the same time, neither Berlin nor Paris have fully grasped the need to breathe new life into the Franco-German political partnership despite the economic differences pulling it apart. German politicians must understand that greater flexibility on debt levels and growth mechanisms is needed for France, and their French counterparts must understand that promising structural reform without delivering it cannot be tolerated indefinitely in Berlin.

The EU framework offers France's leaders the political alibi they need to introduce tough reforms, even though they have still to avail themselves of it. Once again, Eurosceptic pressures are in play. Europeans must therefore revive their lapsed faith in cohesion; the EU's richer northern members have to redouble their efforts to help southern Europe's economies recover, however much they may resent the profligacy that led to those countries' sovereign debt crises.

The guiding spirit of EU policymaking has long been to foster growth in poorer countries and neglected regions with the aim of uniting the people of Europe through shared prosperity. It was an unashamedly self-interested policy of the rich western European countries, motivated by an awareness that their own security depended on the political stability of their neighbours. The far-sighted strategy for bringing the struggling post-communist countries of central and eastern Europe into the EU was based entirely on that thinking, and its success has been indisputable. Living standards in the newcomer EU states may still be catching up, but they have a renewed dynamism and rising productivity that western Europe not only envies but is profiting from.

## Searching for a 'Grand Strategy' ... or Even a New Narrative

The reforms required for a productivity push capable of kick-starting economic growth need EU-wide backing. Yet Europe's political paralysis seems incurable. European governments do not dare, or even wish, to use the framework of a stronger and more collaborative EU to introduce the stringent reforms that could reunite north and south. Norbert Walter, who was for many years Deutsche Bank's chief economist, has commented that if the EU made the most of the competences it already has, and governed more effectively in areas like energy efficiency, alternative energies, environmental issues and liveable cities, it could help the EU as a whole to achieve faster economic growth for at least the next decade, with 2.5 per cent a year certainly not out of reach. Meanwhile, the uneven way that different countries in Europe are beginning to recover from the shock of the 2008 financial crisis and near-meltdown of banks and markets is doing much to reshape the debate over the EU's future.

The gulf separating the prodigal countries that had been living far above their means and those that were not presents a major challenge, even if it's not generally recognized. The argument that only stronger EU-level action can meet that challenge is widely shared amongst policy analysts across Europe and a good many politicians, but features hardly at all in the national political debates that shape public opinion. The Brussels commission's concern to emphasize good news from the EU rather than stimulate interest by generating debate has reduced it to being more a spectator than a player.

That doesn't alter the fact that Europe needs a shot in the arm. Some advocate a 'grand strategy' capable of seizing people's imaginations that would also cover detailed policy areas where a collective approach would pay dividends. That could mean falling back on the old dream of a federal Europe, while others see the first priority as a strengthening of what in the Brussels jargon is called 'the community method', meaning decision-making in which the interplay between the European Commission and Parliament would be stronger and much less eclipsed by intergovernmental deal making.

Emma Bonino, the straight-talking, no-nonsense Italian politician whose stint some years ago as the EU Commissioner in charge of humanitarian aid did much to burnish the EU's image, advocates what she calls 'federalism-lite'. Far from creating a superstate, her thinking is that by raising the EU budget from its modest one per cent of Europe's GDP to five per cent it would be possible to finance the long-term programmes needed to get Europe back onto a growth path.

Fears that the power of the EU's intergovernmental mechanisms is reducing rather than strengthening Europe's ability to resolve its problems have been persuasively summed up by Jacques Delors. His ten years at the head of the European Commission are looked back on by many as the halcyon times of European integration, for when he stepped down in 1995 the EU's future seemed golden. Much of the single market project had been accomplished, the eastward enlargement to 'reunite' a Europe whole and free was under way, and the single currency was taking shape.

Two decades on, Delors doesn't hide his disappointment. In a widely reported address in the European Parliament to fellow socialists, he urged the need 'to think about a new model of development, investment, job creation, and assets to equip our youth'. Delors's concern is that intergovernmentalism is taking Europe back 'to the Congress of Vienna and nationalistic government attitudes" and he laments that 'when I hear the current leaders say they are not getting rid of the Community method but are keeping it, I am not convinced'.

As well as calling for a more strategic approach, pro-Europe opinion-formers have been demanding a 'new narrative'. The idea is that there should now be a third phase in the project of economic and political integration that people can latch onto and support. The first, back in the 1950s, spanned almost twenty years with the 'no more war' slogan along with the message that however irritating and seemingly unnecessary policies such as the expensive Common Agricultural Policy might be, they were part of a project that made another war between Europeans unthinkable.

The second phase was free movement throughout Europe of goods and business dealings thanks to the single market, of money, of people seeking greater opportunities and even of tourists thanks to 'freedom of the skies' and cheaper air fares. As for students, the leaders of tomorrow, the Erasmus exchange programme that uses EU funding to allow university students to spend time studying abroad has been among the commission's proudest achievements. It has nurtured a new generation of Europe-minded younger people whose influence may yet help turn around the EU's fortunes.

What a third phase might consist of no one can tell. In the wake of the eurozone crisis, with all the ingredients for further turmoil still present in Europe's national economies, it's hard to identify a new theme that would once again rally public opinion to a common cause. It may be beguiling but it is also fruitless to think that a slogan can do the trick when what's really needed is political courage.

Europe's salvation is more likely to be found in EU officials who are unafraid to speak out and defy national governments whenever they are wrong-headed. In an aside during his speech in the European Parliament, Jacques Delors gave a glimpse of the steel that's needed from a commission president. 'If I had not brandished the right of initiative', he reminisced, 'there would never have been the Erasmus programme. The governments were afraid that I would announce publicly that it was due to their refusal that we could not allow millions of students to discover another country, to have another university experience'.

That willingness to name and shame recalcitrant member states gave him enormous leverage in his dealings with heads of government, but also proved politically costly at times. Britain's difficult and fractious relationship with Brussels has many causes, but it's certain that Margaret Thatcher, the handbag swinging prime minister who secured a special budget deal for the UK, never forgave Delors for the critical speech on her social policy he made at an annual conference of the UK's Trades Union Congress.

Successive EU commissions have since been much more muted in their criticisms, with individual commissioners' barbs usually couched in general rather than country-specific terms. Their reward has been a steady erosion of their own powers. The discretion exercised by commissioners may reflect a mature awareness that public rows rarely advance negotiations, but also the reality that their future careers are often in the gift of fellow politicians back home. Joaquin Almunia is among those veterans of the EU scene who bemoan this weakness, he says. 'Much of the problem has been poor leadership—there's a job opportunity for someone. Our political leaders need to explain the very real challenges of demographics; we will need millions of foreign workers, but we also need to create a more cohesive society. It's a perfect opportunity for arguing in favour of a common European political space'.

Discussion on where the EU is headed might be beefed-up if the commission were itself seen as a starting point for radical change and sacrifice. It seems not to have occurred to the EU's highly paid senior officials that their own cosseted employment conditions are resented in the outside world.

Any formula for injecting new life into the commission and attacking its image of undemocratic privilege should begin with the tearing up of the *statut européen*, the charter defining EU civil servants' rights and responsibilities. It makes them virtually unsackable and has helped foster a culture of arrogance and inertia that can be the despair of the commission's own senior officials as well as a source of out-siders' dislike. Ideas for overhauling the commission's structures and working conditions are not greatly encouraged in Brussels; two past commissioners—Neil Kinnock from the UK and Finland's Erkki Liikanen—tried, but their efforts were to a large extent frustrated by the stubborn opposition and strike threats of the Eurocrats' trade unions.

Reform of the commission has so far meant little more than the fairly frequent reshuffling and reorganization of its directorates-general (DGs), and the swiftly abandoned measure of relocating com-missioners' offices to those of the DG for which they were responsible rather than grouping them together in the commission's Berlaymont headquarters building.

A genuine streamlining of the commission should have two parallel objectives; an internal goal of revitalizing its culture, and an external one of banishing criticisms that it's a bastion of privilege and answer-able to nobody. Ideas for shaking up the Eurocracy range from the fairly modest, which run the risk of being merely cosmetic, to the truly radical that would shatter the commission's complacency but risk disrupting its ability to function.

A first step would be to attack the institution's 'silo mentality'. Its specialist directorates-general have great difficulty in communicating with one another—in large part because of their own turf wars—and would benefit from a thorough shake-up. Some senior officials talk of 'joining up the dots' so that people working on a specific topic in one directorates-general would collaborate with relevant opposite numbers in others.

Introducing such a spirit of flexibility into the commission isn't that easy. The rigidities that have grown up over the years are ingrained features of the commission's culture. Although they are not necessar-ily beyond reform, it will take a determined assault by the entire College of Commissioners to break down the opposition to change championed by its in-house trade unions.

The inefficiencies of the directorates-general that have become commissioners' jealously guarded fiefdoms is one problem, and an even greater one is the EU executive's lack of communications savvy. Its inability to get its messages across is an abiding weakness, and is shared by all the EU institutions. The European Commission and the secretariats of the European Parliament and the Council chiefly employ lawyers and economists, and only in recent years have they taken on a handful of journalists and communications specialists, who as spokespersons are mostly kept on very short leashes.

If Jean-Claude Juncker and his fellow members of the College of Commissioners could be persuaded to kick over the traces and defy the Eurocrats' culture of non-communication, there's a fairly easy way they could do it. All the EU officials need to do is to stop trying to manage news themselves and instead hand over everything of media interest to a wholly independent operation run by and for journalists.

'Newsroom Europe' would be an ambitious project for getting more coverage of EU policy issues into the media around Europe and worldwide. But in contrast to Brussels' long standing and generally frustrated efforts to promote the anodyne fare that they see as good news, it would operate like any other independent news-gathering organization. A newsroom staffed by print and broadcast journalists from across Europe would cover all aspects of EU activity, but under the direction of editors and not of EU officials. With today's online media revolution increasing the hunger for newsworthy material, Newsroom Europe would supply a steady stream of stories that went out untouched by EU censorship or even influence.

The number of EU-accredited journalists in Brussels has been falling steadily ever since the economic crisis combined with the impact of digital media. On the other hand, the market for stories about Europe's difficulties and their solutions has been growing. Regional as well as national media have a hunger for information, but stories need to be in the local language, in the appropriate journalese (a term of reproof amongst Eurocrats), and tailored to local tastes. In other words, a massive editing and translation effort, with reporting tailored to what national readerships are interested in rather than what EU officialdom considers appropriate. It would be expensive, but beyond price when set against the rising political costs of non-communication.

At the more modest end of the spectrum of ideas for addressing the weaknesses of the EU bureaucracy, there are reforms that could work quite quickly while delivering a useful shock to the system. There should be greater internal rotation to move younger and lower-grade Eurocrats more speedily from one directorate-general to another. And there should also be a more stringent career review mechanism to fast-track the best and brightest while quietly 'letting go' the time-servers and the self-satisfied.

The example set by the anti-trust watchdogs in the directorates-general for Competition of establishing 'devil's advocate' teams should be adopted as widely as possible throughout the commission. Their function is to challenge the accepted wisdom of commission policies, and it's an approach that's also badly needed in those departments that administer the Brussels executive's more inflexible and self-protecting regulations.

Moving across the spectrum towards those truly difficult innovations that require member governments' cooperation, the ranks of EU officialdom have to become more porous. That means bringing in national civil servants, especially high-flyers, on temporary assignments, and it also means overhauling or even scrapping the quota system that guarantees each member state a given proportion of top jobs. For the last ten years this has reserved the lion's share of promotions for the new member states, and though well-intentioned has acted as a strong disincentive to other ambitious younger Eurocrats seeking to advance their careers.

Even more revolutionary suggestions for electrifying what is widely seen as the faceless bureaucracy of the EU should at the very least be publicly discussed. One idea might be to leave the Eurocrats' attractive and virtually tax-free pay grades and perks intact, but to end the concept of an EU post being a job for life. The standard contract for relatively senior EU officials could, for example, be set at five years, the span of each commission's mandate. Only three-quarters of them, say, would be renewed, so that underperforming officials would not survive. They would have to find work elsewhere, with their own national government or the private sector, but would be able to reapply after an absence of at least five years.

It's not certain, of course, that making employment by the European Commission more precarious and uncertain will necessarily attract greater talent or more original thinkers. On the other hand, those market forces are the conditions that prevail in the private sector, whereas creating special privileges for EU officials has introduced unwelcome rigidities. What is certainly needed is a further updating of the commission's entrance exam—the 'concours' that still demands knowledge of recondite and arcane EU history—and greater transparency of its promotion methods. Appointments to key posts should not be in the gift of individual commissioners but decided by independent panels.

The effect of any of these shake-ups of Brussels' comfortable bureaucracy would be to oxygenate the EU's thinking and improve its external image. The greater goal should be to loosen up discussion of the main policy blockages standing in the way of a more flexible approach to Europe's biggest problems. Economic cooperation and industrial innovation are not the only issues of concern; just as important are the policies that relate to immigration, energy, and security. By embracing its own reform, EU officialdom could do much to signal the need for far-reaching changes in the way the union is run.

## Reforming the EU: Great Debate or Timid Nibbling?

There's a general view across Europe that the EU is in need of reform, but little clarity about exactly what sort of reform. The clearest element of this debate is that there's a vitally important distinction between reform ideas that involve treaty change and those that don't.

Ideas that would demand a reopening of the treaties to which EU governments have committed themselves are obviously more ambitious and fundamental than those that would not. They also, of course, have the major disadvantage of demanding widespread agreement between governments while running the risk of being overturned by voters in countries where a referendum would have to be held. That happened in 2005 when French and Dutch voters rejected the idea of a European constitution.

The proposed EU constitution would have settled a good many of the arguments that still rage, but in retrospect its name was provocation enough to ensure it would be torpedoed. In Germany and much of northern Europe it was seen as a 'basic law' that tied up legal loose ends and set out a coherent political framework. Elsewhere it looked like the dread hand of the European superstate.

The fate of the EU's constitutional treaty is seen by many as a warning. It tells them, they believe, that Europe's leaders can either cobble together something as complex, unreadable and anodyne as the Lisbon Treaty that rescued elements of it, or incur the wrath of increasingly Eurosceptic electorates. The result is a wariness that leads them to package EU reform in such a way that treaty change would be avoided. Ideas that don't demand the reopening of its treaties are therefore much more likely to figure prominently when the reform agenda takes shape. The truth, meanwhile, is that the workings of the EU could be greatly improved by a strong dose of common sense rather than constitutional tinkering.

A plea for common sense came from the unexpected quarter of the Vatican when Pope Francis briefly visited Strasbourg to address the European Parliament in November 2014. 'Europe seems somewhat elderly and haggard', said the pontiff, 'feeling less and less a protagonist. The great ideas that inspired Europe have been replaced by the bureaucratic technicalities of its institutions'. He warned of European citizens' growing mistrust of EU institutions 'they consider aloof and engaged in laying down rules perceived as insensitive to individual peoples, if not downright harmful'.

The commission's hidebound approach to policies that no longer work and its insistence on inflexible rules and lengthy procedures are problems that can quite easily be fixed. To its credit, the commission is aware of that and has introduced a review called REFIT—an acronym for Regulatory Fitness and Performance programme—to winnow out the sillier bits of EU activity. Among the more hilarious of the hundred or so nonsensical and outdated matters it has tackled was a proposal that hairdressers should be forbidden to wear high-heeled shoes!

REFIT and other streamlining efforts are just a sideshow; the main aim should be to identify reforms that restore the EU's dynamism and credibility while recovering its lost public support. The EU's member governments are the key players, and so far they have all been careful to hold their cards close to their chests. The UK government, pushed by vociferously Eurosceptic conservative MPs seeking shelter from the UKIP 'independence' party, has claimed that its ideas for reform are backed by a growing number of other governments. It did not, though, seize the opportunity of the mid-2014 European elections to detail those ideas.

The 'seven-point reform plan' that prime minister David Cameron repeatedly spoke of refers vaguely to cutting red tape, removing the hidden barriers to trade within Europe, and completing the single market in services and other areas. These are so general as to be uncontentious, and some national leaders, such as Alexander Stubb when he was Finland's prime minister, have endorsed them. It's hard to see how they can satisfy anti-European backbench Tory MPs and their constituents, who are baying for the 'repatriation' of many of the powers held by Brussels.

There's a wide gap between the emotional arguments advanced by Eurosceptics in Britain and elsewhere and the discussion taking place between experts who understand the complexities of the reform debate. Some very sensible suggestions have been advanced in the UK by the Centre for European Reform (CER), an independent pro-EU think tank. It has produced a long list of ideas that don't require treaty change, and a shorter list of those that do.

In a report entitled 'How to build a modern European Union', CER researchers advocate changes that most people would probably be amazed were not automatically introduced as the EU moved forward. They suggest that the commission, parliament, and council should agree on a common working programme for each five-year mandate, and they ask for external experts to be appointed to take part in the commission's impact assessment studies of proposed policies. They add that both parliament and council should carry out their own impact assessments when significant changes to EU law are being discussed.

Other common-sense ideas range from non-eurozone countries having observer status at Eurogroup finance ministers' meetings to establishing a new single market council made up only of ministerial heavyweights. Another useful innovation would be an EU standing committee on immigration and labour needs capable of feeding objective information into this heated debate. On the EU budget, which for some is far too large at a trillion euros over five years, or far too low at only one per cent of the EU's GDP, the CER team proposes a strategic review that by 2020 would shift funding away from farm support and regional development, especially in richer countries, to cross-border projects such as energy and transport.

Various reform suggestions from other sources—notably from individual analysts rather than political parties in or out of government—include ideas that astonishingly are still absent from a decision-making arrangement that has any claim to be democratic. Philippe Legrain, who followed his stint in the European Commission's in-house think tank with a widely praised book *European Spring*, has joined the calls for Council of Ministers meetings to be opened to the public, and especially the deliberations of finance and economy ministers in the EcoFin council and the Eurogroup. Another book, *Unhappy Union* by John Peet and Anton La Guardia, two former EU correspondents of *The Economist*, suggests that the powers of the European Parliament should be downgraded to permit a greater role for national MPs.

There's certainly a growing consensus that the EU's member governments should no longer operate in the cosily secretive fashion of years past. And ideas abound for bringing national parliamentarians into the picture, either through beefing-up the yellow and orange card system for challenging regulatory proposals, or by creating special committees as an integral part of EU decision-making. The drawback is that these would need treaty change. It would be easier to introduce throughout the EU a similar arrangement to that now common in the Nordic member states; hearings by relevant parliamentary committees scrutinize ministers' intentions before they leave for Brussels, thus shaping their positions instead of hearing the results afterwards when it's too late to change anything.

The German government has been keeping a low profile on EU reform, doubtless because it wants to avoid pouring oil on the flames of popular resentment in Germany against eurozone bail-outs. France, for many decades the principal source of innovative thinking on Europe's future, has also been discreetly silent. The Netherlands, though, has produced a number of ideas that don't demand treaty change, including the introduction of a 'subsidiarity court' that could rule on whether an activity should be conducted at national or EU level. Some Dutch politicians are keen to ensure that the European Parliament is unable to 'dictate' the EU's policy agenda, and others want new mechanisms that would limit the European Court of Justice's power to impose as law its rulings on legal disputes.

These ideas have none of the shrill anti-European tone of so many of the British contributions to the reform debate. The demand by some Eurosceptics on the right wing of the UK's Conservative party for the goal of 'an ever-closer union' to be removed from the EU's founding treaty is particularly absurd because that text doesn't refer to the governments of Europe. Written barely a decade after the end of Second World War, it expresses the well-intentioned sentiment that the peoples of Europe should become more closely united.

More to the point is the pressure now being exerted by Britain's Tories for the return to Westminster of powers held by the EU. This is already the focus of much discussion in the UK, even though when examined point by point there seems little room for tinkering. On matters such as the free movement in Europe of EU nationals to live and work where they please, there is no room for negotiation. In other areas ranging from police cooperation to social protection, the truth is that British interests would suffer from major changes.

The UK has in any case already won opt-outs on the euro and from the EU's free travel Schengen regime, can pick and choose on justice and policing issues, and is protected by unanimity voting from any unwelcome taxation or foreign policy ideas. The limits to London's room for manoeuvre have been set out in a book entitled *Britain's Future in Europe: Reform, Renegotiation, Repatriation or Secession?* edited by Michael Emerson of the Centre for European Policy Studies think tank in Brussels, together with twelve other contributors. EU expert Tony Barber hailed the book in the *Financial Times* as deserving congratulations for setting out the arguments on reform with clarity and common sense.

France and Germany have already dashed the hopes of the Conservative-led UK government of involving them in its 'audit' of EU powers that might be repatriated, and they have made it plain that unpicking the treaties that bind European countries finds no favour in Paris or Berlin. Guido Westerwelle, who was German foreign minister and vice-chancellor from 2009 to 2011, summed up Berlin's view when he said: 'Cherry-picking is not an option. Europe isn't the sum of national interests but a community with a common fate in difficult times'. More bluntly, the same message has been conveyed by former Swedish prime minister Carl Bildt. 'Flexibility sounds fine', he commented of various reform ideas, 'but if you sign up to a twenty-eight-speed Europe, at the end of the day there's no Europe at all. Just a mess'.

## What *Do* Europeans Think of Twenty-First Century Challenges?

More than sixty years ago, Belgian statesman Paul-Henri Spaak said of the early stirrings of European integration: 'There are only two types of state in Europe; small states, and small states that have not yet realized they are small' Spaak was among the founding fathers of the

Common Market and was NATO's second secretary-general, but his prescient remark about European countries' diminishing weight in the world has not, with hindsight, been taken to heart by successive generations.

No one knows whether people in European countries truly believe that their own governments and their national decision-making systems are capable of handling the challenges of the twenty-first century. Opinion polls suggest, though, that far from understanding the way global change is rapidly reducing even the biggest EU members to impotence and irrelevance, most Europeans still see the making and implementation of national policy as quicker, more democratic, and more effective than EU policymaking.

And they're right; to a great extent that is certainly the case. National decision-making is faster than the EU's ponderous consensus-building, and political cultures built around a shared language and national media obviously exert a stronger influence than noises from faraway Brussels. But these national bonds are weakening the EU's chances of becoming more effective, and have the effect of compounding global threats to Europeans' living standards and to their future security.

There's no quick fix for Europe's problems. To restore the European Union's external clout, its members need first to address their internal difficulties. Culturally similar though the countries of Europe are, it is striking how different are even neighbouring countries' political debates. The legacy of history is Europe's very different national democratic structures. That shouldn't, however, prevent Europeans' elected representatives from creating a common political culture to confront the global challenges ahead.

Whether it's jobs and immigration, schooling and skilling, pensions or healthcare, all European countries share to varying degrees the same structural and demographic weaknesses. Europe is shrinking in a world where size matters, and although for many centuries a scientific and intellectual powerhouse, it has been complacently unaware of how rapidly other parts of the world are catching up and even overtaking it.

The narratives of national politicians throughout Europe reflect little of the common nature of these challenges. Quite the contrary; European issues tend to be portrayed in competitive terms—eurozone debt as a zero-sum game in which there are winners and losers, or industrial competitiveness where northern Europe seems pitted against the south. These are false ideas, for as Benjamin Franklin famously remarked in 1776 when America's Declaration of Independence was signed: 'We must all hang together, or most assuredly we will all hang separately'.

The place to start is at the grass roots. The grand strategies for R&D and innovation so beloved by EU officialdom in Brussels are certainly important, but they are too technocratic to strike any sort of chord with European voters. Jobs and housing and the opportunities available to people's children are the issues that engage their interest and support. That in turn means agreeing common political narratives. They won't be the same across the left–right spectrum, but a first step would be for national politicians to evoke the shared nature and pan-European character of these problems.

Only the most die-hard Eurosceptics would deny that the integration of Europe's nation states has been a remarkable achievement. It has also been a very subtle process, perhaps too subtle. Apart from greater ease of travel and the introduction of an increasingly controversial common currency, the creation of the EU's pan-European political mechanisms has not impinged greatly on people's everyday lives. It hasn't been done by subterfuge, but it has been done with such discretion that it is scarcely surprising that voters neither understand it nor see it as crucial to their future.

Europe's decline is gradual enough to be almost imperceptible to public opinion. Without stark choices on the horizon that could jolt national electorates out of their somnolence, each successive year will see an almost invisible narrowing of the available options. This isn't inevitable, just probable. To counter it, perhaps even defy it, Europe must shake itself out of its stupor and awaken to the many different measures to be taken. That means greater courage and imagination from the EU and its institutions, but also the spirit of self-sacrifice by national politicians that has been so signally lacking.

Like Jean-Claude Juncker, most national leaders across Europe doubtless know what needs to be done. They also know that the reforms to be introduced and the mindsets to be challenged will in the short term provoke anger and resentment, and will cost them votes. They must summon the courage to do what needs to be done, even if that means they are not re-elected. That is, after all, the difference between a politician and a statesman. The compensation is that the former are soon forgotten, while the latter are remembered and may even come to be revered.

# 12

# No Master Plan for the EU, but an Urgent 'To Do' List

*A 'master plan' for Europe is tantalizingly out of reach, yet many of the building blocks for recovery and a more constructive future are at hand. The key will be getting European Union governments to pay more than lip service to working together in areas where they still believe they have different, even rival, national interests. This chapter sets out the substantial list of projects and policy areas where the European Union could, if so minded, deliver progress and concrete results.*

There's no magic wand to be waved over the politics of Europe. Problems that reflect decades of complacency and neglect are crowding in, and the founding Treaty of Rome's vision of a united Europe has been eclipsed by nationalist pressures and populist opportunism. European integration has given way to fragmentation, making it more difficult than ever to talk believably of a recovery strategy that would reverse the EU's downward path.

On foreign and security policy, Europe needs to be much more coherent if it is to be respected. Reacting piecemeal to events around the world isn't the way forward. Conflicts in northern Africa, the Middle East, and eastern Ukraine, and the arrival of boatloads of refugees in Europe's Mediterranean ports underline the pressing need for a recognizable EU external strategy. Europe is seen around the world as a moral force for good, but that has to be capitalized on through collective policies rather than competing and at times contradictory national ones. The adoption of the EU's Common

Foreign and Security Policy (CFSP) was a start, but it must be seen as only the basis for a wider strategy embracing such disparate issues as global governance, trade, development assistance, and Europe's security outreach.

It's a different story within Europe. A more tactical approach rather than some overblown 'EU master plan' stands a better chance of slowing or even reversing our decline. That means identifying measures that command public attention, and signalling to voters that Europe still has the answers to their own problems.

This closing chapter looks at the options open to decision-makers. It aims to separate these from the giant political strides which, badly needed though they are, will not be achievable in the short term until an improved economic climate helps to win back people's confidence in more ambitious long-term measures.

As well as being impossible to realize politically, the sort of master plan some visionaries dream of would through its failure risk further alienating public support. That doesn't mean inaction and EU-style muddling through is the alternative. What's called for is a more intelligent and collaborative approach by EU governments consisting often of low-profile initiatives that won't excite controversy.

Technically complex measures of this sort are crucial to economic recovery, and have the added advantage of being unrewarding for grandstanding politicians. Populists who use emotion-charged issues such as immigration and 'benefits tourism' to fan the flames of Euroscepticism will find little fuel in topics such as fiscal coordination, investment guarantees and incentives, pension improvements, youth training and reskilling, cross-border mergers, and energy and transport links.

The first hurdle to be overcome is not so much Euroscepticism as inertia. There is a palpable sense of drift in Europe, with the EU's twenty-eight governments seemingly content to await developments and then to react. They don't seek to set the international agenda, and have no plans for rallying Europeans to a common cause. Yet that doesn't mean all is lost—thirty years ago much the same rudderless mood was banished by an initiative that galvanized people into action with a spirit of renewed enthusiasm and purpose.

Flashback three decades to autumn 1984. Up in Brussels from Paris on a familiarization tour, Jacques Delors looks more like a country bank manager than the president-designate of the European Commission. Dressed in a brown tweed suit and perched on the edge of one of the twin beds in his modest room at the Amigo Hotel, Delors seems from another world than that of the elegant and cosmopolitan EU officials he will be directing. He is, however, nursing a plan to revitalize the commission and the whole European integration project.

Delors has agreed to a one-on-one press interview about his intentions once he takes the reins of the commission in January. Then as now, Europe was in the doldrums and newspaper headlines spoke of 'Eurosclerosis', so few hopes were being pinned on this former French finance minister who had unexpectedly won the job of heading the next commission.

When asked for his main policy thrust, he said that it would be to complete the single market. It was hard to suppress an ironic smile, for the single market had become more than a notoriously tough nut to crack; it was widely seen as Mission Impossible. European governments had long promised unhindered free movement of goods, people, and capital, but these objectives were far from honoured. Europe's business leaders could only look longingly at the benefits their American competitors enjoyed with their continental-size home market.

The member of the outgoing commission responsible for removing all the barriers blocking business between European countries was outspokenly frustrated by the resistance of national governments. Karl-Heinz Narjes had been a U-boat commander during the Second World War and did not suffer his setbacks in silence. But denouncing intra-European protectionism had yielded little progress.

So how did the Delors Commission succeed where its predecessors had failed? In 1992, towards the end of his second four-year term, Delors was able to announce a genuine single market in goods and services. There remain to this day glaring holes in it, but Delors's achievement stands as an example of how to get things done though they had long been dismissed as impossible.

The unsung hero of the commission's success was a middle-ranking UK diplomat on secondment to Brussels. Adrian Fortescue was *chef de cabinet* to Lord Cockfield, a former British business leader sent by Margaret Thatcher to take over the single market portfolio from Narjes. Fortescue's thinking, which Arthur Cockfield and Delors readily adopted, was that the complicated and disorganized process of ratification by the then twelve national parliamentary bodies constituted the chief obstacle to be overcome.

The member governments of what was still the European Economic Community could conceivably be bullied and cajoled into accepting a structured trade liberalization package, but their parliaments' different procedural hoops and time lags would quite quickly unravel everything. To overcome this, Fortescue studied the intricacies of national parliaments' procedures, and with Cockfield's backing devised a matrix of liberalization measures and ratification deadlines that brought order and clarity to an unruly tangle.

Delors' single market slogan of '300 measures by 1992' not only revived the fortunes of the Brussels commission but the whole dynamic of European integration. Its easily understood message reached out to the media and public opinion, while the liberalization measures and the need for common rules triggered a much-needed debate on industrial policies.

There's undoubtedly a leaf to be taken from the book of the Delors commission for tackling today's morass of political, economic, and cultural differences. The challenges that confront Europe today have changed beyond all recognition, but a wide-ranging plan capable of acting as a catalyst and introducing a sense of purpose could be just as effective.

The magic ingredients for such an initiative are ambition and theatre; ambition to seize the imagination of Europeans, and theatre to fire their enthusiasm. 'Relaunching' or even 'reinventing' Europe should be the watchword, with a scope so broad that it visibly reaches out to improve the lives of all.

## EU Reform Risks Being a Recipe for Trouble

Any new approach to curing Europe's ills is certain to fall under the general heading of EU reform. It is a term that's bandied about increasingly, partly because of strident criticisms from Britain and elsewhere, and also because the feeling is widespread that the European project and its rulebook were born of a different era and need to be brought up to date.

What's meant by the term EU reform depends on who is calling for it. Some say it is the European institutions in Brussels that are at fault, and must be reformed. That may indeed be the case, but the greater problem is the refusal of many of the member governments to accept that it is their own deadlocks on a variety of issues that bar the way to constructive change.

The EU's three largest countries offer good examples of this, and these are just the tip of the iceberg. In the UK, there's the ill-informed but widely held view that London should block closer integration because it 'signed up' only to a free trade area. That free trade demands common rules and standards, which in turn require effective political mechanisms, is a common-sense argument that seems lost on fanatical Eurosceptics in the Tory party, let alone on supporters of UKIP.

Then there's France's refusal to discuss any sort of change to the institutional structures of EU decision-making. That's because it would open the Pandora's box of political union, which would weaken the presidential powers of the Fifth Republic created by Charles de Gaulle, and it has also to be set against the background of growing French Euroscepticism.

For Germany, the debate is more complicated. Ensuring the eurozone's long-term sustainability would mean turning the European Central Bank into an economic and fiscal policy instrument akin to the US Federal Reserve. Germany clings to the ECB's limited mandate, modelled on its own Bundesbank, of maintaining price stability through its control of monetary policy; that's because anything else would demand EU political union of such a revolutionary nature that although perhaps acceptable to federally minded Germans is anathema in most other European capitals.

Until these and other barriers can be overcome there appears little chance of a strategic plan for the EU. Rather than admit that their conflicting views stand in the way of change, the unspoken consensus between national capitals is that reforming the EU is about cutting away Brussels' wastefulness and inefficiency. Yet another 'war on red tape' is to be mounted by the European Commission, and as before it will doubtless trim some of the outdated and superfluous regulation that is inevitable at a time of rapid technological change.

The idea that the commission is itself the author of the EU's ills flies in the face of reality. The EU executive is nowadays little more than the creature of its member governments. The original dream of an independent and autonomous body that would wield the EU's treaties to defend the interests of all is fading fast. Today's Eurocrats are not exactly at the beck and call of national governments, but they are less and less independent of them. Something like four-fifths of the EU's directives and regulations originate as suggestions and sometimes outright commands from within the Council of Ministers. Commission officials do the donkey work of drafting and consultation, and formally propose the results to member governments' ministers, but as often as not it's the governments that call the shots.

Does that mean we must forget any ideas that EU reform could be the answer; should we abandon all hope of solutions to the EU's low-growth, no-growth problems and to its shrinking global influence? Of course not; Europeans' resilience in the face of adversity is beyond question, even though it has in the past been in response to much clearer challenges, like the aftermath of war.

The reform agenda has to be handled with care; it could be a recipe for greater trouble ahead. The danger is that it could set member states on collision courses over policies that had been thought largely resolved, ranging from farm subsidies to energy security, and including social benefits, trade protection, monetary policy, and yet more belt-tightening economic austerity. Europe's northerners may find themselves more at odds than ever with southerners, the larger EU nations with smaller ones, and the union's founding western European governments with those of the eastern newcomers.

Getting the balance right on the reform agenda is so tricky that the temptation will be to make it so modest as to be almost valueless. That would leave Europe still burdened with the many shortcomings that threaten living standards and social cohesion.

Can lessons be drawn from the EU's own history? In retrospect, the most salient feature of the single market programme three decades ago was not so much the immediate economic impact as the fact that it was so widely understood. Compared to present day misconceptions about the EU and its doings, the single market was quickly accepted by public opinion across Europe. There were disagreements between different interest groups and industries about the nature of its liberalizations, but in general terms the value of creating a single marketplace for businesses everywhere was unchallenged.

That was not just because the concept of tearing down trade barriers within Europe was simple and straightforward. It was also because the European Commission made an important commitment to conveying key messages to the public. An in-depth report in 1988 by senior Eurocrat Paolo Cecchini on the economic disadvantages of trade fragmentation—the cost of non-Europe, as he termed it—was quickly boiled down into a paperback version that, as EU-related publications go, was a bestseller.

The value of putting, as Cecchini did, some figures on the benefits to the European economy of embracing the single market's disciplines has not been lost on today's Eurocrats. A report published in mid-2014 under the aegis of the European Parliament entitled 'Mapping the Cost of non-Europe' reckons that a really determined drive to create a digital single market would be worth an extra €990 billion to the EU economy.

Analyses like this, along with the ideas featured in previous chapters of this book, add up to some useful suggestions. But their sheer variety risks confusing rather than clarifying public understanding of the issues at stake. These different suggestions make up a babble of opinions and counter-proposals that have so far made little dent in the arguments of the Eurosceptics. What's needed is to marshal these various policy proposals into a simple and straightforward menu.

## Better to Fashion a Flexible Menu of Policies than an Unrealistic 'Master Plan'

The events of 2003 have long faded into the mists of EU history, but at the European Convention of that year its 105 delegates engaged in protracted and often stormy discussions to thrash out a draft 'constitution' to take the EU into a new era. Now, when looking forward once again to ways that the European Union should try to reconcile so many conflicting pressures, it is instructive to look back at that failed attempt.

Perhaps the first lesson to be drawn is that public perception is everything. An important feature of the constitutional treaty proposed in mid-2004 was that it very plainly said the EU could never encroach on the powers of national governments. Yet the constitution's downfall was that so many voters saw it as doing exactly the opposite, leading to the creation of a 'superstate'. Within a year, French and Dutch voters said 'No' in national referenda, and because a new treaty needs the unanimous ratification of all member states, that was that.

The rescuable parts of the abandoned constitution—and needless to say, it was calling it by that name that had raised fears of an EU superstate—were cobbled together into the Lisbon Treaty of 2007. This introduced majority voting by governments in almost fifty key areas where unanimity would no longer be needed and strengthened the European Parliament's role while launching the EU's own diplomatic service.

What Lisbon didn't fix, of course, was the key question of whether European governments should further strengthen the EU by ceding more of their sovereign authority in specific areas. Those discussions took place in the calm before the storm that was soon to break with the 2008 global financial crisis and the ensuing economic recession. Events since then have done nothing to persuade EU governments, and especially those in the eurozone, to favour a greater centralizing of power. The opposite has been the case, with many member governments even less inclined than before to pool their powers and resources.

European public opinion could conceivably alter the political calculus. The example of how Jacques Delors rallied support for his 'great adventure' of the single market suggests that an electrifying clarion call might conceivably turn the Eurosceptic tide. The call would need to convince people that Europe must make headway on ten goals ranging from the neglected to the widely contested if it is to regain its lost ground and gear up for the tougher global conditions that lie ahead. These range from the more tactical policy areas mentioned at the beginning of this chapter to the three enormously ambitious political challenges that although seemingly unattainable must not be shelved indefinitely. These span the creation of a genuinely pan-European 'demos', the arming of the European Central Bank with far greater powers to stimulate and balance growth in the eurozone, and a political union that would be a new EU-level governing mechanism.

The contrast between today's political climate and that of the European project's early years is inescapable. In the wreckage and misery of post-war Europe, radical change was attractive because it held out the promise of reconciliation, reconstruction, and economic recovery. Now the mood is that the EU represents costs and not benefits. The bruising recession has led many people to believe the EU oversold itself, engendering hostility to the measures that urgently need to be taken.

This book opened by challenging ten myths hastening Europe's decline. It draws to a close with a daunting list of ten elements that must be tackled sooner or later if Europe is to regain its forward momentum. In terms of practical politics, the list begins with the wholly possible and winds up with the improbable, not to say impossible in terms of the current political outlook.

**1. Europe needs a more determined strategy for modernizing and expanding basic infrastructure, especially transport, to boost competitiveness and spur growth.**

Improving competitiveness with new infrastructure to speed goods across Europe and unclog the traffic jams paralysing many cities is becoming such a high priority that concerted action may now be on the cards. It's certainly very badly needed.

Ambitious proposals for cross-border transport links have met with only limited success in years past. They were apparently too ambitious, so their eye-watering price tags saw them flatly rejected by most governments. Now, Jean-Claude Juncker's commission is championing a €315 billion infrastructure strategy that it says could do much to kick-start European economies, but the EU still has to persuade taxpayers and finance ministers of the benefits.

There's disagreement on how to finance this without saddling future generations with more debt, and the experts argue over whether it would really make that big a difference. The 'financial engineering' involved in leveraging the mere €20 billion or so the EU can command in cash draws much criticism, and it's far from certain that private sector investors such as pension funds will sink huge amounts into an EU gamble without cast-iron guarantees from member governments—a question that will reawaken the 'moral hazard' debate that raged in the aftermath of 2008 over the bailing-out by taxpayers of 'too-big-to-fail' banks that had behaved irresponsibly.

Juncker's idea, whatever the drawbacks, at least amounts to a plan that can help to restore Europe's momentum. If anything, it probably needs to be expanded and placed in the hands of a new EU institution comparable in some ways to the various 'New Deal' agencies created in the US by president Franklin D. Roosevelt to pull America out of the Great Depression in the 1930s. Matheusz Szczurek, Poland's finance minister, spoke for a good many experts and observers of EU policy-making when in autumn 2014 he suggested that the target figure for an investment drive should be more than doubled to €700 billion.

The infrastructure strategy is now moving ahead under the auspices of the EU's Luxembourg-based European Investment Bank, and is attracting a growing number of candidate projects both large and small. But the key to moving forward with such an ambitious Keynesian pump-priming effort is in the hands of the EU's member governments, not with the European Union itself. That will in turn demand an acceptance of increased borrowing at a time when the extent of governments' indebtedness is such a divisive issue.

It would in any case be a mistake to put all Europe's Keynesian eggs into only the EU's basket. Housing shortages across Europe are already a serious brake on economic growth and on job-seekers' mobility; the obvious answer to the economic doldrums now threatening deflation and a return to a 1930s-style Great Depression is for EU member governments to launch national house-building and infrastructure drives. The 120,000 new homes being built yearly in the UK, for instance, are reckoned to be roughly half the number needed to address severe housing shortages and to prick the country's dangerous property prices bubble.

## 2. The EU should have a more realistic budget than its tiny one per cent of the EU's €13 trillion economy, and it should scrap spending where national supports are more appropriate farm subsidies, say—while boosting cross-border funding for research and innovation.

Hopes of increasing the EU's budget from one per cent of EU countries' combined GDPs were dashed in early 2014 when member governments decided to peg the 2015 to 2019 budget to its previous level, which in practice means cutting it.

Opposition from France and some others to a progressive renationalization of farm subsidies so as to curtail the EU's top-heavy Common

Agricultural Policy spending will not easily be overcome. Farm subsidies continue to mop up around four-tenths of the budget's €140 billion-plus yearly outlays. On the plus side, if the EU reform bandwagon were really to pick up speed, then calls to fund more ambitious cross-border R&D and business-oriented projects could start to unlock the coffers of the richer member states.

The European Commission has long tried to increase EU governments' financial support for key industrial and research projects, but without much success. Its handicaps include unfair criticisms of its own financial probity, even though the EU Court of Auditors is usually so slow to clear the accounts for technical and not criminal reasons. The perception that the commission unhesitatingly funds its own pet projects, however dubious their economic value may be, is more justified and tighter public supervision of these would be useful.

The lion's share of EU spending is disbursed by national authorities rather than by Brussels, so when there's fraud it can rarely be laid at the Eurocrats' door. That doesn't mean the EU shouldn't be making a much more determined effort to ensure total transparency of its budgetary mechanisms. The watchdog role of the European Parliament, coupled with commission officials' paranoia about being vulnerable to criticism, makes it unusual for the EU itself to be guilty of financial mismanagement or worse.

The stigma of fraud resulting from a few rare scandals has been hard to erase, and is overshadowed by perceptions that too often EU budget funds are squandered. A plain guide to EU spending, and to how member governments decide on the allocation of funds, would be a useful contribution to a Europe-wide public debate about the future size of the EU budget and its priorities.

**3. The strengthening of EU foreign policy mechanisms should see Europe setting the international agenda, notably on global governance and security issues, instead of merely reacting to events.**

Brussels must raise its game as a foreign policy player, but the ball is in the court of the EU's member governments. The European diplomatic service created by the Lisbon Treaty of 2004 reflected EU governments' awareness of the need to 'speak with one voice', and saw the introduction of an EU 'foreign minister'—the High Representative—at the head of the new European External Action Service (EEAS).

The activities of the EEAS have so far centred chiefly on trade and economic relations, but not on the lengthening list of security threats. New as it is, it needs both an internal shake-up and a showdown with EU governments. These, especially the Big Three, have shown no signs of accepting that Europe badly needs common foreign policies in the light of events in the Middle East and Ukraine. The smaller EU countries often lack experience in foreign affairs at a geopolitical level and have been slow to back the EEAS as an instrument for creating consensus on external policies, and it's time they did so.

The European Union's external policy outreach is patchy, yet it could potentially be a powerful diplomatic and economic instrument. The failure of Europe to react quickly and buttress the countries of the Arab Spring with immediate economic assistance has contributed to the conflicts that threaten so much of the Middle East. An ambitious and high-profile Africa strategy along with a more coherent and structured approach to Asia would be welcomed in those regions and would also resonate with people in Europe who ask 'what's the EU for?'.

Enhancing Europe's foreign and security policies means a lot more commitment and work than has so far been the case. That demands increased financial resources from the member states and a greater willingness on the EU's part—in other words, political courage—to draw attention to backsliding or even outright refusals by member governments to agree on common positions. All twenty-eight accept the principle of speaking with one voice, and now they must allow Brussels to put it into practice.

The EU and its officials must for their part earn the respect of national governments that have for centuries conducted their own foreign policies. Europe's diplomatic service must learn to behave like a real foreign ministry rather than an adjunct of the European Commission. There should be more emphasis on scenario planning and the concerting of member states' positions in advance of a crisis, not afterwards.

The early years of the EEAS have been marked by slow reaction times, and by a failure to prevent member governments from breaking ranks and undermining the common EU position. Those governments must for their part send more of their own diplomats to bolster the EEAS and water down the numbers of seconded commission officials whose focus is on trade and commercial matters.

**4. Europe has to overhaul its social and fiscal policies so as to buttress its claim to be a 'caring society', and it must adapt more swiftly to the pressures of an ageing population.**

Taxation cannot continue to be a no-go area for EU policymaking. Governments and political parties across Europe have jealously guarded their fiscal sovereignty, and in the absence of new and unifying political structures there still seems little likelihood of a major breakthrough on tax harmonization. Yet common tax policies are vital to Europe's future; they can help prevent 'races to the bottom' in which EU countries compete through giveaway investment incentives and can also do much to support broader social policy objectives.

Few people would deny the importance of raising skills and educational levels to achieve greater economic convergence and boost EU competitiveness, and rethinking tax policies could make a valuable contribution. Problematic tax havens and the ratcheting up of fiscal competition between EU countries are increasingly controversial, and touch a raw nerve amongst voters who have suffered from austerity cutbacks.

If that forces an overhaul of national fiscal policies, these should be accompanied by renewed emphasis on social policies, especially those related to ageing and to underprivileged young people. A shift away from taxes on labour that discourage employment to a greater taxation of capital would help Europe's 'lost generation' of unemployed young people to find work. Ideas like a sweepingly global and and therefore potentially unworkable 'Tobin tax' on the profits of financial transactions led many EU governments to dig in their heels against concerting their tax policies. That doesn't necessarily mean they will never sign up to complementary tax structures that remove unfair incentives.

Fiscal readjustments in EU countries could also be directed towards social objectives such as tackling housing shortages and educational and skills goals. The immigration needs of many European countries demand major investments to accommodate, educate, and integrate the newcomers and ensure their future contributions to society and the economy.

**5. The EU must capitalize on the linked areas of energy security and climate change if it is to allay fears over the vulnerability of oil and gas imports while reasserting its global leadership on environmental protection.**

Force of circumstances may yet push European governments into scrapping their cherished and often protectionist national energy policies. Falling oil prices distort the picture, but in many EU countries the reality is a looming energy crunch. Caused ostensibly by deteriorating relations with Russia and growing uncertainty over gas imports, the much more significant threat is the standstill in new power station construction. These combined factors may yet break the long-standing deadlocks that have prevented a common EU energy policy.

A shared energy policy has eluded Europe for many years. EU governments have long paid lip service to the idea, but usually for electoral reasons pursue very different policies on energy supply, including imports, and on subsidies to address climate change by encouraging renewable sources of energy.

Energy stands high among the EU's attainable goals, and a common energy policy could be a rallying cry for Europe's consumers. The

Brussels commission should transform the tangle of technical questions surrounding energy pricing and security of supply into a clearly defined political issue and then lead a crusade that places the onus for energy reform and collaboration squarely on the national capitals.

The complexities of energy supply and demand are such that a coherent and easily understood public debate is hard, but not impossible. The Brussels commission often lacks the appetite and the skills to launch an effective public debate, but that is precisely what it must do.

**6. Brussels must fire people's imaginations to secure a turnaround in Europe's slow and patchy adoption of digital technologies and recover its global competitiveness.**

The EU's industrial policies have long been neglected and allowed to drift lower and lower on the priorities list. Many of them are nevertheless within reach, and need to be addressed urgently and with far greater determination. As the digital age accelerates, Europe risks lagging forever behind the United States, and is even finding itself overtaken by high-tech competition from Asia. EU governments have for more than twenty years talked about a European innovation strategy, but most have yet to put their money where their mouths are.

Much lost ground could be recovered if the concept of 'national champions' in key sectors were to be ended. Governments should abandon the 'golden shares' they often use to keep control of industries they see as vital to the national economy. They have preferred the painless solution of hoping cross-border R&D cooperation will fix European companies' waning global competitiveness, but their dwindling international market shares in many key sectors show that's simply not enough.

The EU should publish a clear analysis naming names in the industrial sectors where corporate Europe is being overtaken by international competitors. This should also suggest where inter-European concentrations and mergers would be the answer. The EU's failure to put its weight behind the proposed merger of the Franco-German EADS civil and military aviation group with the UK's BAe Systems aerospace giant to create a European defence behemoth was hopefully a never to be repeated mistake.

The Brussels commission's reluctance to name and shame those member governments that haven't honoured their commitments to agreed innovation policies and R&D spending increases has been a feature of the EU's growing impotence since the signing of the Lisbon Treaty at the beginning of this century. Its overblown promise to make Europe the world's most technologically innovative region made headlines, but it was so widely flouted that the EU's own credibility was sapped. What's now needed is a fresh and more hard-headed start in which Brussels would summon the courage to draw up and publicize league tables of winners, losers and backsliders.

**7. The EU needs to take an unambiguous stance on immigration to staunch the shrinkage of its workforce.**

The ageing and shrinking of Europe's population is incontrovertible. It means that almost all EU countries will within a generation badly need the economic security of increased immigration. It's hard when Europe is in the throes of its unanticipated refugee and migrant crisis, and with the climate of recession still lingering, to persuade large sections of public opinion that this is the case. But political leaders nevertheless need to confront the resistance to immigration that is being stoked by opportunists, and not only in the fringe parties of the far right.

There has already been a steady move away from any common EU policy on immigration, and the strains of the refugee crisis make it recede further still. The polarization of opinion in Germany and Scandinavian countries that have been most open to immigration is now being magnified elsewhere in Europe. The European Commission, like the OECD, has conducted authoritative studies on demographic shifts, and could be much more forthright in urging EU countries to get real about their labour shortages and immigration needs. It should do more to publicize its own forecast that Britain's economy can can look forward to a sustained boost thanks to immigration, so much so that by mid-century it will overtake Germany as the EU's most populous country. Although there's a widespread view in Britain that being outside the eurozone has fuelled Britain's higher economic growth rate, the more likely explanation is that it's the influx of foreign workers to swell the workforce that has done the most to stimulate greater activity.

As well as being more outspoken about immigration, Brussels should actively encourage the copying of Scandinavian practices for delaying retirement. In Sweden, almost three-quarters of people in the fifty five to sixty-four age bracket stay at work, whereas the EU average is only half. Governments should understand that keeping older people in work is a win-win proposition, lowering overall pension costs while enabling the state to pay more to those people who take late retirement.

These crucially important elements are already shaping Europe's economic outlook, and they are blighting the prospects of young people in the decades ahead. Prejudice and misinformation about Europe's multicultural future are fuelling Euroscepticism, and the EU's inadequate policy response must be boldly reversed.

### 8. The EU must move to a more democratic institutional balance that makes decision-making less distant and unaccountable.

Democratic legitimacy is the key to the two most important but most distant goals on this 'to-do' list—a far more powerful European Central Bank and some sort of 'political union'. But unless voters feel that they have a voice in the way a more coherent and centralized EU is governed, neither of these goals will ever be attained.

We live in an era of doubt and dissatisfaction with politics and politicians. Whether involved in their country's politics or simply as voters, not many people nowadays seem to believe their own national form of parliamentary democracy is satisfactory. This may be less true of formerly communist countries in eastern and central Europe, but by and large, doubts abound over questions such as the role of an upper house, the fairness of the voting system, constituency bound-aries, and the selection of parliamentary candidates.

So perhaps the time will come before too long for a serious re-evaluation of democracy in Europe. There's a need to establish much clearer democratic rules and responsibilities for governing EU decision-makers—the power of the governed to oust their govern-ment. The EU will sooner or later have to develop a system that calls decision-makers to account and ensures they can be replaced.

But what democratic mechanisms would deliver legitimacy and efficiency while at the same time bringing complex EU-level politics closer to faraway voters? There's no consensus between the cham-pions of competing systems and ideas, and the established political parties in EU countries on the left and the right have shown no signs of wanting to find common ground.

With no acceptable model in sight that could reconcile the inter-ests of big and small countries and richer and poorer ones, a more modest form of democratization could be the first answer. A greater involvement of national parliamentarians in EU decision-making by dovetailing the 'Europe committees' of national MPs with their MEP counterparts would help to satisfy criticisms of the democratic deficit.

At the same time, the further democratization of the EU could become a double-edged sword that cuts both ways; making the commission more accountable could strengthen criticism that it is a stealthy move towards political union, especially if 'federal' arrange-ments for economic governance were involved. It's not a non-starter, but it certainly isn't within easy reach. An initial step could be to make the commission less monolithic by hiving off some of its more its fairly autonomous administrative functions away from Brussels and distributing them to cities around Europe. Decentralizing EU decision-making would help to counter anti-Brussels prejudices, and in this information age the concentration of EU bureaucracy in a single place seems less and less justifiable.

The European Commission is the place to start, and the heterogeneity of its functions makes it relatively easy to break up. Its 'competences'—the independent powers it has on things such as anti-trust competition policy or international trade negotiations—could be hived off and entrusted to newly created EU bodies. These 'honest broker' functions where the commission is trusted to be completely neutral in its decisions are often at odds with its increasingly 'political' role in areas such as economic supervision of member states and the creation of a more muscular EU industrial policy.

The answer could be to review the commission's present structure and place those responsibilities that are appropriate to decentralization into EU agencies that would be responsible to the commission but functionally autonomous. There are already some thirty EU agencies scattered around the member states, and adding new heavyweight agencies to their number would do much to dilute fears of Brussels as the heart of the 'EU superstate'.

**9. The European Central Bank should, like the US Federal Reserve, have the powers to promote growth and jobs as well as price stability.**

Europeans have learned to their cost that the euro is suited to fair weather, not foul. Its design dates back twenty-five years, when the gaps between eurozone members' national economies were far less evident. The challenge now is to find a eurozone governance formula that can reconcile their different needs and interests while also wielding the policy instruments to rekindle growth. That points to greatly beefing-up the Frankfurt-based European Central Bank and giving it a broader role akin to its US counterpart, the Federal Reserve.

Tinkering with the ECB is fraught with difficulties; there's already much debate about what the eurozone central bank's function is, and what it ought to be. Should the ECB play a key role in supporting national economic policies and serve as a lender of last resort for their debt? These roles are not enshrined in the EU treaty, which explicitly outlaws the monetary financing of governments. But were the goal to be a more federal system of economic governance, the EU would have to press the restart button and overhaul the powers of the ECB along with those of the European Commission and the Eurogroup, the body made up of eurozone finance ministers.

The idea of a strengthened European Central Bank whose role in the eurozone would be more like that of the US Federal Reserve is attractive for a number of reasons. First, there's the question of jobs; the ECB's mandate is limited to maintaining price stability, whereas that of the Fed extends to promoting economic growth, including employment. Set up just over a century ago in response to a number of banking panics and financial crises, the Federal Reserve System was further strengthened at the time of the Great Depression and mass unemployment in America. Its history points up some obvious parallels with the eurozone's own difficulties.

Advocates of stronger and more effective economic governance for the eurozone see the Fed as a desirable model. A Fed-like ECB would therefore have the same broad mandate of promoting economic growth and employment. Its primary role at present is fighting inflation, even though it is the spectre of deflation that is haunting so many of Europe's national economies. That focus on price stability is seen as less and less relevant by those who fear that if prices and incomes become trapped in a downward spiral, Europe's ensuing depression will be so deep that it could take many years to climb out of it.

The main argument of those who want a much more powerful ECB is the need to prevent the eurozone from breaking apart. When the euro was being launched in the late 1990s, the economies of those countries intending to join were converging. The single currency was seen as a mechanism to promote still closer economic convergence, and for several years that proved to be the case. But now the indebtedness of southern eurozone countries—especially Greece—has cast the euro in the very different light of exacerbating their divergence from its northern members. In other words, the disciplines and rigidities of the single currency are pulling them apart. The idea is that a Fed-like ECB could do much to stimulate growth in the euro's weaker economies and bring about a return to eurozone convergence. By doing so, the catastrophe of a failed euro would be averted.

Germany is at the heart of this discussion. It had originally insisted that price stability should be the ECB's chief responsibility, and has been sceptical of the ECB's measures to reinvigorate economic activity through its policy of 'quantitative easing', the jargon for what in effect is printing more money by pumping new funds into the eurozone banking system. Like other EU members and governments around the world, Berlin recognizes that the euro is in great danger, but that doesn't mean there's a rescue plan.

Along with other northern European member states, Berlin would only accept a huge expansion of the ECB's remit if it were to be paralleled by new political mechanisms to prevent any repeats of the irresponsibilities in some southern eurozone countries that led to the sovereign debt crisis. In short, federal economic governance. The only acceptable trade-off would be that the eurozone's stronger members would give unprecedented structural support to its weaker economies, but must have a major say in their economic policymaking.

The decoded version of all this is that a major overhaul and expansion of the ECB would add up to the creation of a new European economic governance mechanism, and doing that would require political union. The idea of a eurozone 'finance ministry' has been kicking around for some time, but so far with no takers. When France's Jean-Claude Trichet was president of the ECB he used the occasion of being awarded the prestigious Charlemagne Prize in 2011 to call for a body with the power to exercise control over eurozone members' national budgets. His proposal fell on deaf ears.

Saving the euro is much cheaper and easier than the nightmare of picking up the pieces, to say nothing of the unforeseeable consequences of its collapse for all of Europe and for the global economy.

Nobody disputes that, but there's no agreement on how in practice the single currency can be safeguarded without radical change. The concessions a sustainable solution would demand from national governments that no longer trust one another seems to rule out a 'new deal', not just within the eurozone but also for the nine EU countries outside it.

For all that, some sort of forward movement is needed. A first step towards shoring up the euro could be to create a eurozone budget as an instrument for monitoring and overseeing national spending plans. It would offer the ECB, the European Commission, and other relevant authorities the means to coordinate policymaking without resorting to the heavy-handedness of the bail-outs that turned the sovereign debt crisis into an EU-wide political crisis.

What a eurozone budget might look like nobody knows. There already exist mechanisms for the European Commission to scrutinize member governments' national budgets and discipline their debt levels, but a eurozone budget should go further and be the means for transferring funds from northern countries to the south. As well as strengthening controls over indebted countries' spending it would act as an instrument of greater solidarity. A relatively uncontroversial beginning could be made by arming the new eurozone budget with what economists call 'countercyclical' instruments for helping countries to weather the storms of recession— for instance with special funding for unemployment benefits or skills training.

The sticking point in all this isn't necessarily the North–South tensions between the eurozone's debtors and creditors. It is just as likely to be the resistance of all European governments to handing greater powers to the EU. Recent years have seen a number of ideas for making economic and monetary union less divisive and more cohesive, and all have somehow been torpedoed by EU member states' reluctance to hand over greater powers to either the European Central Bank or the European Commission. That doesn't alter the fact that the eurozone cannot remain as it is or go back, so must somehow move forward.

**10. The EU must not abandon the 'political union' that could prevent its own unravelling, save the euro, and and keep Europe's seat at the global top table.**

This is 'The Big One'—the question of whether a totally new departure for EU decision-making is possible, desirable, or just plain madness? And what is meant by political union; would it be the European superstate that Eurosceptic nationalists decry when rallying their supporters, or could it be—despite so much opposition—the rational next development in Europe's slow but certain history of cooperation and centralization?

An EU polity that enables Europeans' political representatives to agree on common policies is the logical key to forging a pan-European economy and to the euro's long-term survival. It is also deeply repugnant to most EU governments. Of the Big Three— Germany, France, and the UK—only Berlin favours eventual political union, and it does so in the face of stern opposition from London, Paris, and elsewhere.

It is hard to find senior political figures in EU countries who openly back political union, and harder still to find agreement on what they might mean by the term. The more Europe-minded are the clearest, seeing a federated EU as essential if Europe is to be a coherent force in the world. They argue that the rise of new economic giants such as China, India, and Brazil, the volatility of so much of the Middle East, and Russia's renewed assertiveness, underline the European Union's divisions and its incoherence and therefore make unity more essential than ever.

For now, though, anything that amounts to a 'European government' must be ruled out. A political union with the right democratic underpinnings could be the only mechanism for transferring funds from richer to poorer countries and averting the threat of a eurozone collapse, but it's not going to happen anytime soon.

The implications of political union are so far-reaching that the EU's present institutional arrangements would have to be largely scrapped.

Today's so-called executive commission would need to be streamlined into a politically legitimate governing body headed by universally elected politicians, with both its statutory powers and its more humdrum responsibilities hived-off into EU agencies.

A working majority in the European Parliament would be needed to support this new 'EU government', and if ever it were to be defeated there would be fresh elections. In some instances these would be for membership of the College of Commissioners, in others to the parliament itself. National governments and their parliaments would take a backseat. Die-hard federalists have long urged this, and make an attractive case for root-and-branch reform that would create a new and more progressive Europe. It is also impossible to deny there's a risk of creating a pan-European system that is potentially so volatile it might greatly exacerbate Europe's difficulties.

## Here's What Can be Done Without Plunging the EU into a Political Furore

Europe's policymakers face a tricky paradox. The difficulties that since 2008 have been piling up one on top of another would be best resolved by ambitious and sweeping policy initiatives; but tempers are now so frayed that extensive policy initiatives could trigger an EU political furore that would make matters worse.

Even if the cumulative effects of low-profile tactical policies were to deliver results by 2020 or so, the European Union would still face a chicken-and-egg question: should EU countries first agree on new political mechanisms that can deliver effective economic policies, or should they concentrate on economic policies that open the way to better political mechanisms?

The tensions that have led to the widespread decline of electoral support for the EU mean this conundrum won't be easily resolved. That's no reason to sit back and watch helplessly as the European Union descends into chaos and irrelevance. There are many areas where Europeans are working on cross-border projects, and political leaders across large swathes of the left–right spectrum can agree on many of the policies needed to revive Europe's fortunes.

So what's to be done? To begin with, European decision-makers must recognize that austerity measures for tackling southern European governments' indebtedness can co-exist with the overall streamlining of the EU. Balancing the books so as not to handicap future generations with past debts is desirable, but not urgent. Interest rates look set to remain low for years ahead, making the cost of servicing public debt relatively modest, so it is more reckless to ignore the urgency of tackling the North–South gap. It is widening at a runaway speed that now poses the greatest of all threats to Europe's future wealth and stability.

The austerity preoccupations of Germany and other northern EU governments don't necessarily mean they oppose structural measures for strengthening the EU economy. It is up to the EU institutions' new leaders to promote spending that is an investment in Europe's overall competitiveness but won't be a financial cushion enabling southern eurozone governments to delay structural reforms.

It is not only they who need to reaffirm their commitment to Europe. The wealthier and bigger member states must redefine what they see as the common interests of the EU, and then invest in them. The track record of too many governments has been to sign up to shared commitments only to ignore them. Their fundamental choice is between continuing to relegate the EU chiefly to the handling of minor or relatively uncontroversial matters, or to widen its focus to include big issues such as relations with China and Russia.

That requires a much clearer picture of the direction EU governments and their electorates want to take. A twenty-first century overview that goes beyond the generally incomprehensible technocratic fare served up by Brussels would be the best way to rebut Eurosceptic claims that the EU doesn't address the interests of ordinary people. Europe's largely pro-EU political and business elites know integration has already transformed many people's lives, but it's a message that has to be spelled out much more clearly.

The answer to these problems won't come from Brussels, so the involvement of national governments is essential to any repackaging and reselling of the whole concept of European integration. Europe's capitals must stop using the EU as a political football and blaming Brussels for their own shortcomings.

That doesn't mean EU officialdom has no part to play in recovering people's faith in 'Europe'. The Eurocrats have the organization, the funds, and above all, the know-how to mount an effective information campaign. Unfortunately, they also tend to be happier handling detailed technical issues than larger geopolitical questions, and are poor and sometimes reluctant communicators. For the EU to prosper, and maybe even survive, it must promote a truly far-sighted view of Europe's worth, shifting the focus from regulation and pettifogging minutiae to Europeans' global interests. EU officials have tended to set their sights on short-term goals for bringing member countries into line on common policies, but now the tectonic shifts in the world economy demand a long-term view.

This should begin with a thoughtful analysis of the global governance issues that will affect the development of the international political economy in the medium term of, say, a quarter century. It's not just a European interest but also a transatlantic one. Brussels and Washington should be thinking jointly about reshaping the global rulebook on trade, investment, judicial matters, and intellectual property protection in ways that will satisfy the aspirations of the emerging economic giants while also defending Western interests.

These are questions that no single European country can hope to influence, and a clearly defined EU global governance agenda could help to persuade public opinion of the value of Europe's international role. Europe should be doing more to use its development aid to those countries in Africa and Asia that will be truly global players within just a few generations to forge a collectively 'European' relationship with these coming powers. So far, individual European countries pursue competing trade promotion efforts, yet it is the wider EU relationship that African and Asian governments and businesses most value.

The widespread prejudice that the EU is already some sort of superstate seems unassailable, making it tougher than ever to convince public opinion that Europe must fix its internal problems so that it can exert global influence. The thread running through this work is that far from being an increasingly uncontrollable supranational power, the EU's authority has been steadily sapped. The European Commission is meant to act as a neutral referee to prevent governments as well as big corporations from abusing their power, but in some key areas it has become more neutered than neutral.

Calls for EU-level action inevitably stir fresh criticisms that 'Europe' is exceeding its remit. As with so many of the EU's complex and often controversial activities, poor communications and negative perceptions are a fundamental problem. The preference of commission officials for 'good news' about the EU has proved devastatingly counterproductive, and has led to the EU rather than its member governments being blamed for economic austerity, rising unemployment, and even unrelated problems such as illicit immigration.

There has at the same time been a sense from Brussels of 'crisis, what crisis?' The unchanging TV news pictures of shiny black limousines disgorging complacent-looking political leaders at EU summits are a far cry from the hardships of austerity suffered by so many, not least by the twenty-five million or more people who are unemployed. Europe's jobless seem too young or too old to compete successfully for work in today's fractured labour markets, but are entitled to feel keenly that they deserve better from an ambitious political experiment that once promised so much.

Getting Europe's political economy back into high gear is the immediate priority, but it's not the greatest goal. That will be to persuade public opinion that we must rethink our comfortable and cherished assumptions about Europe's privileged place in the world. A realistic picture of the rapid changes taking place in the twenty-first century is essential to finding the right policy responses. Whether or not we accept that reality will make all the difference between a soft or a hard landing.

# BIBLIOGRAPHY

Alesina, Alberto and Giavazzi, Francesco. *The Future of Europe—Reform or Decline* (MIT Press 2006).

Arbuthnott, Tom and Leonard, Mark. *European Democracy: A Manifesto* (The Foreign Policy Centre, London, and the British Council 2003).

Bindi, Federica (ed.). *The Foreign Policy of the European Union* (The Brookings Institution 2010).

Bongiovanni, Francesco M. *The Decline and Fall of Europe* Palgrave (Macmillan 2012).

Calleo, David P. *Rethinking Europe's Future* (Princeton University Press 2001).

Claes, Willy. *Messages pour le 21eme siecle* (Editions Labor 1998).

Cremer, Marjolein and Mors, Susanne (eds). *The Dwarfing of Europe?* (The European Cultural Foundation, Amsterdam 2014).

de Ruyt, Jean. *Le Leadership dans l'Union européene* (UCL Presses Universitaires de Louvain 2015).

Dixon, Hugo. *The In/Out Question—Why Britain Should Stay in the EU and Fight to Make It Better* (Scampstonian 2014).

Emerson, Michael (ed.). *Britain's Future in Europe—Reform, Renegotiation, Repatriation or Secession?* (Rowman and Littlefield 2015).

Esper, Philippe, de Boissieu, Christian, Delvolvé, Pierre, and Jaffrelot, Christophe. *Un monde sans Europe?* (Editions Fayard 2011).

Friedman, George. *The Next 100 Years—A Forecast for the 21st Century* (Anchor Books 2010).

Giuliani, Jean-Dominique. *Un Européen tres pressé* (Editions du Moment, Paris 2008).

Guérivière, Jean de la. *Voyage a l'Interieur de l'Eurocratie* (Le Monde-Editions 1991).

Hamilton, Daniel S. *Europe 2020—Competitive or Complacent?* (Center for Transatlantic Relations, Washington, DC, 2011).

Hammond, Ray. *The World in 2030* (Editions Yago 2007).

Hill, Steven. *Europe's Promise: Why the European Way is the Best Hope for an Insecure Age* (University of California Press 2010).

Herzog, Philippe. *Wake Up, Europe!* (Editions Le Manuscrit 2014).

Laqueur, Walter. *After the Fall—The End of the European Dream and the Decline of a Continent* (St Martin's Press, New York 2011).

Legrain, Philippe. *European Spring—Why our Economies and Politics are in a Mess, and How to Put Them Right* (CB Books 2014).

Marquand, David. *The End of the West—The Once and Future Europe* (Princeton University Press 2011).

McRae, Hamish. *The World in 2020—Power, Culture and Prosperity* (Harvard Business School Press 1994).

Orbie, Jan (ed). *Europe's Global Role—External Policies of the European Union* (Ashgate Publishing 2008).

Peet, John and la Guardia, Anton. *Unhappy Union—How the Euro Crisis, and Europe, Can Be Fixed* (The Economist 2014).

Perchoc, Philippe. *Correspondances européennes* (UCL Presses Universitaires de Louvain 2014).

Piris, Jean-Claude. *The Future of Europe—Towards a Two-Speed EU?* (Cambridge University Press 2012).

Priestley, Julian. *European Political Parties—The Missing Link* (Notre Europe, Paris 2010).

Ross, George. *Jacques Delors and European Integration* (Polity Press 1995).

Siedentop, Larry. *Democracy in Europe* (Penguin Books 2000).

Techau, Jan (ed.). *Strategic Europe* (Carnegie Endowment for International Peace 2012).

Tsoukalis, Loukas. *The New European Economy—The Politics and Economics of Integration* (Oxford University Press 1991).

Van Miert, Karel. *Le Marché et le Pouvoir* (Editions Racine 2000).

de Vasconcelos, Alvaro. *What Ambitions for European Defence in 2020?* (EU Institute for Security Studies, Paris 2009).

Vibert, Frank. *Europe Simple, Europe Strong—The Future of European Governance* (Polity Press 2001).

Weiler, Joseph H. H. *The Constitution of Europe* (Cambridge University Press 1999).

Wall, Stephen. *A Stranger in Europe—Britain and the EU from Thatcher to Blair* (Oxford University Press 2008).

# INDEX